GERMAN OPERA LIBRETTI

The German Library: Volume 52
Volkmar Sander, General Editor

GERMAN OPERA LIBRETTI

Edited by James Steakley

Foreword by Jost Hermand

CONTINUUM • NEW YORK

1995

The Continuum Publishing Company
370 Lexington Avenue, New York, NY 10017

The German Library
is published in cooperation with Deutsches Haus,
New York University.
This volume has been supported by Inter Nationes and by a grant from
the Marie Baier Foundation.

Printed in the United States of America

Library of Congress Cataloging-in-Publication Data

German opera libretti / edited by James Steakley ; foreword by Jost
Hermand.
    p.   cm. — (The German library ; v. 52)
    Translated into English.
    Contents: The magic flute / Wolfgang Amadeus Mozart ; libretto by
Emanuel Schikaneder — Fidelio / Ludwig van Beethoven ; libretto
from the French of Jean-Nicolas Bouilly by Joseph Sonnleithner,
Stephan von Bruening, and Georg Friedrich Treitschke — Parsifal /
Richard Wagner — The rose cavalier / Richard Strauss ; libretto by
Hugo von Hofmannsthal — Moses and Aron / Arnold Schönberg.
    ISBN 0-8264-0738-2 (hardcover : acid-free paper). — ISBN
0-8264-0739-0 (paperback : acid-free paper)
    1. Operas—Librettos.   I. Steakley, James D.   II. Series.
ML 48.G46 1995 <Case>
782.1'026'80943—dc20   94-31993
                                                         CIP
                                                         MN

Acknowledgements will be found on page 285,
which constitutes an extension of the copyright page.

Contents

Foreword

The question whether the music, the text, the cast of singers, or the stage set is the most important feature of an opera has been asked for the last 400 years. And each epoch—in keeping with its social and aesthetic outlook—has given a different answer. Around 1600, in the realm of the Florentine camerata, major emphasis was placed on the text. Here opera was understood primarily as a recitative *dramma per musica* that ought to correspond to the performance practice of the tragedy of classical antiquity. But as early as the middle of the seventeenth century, especially in the works of Claudio Monteverdi, the music took on growing importance. Indeed, in mid-century Italy the stage setting, singing style, and ballet interludes took on such "baroque" forms that the text became ever less important. What had begun as a relatively strict, classicizing genre now turned into a festive spectacle involving all the senses of human perception. Opera presentation did not become any simpler until about 1700, when so-called aria opera came to the fore in Naples and rapidly began its victory procession through all of Europe. But here, too, music continued to be the dominant force, while the libretti provided only a pretext for the greatest possible wealth of affects. Plots were generally constructed so as to allow all the singers, including many castrati, to demonstrate their brilliance in a wide range of arias thematizing love, yearning, triumph, envy, hatred, and vengeance. The virtuosity and melodic wealth of this still relatively novel genre brought it enormous popularity.

And it was also about this time that interest in the opera arose in Germany. In the 1760s, the courts in Vienna, Munich, and Dresden were the first to import the Italian opera, along with the accompanying music directors and singing stars. The operas they commissioned, at first sung entirely in Italian, had rather inferior texts relating adventurously spun-out stories based on historical events and mythological stories drawn from classical antiquity. Numerous ballet interludes, water spectacles, and other divertimenti often stretched these operas by many hours. Around 1700, the German courts embraced the Neapolitan aria opera, leading to a pronounced cult of stars. At the same time, some of the wealthier commercial cities also began to show interest in this à la mode product called opera. The first of these cities was Hamburg, whose patricians had built an opera house in the year 1678 at the Gänsemarkt. The works staged here, often based closely on Venetian and Neapolitan type of opera, were for the first time sung in German. Rather significant composers, such as Johann Mattheson (1699), Reinhard Keiser (1695–1706, 1709–16), and Georg Friedrich Händel (1705–1706), were active here. Noteworthy libretti, however, remained extremely rare. Indeed, some of the Hamburg composers did not hesitate to insert Italian arias into the middle of German texts in order to offer touring stars from Venice or Naples the opportunity for a virtuoso performance. Thus most of their operas have neither a German nor a bourgeois character, but strike us instead as arbitrarily jumbled pasticcios. They could not but bore the audience of Hamburg merchants, who after 1700 pushed ever more strongly toward a rationalistic view of art. In the face of this development, the Hamburg opera at the Gänsemarkt finally had to close its doors in 1738.

In the ensuing decades, the opera was able to thrive in Germany only at the courts, where the aria opera sung in Italian—be it in the form of the *opera seria* or the *opera buffa*—continued to be regarded as the highest, if not the only form of opera. The bourgeois Enlightenment, under the leadership of its Leipzig preceptor Johann Christoph Gottsched, scorned the opera as a courtly and artificial creature, fantastic and nonsensical, and even in the realm of drama demanded the elimination of all flights of fancy that violated reason by venturing into mythology or the fairy tale. This led to an unanticipated flowering of the drama in Germany that culminated in the works of Gotthold Ephraim Lessing, Johann Wolfgang Goethe, and Friedrich Schiller, but not to a flowering of the opera. Händel departed for England, while Christoph Willibald Gluck, perhaps the most important German opera composer between 1750 and 1780, was active first in Italy and later in Paris. Whereas Händel in London held on to the Neapolitan aria opera, Gluck—hearkening back to the Florentine *dramma per musica* and the tragedic style of French classicism—developed in his late works an operatic style that aimed to reduce the preponderance of music and the cult of the individual singing star in favor of the dramatic *recitativo*. In Gluck's works, the libretto once again became the most important

component. Yet these libretti were composed in Italian or French—
and therefore fall outside the history of German opera texts.

The German-language opera gained new impetus only in the
1780s. Of particular importance were the reform efforts of Emperor
Joseph II in Vienna, who was determined to establish German as the
sole official language of his polyglot Danube empire and therefore
fostered the use of German within the arts. It was for him that
Wolfgang Amadeus Mozart, who until this time had produced only
Italian operas, composed in 1782 *Die Entführung aus dem Serail*
(The Abduction from the Seraglio), a German *Singspiel*. The
emperor remained rather dissatisfied, however, because it contained
"too many notes," i.e., not enough text. And so this initiative failed,
and Mozart returned to the *opera buffa* or *dramma giocoso* sung in
Italian with *La nozze di Figaro* (The Marriage of Figaro, 1786),
Don Giovanni (1787), and *Così fan tutte* (All Women Do the Same,
1790). Of his last operas, only *Die Zauberflöte* (The Magic Flute,
1791) has a German-language text, composed by his fellow
Masonic lodge member Emanuel Schikaneder. In it the wise
Sarastro and his Priests of the Sun vanquish the sinister machinations of the Queen of the Night; ideologically speaking, this signaled
the victory of Enlightenment over absolutism, and it was interpreted
by some contemporaries—in view of the French Revolution—as the
victory of the Paris Constituent Assembly over Queen Marie
Antoinette. Despite its seeming naivete, this libretto therefore has a
powerful political and philosophical message that inspired even
Goethe to such enthusiasm that he immediately started a continua-
tion of *Die Zauberflöte*, which remained, however, fragmentary due
to Mozart's death shortly after this work's Vienna premiere.

The German-language opera received its next boost only after
Napoleon and his armies invaded Germany, introducing to the
German stage the operas of the French Revolution and the Empire,
i.e., the works of Luigi Cherubini, Jean-François Le Sueur, Etienne-
Nicolas Méhul, and Ferdinando Paer. The composer most deeply
moved by these works was Ludwig van Beethoven, whose revolutionary sympathies led him to be especially enthusiastic about Jean-
Nicolas Bouilly's libretto of *Léonore, ou L'amour conjugal*, with its
hatred of tyranny and bold deed of liberation. It had been unsuccess-
fully turned into an opera by Pierre Gaveaux in 1798. Once
Schikaneder had drawn Beethoven's attention to this work, he
immediately had it translated into German by Joseph Sonnleithner
and later had it reworked by Stephan von Breuning and Georg
Friedrich Treitschke. Beethoven himself made several revisions in the

final, 1814 version of the text, so that what began as a French libretto was ultimately transformed into a German libretto that bears the unmistakable impress of Beethoven himself.

But with its pathos embracing all of humanity, Beethoven's *Fidelio* (1806), as he called his Leonore opera, remained an exception. The further course of German history, under the sway of a national Romanticism opposed to the French occupation, tended to favor operas with a mythological or fairy-tale character that was specifically German. A clear example of this trend is Ernst Theodor Amadeus Hoffmann's *Undine* (1813), the story-line of which is drawn from the fairy-tale world typified by the Brothers Grimm. Beethoven, too, was offered such a text: the libretto of the opera *Melusine*, which left him, an old adherent of the Enlightenment, entirely nonplussed. But even this national-Romantic wave lasted only a short time and subsided after the 1815 Congress of Vienna, which quashed all hopes for German nationhood by reinstating petty absolutism. The repercussions were evident in the case of such a composer as Carl Maria von Weber, who had ventured to set to music a few of the rebellious texts of the anti-Napoleonic Wars of Liberation. When his opera *Der Freischütz* (The Free Shooter, 1821), based on a text by Johann Friedrich Kind, premiered in Berlin, the royal household was conspicuous by its absence, and Weber found himself denied the position of court kapellmeister he had been hoping for. The libretto of this opera was anything but revolutionary: its conclusion glorified a social order whose highest representatives were the prince and the religious hermit. But this opera accorded significance to the "German forests" in which the Lützow militiamen—celebrated in song by Weber—had taken refuge during their 1813 guerrilla war against the French, and this was still held against him by the authorities in 1821, just two years after the infamous Karlsbad Decrees which criminalized any form of nationalistic strivings.

What followed, even in the realm of opera, was a clear-cut victory of those conservative forces willing to tolerate only the sort of culture later termed "Biedermeier." The strongest link to the old spirit of Romanticism appeared in the gloomy settings of so-called uncanny operas, or operas of fate. In the operas *Der Vampir* (The Vampire, 1828) and *Hans Heiling* (1833) by Heinrich Marschner, for example, we encounter eerie spirits of nature or the elements in the form of Melusinas, Undines, dwarfs, mountain sprites, and Dracula-like figures, who either yearn to acquire a human soul or, as evil spirits, carry out their evil deeds until driven back into subterranean catacombs by representatives of the church or state. But during these years there was also a noticeable trend toward the bourgeois, even petit-bourgeois, idyll. This is documented by such operas as Albert Lortzing's *Zar und Zimmermann* (Czar and Carpenter, 1837), *Der Wildschütz* (The Poacher, 1842), and *Der Waffenschmied* (The Armorer, 1846), which have a decidedly un-Romantic character and occasionally take on a simple-minded, almost operetta-like air.

The sole German composer able to advance beyond this genre of uncanny Romanticism and Biedermeier idyllics to a more demanding sort of opera, which he called musical drama, was Richard Wagner. Wagner, who as a young man strongly sympathized with the rebellious trends of his age—the Young German and Pre-March movements—wrote all his texts himself. After his *Rienzi* (1840), a French *grand opéra* in the style of Giacomo Meyerbeer transformed into a revolutionary opera, *Der fliegende Holländer* (The Flying Dutchman, 1841) and *Tannhäuser* (1845) took up subject matters borrowed from the works of Heinrich Heine, famed for sharp social criticism. Even in his drama *Siegfrieds Tod* (Siegfried's Death, 1848) as well as his programmatic writings *Die Kunst und die Revolution* (Art and Revolution, 1849) and *Oper und Drama* (Opera and Drama, 1851), Wagner remained true to his dream of transforming the prevailing conditions of capitalistic greed into a longed-for utopia of communist solidarity. It was only in Swiss exile, faced with the failure of the 1848 Revolution, that he gradually lost his enthusiasm for socialism and, influenced by his reading of Schopenhauer's work, turned to a fatalism tinged with Buddhism, which found its purest expression in his music drama *Tristan und Isolde* (Tristan and Isolde, 1859). As the drive toward national unification gathered momentum in the 1860s, however, he regained hope and emphatically proclaimed his fealty to the grandeur of "German spirit and art" in his *Die Meistersinger von Nürnberg* (The Mastersingers of Nuremberg, 1867). After that, nothing stood in the way of his return to the German Reich, which he hailed with his "Kaisermarsch," and he was even forgiven his earlier rebellious outlook. The 1876 premiere of his tetralogy *Der Ring des Nibelungen* (The Ring of the Nibelung) in the Bayreuth Festival Playhouse, designed by Wagner himself, therefore figured as one of the cultural high points of the so-called Founders' Years, which favored a national, almost mythical monumentalism in other forms of cultural expression as well. Soon plagued anew by debts, Wagner reverted to raging against the capitalist age with its profit-hunger and imperialistic features of degeneration. His response was the "Stage Dedication Festival Play" *Parsifal* (1882), the text of which is perhaps one of the most ambitious libretti of the entire operatic literature. Here victory is accorded to those noble figures of the Grail Brotherhood who have submitted to the discipline of vegetarianism, cleansing themselves of all the materialistic and sensualistic desires symbolized by Klingsor.

Thanks to Wagner's works, the German-language opera achieved such prestige that even the French, defeated in the Franco-Prussian War of 1870–71, became enthusiastic Wagnerites. This led not only to heightened esteem for the German opera, alongside which French and Italian opera were suddenly reduced to second- or third-rank positions, but also to considerably higher demands on the libretti of operas composed around the turn of the century, most of which were either written by the composers themselves or based on well-known works of contemporary drama. Perhaps the most ambitious of this era's German opera composers was Hans Pfitzner, who authored a libretto for his major work, the three-act musical legend *Palestrina* (premiered in 1917), in which he largely identified himself with the protagonist of this opera and, like Palestrina with his *Missae Papae Marcelli*, attempted to create a work that would testify to the eternal dignity of Frau Musica herself. Following the example of Wagner, Richard Strauss wrote the text of his first opera, *Guntram* (1894), himself and based his *Salome* (1905) on the Oscar Wilde play of the same title. In the following years, the texts for almost all his operas were provided by Hugo von Hofmannsthal, with whom Strauss discussed many dramaturgical details before composing these works; thus he had a direct influence on the shaping of many of these libretti. This is especially true of *Der Rosenkavalier* (The Rose Cavalier, 1911), *Ariadne auf Naxos* (Ariadne on Naxos, 1912), *Die Frau ohne Schatten* (The Woman without a Shadow, 1919), *Die ägyptische Helena* (The Egyptian Helen, 1928), and *Arabella* (1933). In addition to these works, Strauss wrote operas such as *Intermezzo* (1924) and *Capriccio* (1942), for which he and Clemens Krauss wrote the libretti themselves.

With their superb culture of voice and psychological refinement, Strauss's works brought the bourgeois opera of the late nineteenth century to its final great climax. While what followed in the area of stage composition continued to be called opera, it remained largely restricted to the realm of modernistic-elitist sound experiments and proved incapable of entering the opera repertory embraced by the public, which therefore became increasingly fixed on the past. Despite many attempts to breathe new life into the opera, no new Wagner or new Strauss emerged in Germany after World War I, and even in other countries with an established opera culture, such as Italy and

France, no comparable opera composers have come to the fore. Granted, the succeeding years have brought forth a few musical stage compositions that display highest artistic abilities, but their overstated sound experiments ultimately rendered them inappropriate for a genre that aims at theatrical effectiveness, and these works have therefore won only limited recognition from a handful of musical connoisseurs.

This is especially true for the stage compositions of the so-called Second Viennese School. Still highly regarded among specialists in modernistic music, these works remain largely inaccessible for average operagoers, who are in any case drawn largely from the educated upper classes. The most successful of these works, albeit in a limited sense, was undoubtedly Alban Berg's *Wozzeck* (1925), based on the first proletarian drama of the German language, Georg Büchner's *Woyzeck* (1837), a work unsurpassed in its depiction of human misery, which Berg turned into a highly refined sound construct that appeals only to a quite sophisticated audience. Similar discrepancies are characteristic of the opera *Moses und Aron* (Moses and Aron, 1932), in which Arnold Schönberg, under relentless attack from German anti-Semites because of his allegedly "un-German" twelve-tone technique, called upon his people not to mix with other nations and to return to the biblical path already pointed out by Moses. After Schönberg had finished the text and the music for the first two acts in 1932, the National Socialists hounded him into exile, where he worked tirelessly to build up a Jewish unity party but was unable to find the time to complete his *Moses und Aron*.

In the 1920s, somewhat greater success was accorded only those composers who sought to update the opera by introducing topical plot elements and employing a musical language that corresponded to the dominant mood of New Sobriety. This school dispensed with the conventional opera libretti based on famous works of world literature, creating instead an entirely new type of opera text which was intentionally hard-boiled, even cynical. Notable success was achieved by Kurt Weill and Bertolt Brecht with *Die Dreigroschenoper* (The Threepenny Opera, 1928), which became a world-wide hit because of its criminal milieu, seductive jadedness, and partly balladesque, partly jazzed-up music. Drawn by the high literary quality of Brecht's libretti, Kurt Weill went on to set a number of other Brecht texts to music, including *Aufstieg und Fall der Stadt Mahagonny* (Rise and Fall of the City of Mahagonny, 1929) and *Der Jasager* (The Yes-Sayer, 1930). But such divergent composers as Paul Hindemith and Hanns Eisler also based some of their stage compositions on texts by Brecht during these years. Apart from them, only Ernst Krenek with *Jonny spielt auf*

(Jonny Strikes up the Band, 1927), for which he wrote the text himself and introduced the new jazz medium, scored an international success in the field of the topical operas of the New Sobriety.

The 1930s, by contrast, witnessed a rigorous repudiation of the elitist traits of the Viennese School and the topical trends of New Sobriety. Operas and the libretti they were based on underwent a conscious return to German-Romantic fairy-tale motifs and events from German history. Exemplary for these tendencies are the fairy-tale operas *Der Mond* (The Moon, 1939) and *Die Kluge* (The Clever Woman, 1943) by Carl Orff as well as Paul Hindemith's *Mathis der Maler* (Mathis the Painter, 1938), in which he—on the basis of his own libretto—sought to bring to the opera stage the life of the German painter Matthias Grünewald during the Peasant Wars of the sixteenth century. Almost all these works tended toward a half-hearted modernism, which was not only favored or tolerated by the National Socialists but also typical for the musical creations of other countries in the 1930s.

Even in the years after 1945, numerous operas were composed and produced in the Federal Republic of Germany, the German Democratic Republic, Switzerland, and Austria, because these countries—thanks to major state subsidies—were home to more than seventy percent of the world's opera houses. But the stage compositions of Hermann Reutter, Werner Egk, Gottfried von Einem, Paul Dessau, Wolfgang Fortner, Karlheinz Stockhausen, Hans Werner Henze, Aribert Reimann, and Wolfgang Rihm, some of which have outstanding libretti and elicited enormous waves of commentary in the press, were set aside after a limited number of performances. While the opera repertoire of the late eighteenth and nineteenth centuries still enjoys great popularity and is constantly being revived because of its thrilling melodiousness and elaborate stage sets that satisfy the desire for viewing pleasure, the operas of the twentieth century have failed to become established, due in part precisely to their "superior" libretti and exquisitely modernistic music. And thus the opera, which was the music-theatrical showpiece of an era focused on social representation, has increasingly turned into a museum genre of a culture-minded social class which does not want to be sucked into the trivial current of popular commercial music. This attitude may elicit a smile, but it also commands our respect, especially because even the commercial music of our time, such as jazz and rock, despite all its display of youthfulness, has already taken on distinctly museumlike traits.

JOST HERMAND

THE MAGIC FLUTE

Libretto by Emanuel Schikaneder

Wolfgang Amadeus Mozart

CHARACTERS

SARASTRO	*Bass*
TAMINO	*Tenor*
SPEAKER	*Bass*
A SECOND PRIEST	*Tenor*
AN OLD PRIEST	*Bass*
THE QUEEN OF THE NIGHT	*Soprano*
PAMINA, *her daughter*	*Soprano*
FIRST, SECOND, THIRD LADIES OF THE QUEEN	*2 Sopranos, 1 Mezzo-Soprano*
FIRST, SECOND, THIRD BOYS	*2 Trebles (Soprano), 1 Alto*
PAPAGENO	*Baritone*
PAPAGENA	*Soprano*
MONOSTATOS, *a Moor*	*Tenor*
FIRST AND SECOND MEN IN ARMOR	*Tenor, Bass*
FIRST, SECOND, THIRD SLAVES	*Speaking Parts*
PRIESTS, ATTENDANTS, POPULACE, SLAVES, VOICES, APPARITIONS	

ACT 1

A rocky scene dotted with a few trees. In the center stands a temple, to which steep paths lead from either side.

Scene 1

Tamino, dressed in a magnificent Japanese hunting costume, enters over one of the rocks; he carries a bow without arrows; he is pursued by a serpent.

TAMINO

> Oh, help me! Oh, help me! Can nobody hear me?
> The venomous fangs of the serpent are near me.
> O heaven, protect me! I cannot escape.
> Ah, rescue me, help me, save me!

He falls unconscious. At that moment the door of the temple opens, and Three Ladies, veiled, enter, each with a silver javelin.

THE THREE LADIES

> Now we are here: the beast shall die!
> He dies! He dies! The deed is done,
> The battle won. We've set him free.
> We've saved him through our bravery.

FIRST LADY *(looking at Tamino)*

> Handsome stranger, full of grace!

SECOND LADY

> I never saw so fair a face!

THIRD LADY

> Yes, yes, that's true, a lovely face!

ALL THREE

> If I should fall in love one day,
> It will be with this youth, I pray.
> But let us hasten to the Queen now
> And tell her what we've done and seen here.
> Perhaps this good man can restore
> The peace and joy she knew before.

FIRST LADY

> So hurry and begone,
> I'll guard him here alone.

SECOND LADY

> No, no, I'd rather stay.
> I'll watch him through the day.

THIRD LADY
>> There's no cause for alarm,
>> I'll keep him safe from harm.

FIRST LADY
>> I'll guard him here alone!

SECOND LADY
>> I'll watch him through the day!

THIRD LADY
>> I'll keep him safe from harm!

FIRST LADY
>> I'll guard him!

SECOND LADY
>> I'll watch him!

THIRD LADY
>> I'll keep him!

ALL THREE
>> I! I! I!
>> *(each one to herself)*
>> I am to go? Oh no, not so!
>> They'd like to be alone—
>> I know! I shall not go.
>> *(one after the other, then all together)*
>> I'd give up all my hopes of heaven
>> To live with this young man forever!
>> I know he would be good and kind!
>> But they'll not leave, for love is blind.
>> And so I must be on my way.
>> Now lovely boy, I'll say adieu.
>> So dear young man, farewell to you.
>> We'll meet again I pray.

They go toward the door of the temple, which opens and closes behind them.

TAMINO *(awaking, and looking nervously around)*
Where am I? Am I still alive or am I dreaming? The evil serpent lying dead at my feet. . . . Have I been protected by Providence? *(He stands up and looks around. In the distance, panpipes are heard, accompanied quietly by the orchestra. Tamino follows the sound.)* What's that I hear? There's a man coming through the trees . . . or something like a man.
He hides behind a tree.

Scene 2

During the introduction, Papageno comes down a path. On his back he carries a cage of various birds. In his hands he holds the panpipe with which he accompanies his singing.

PAPAGENO

> My trade is catching birds, you know,
> I spread my nets and in they go,
> And all men know me as a friend
> Throughout the land, from end to end.
> I know what ev'ry cockbird likes
> So lure the peahen with my pipes.
> No wonder that I'm happy then
> Since I can catch both cock and hen.

He pipes.

> My trade is catching birds, you know,
> I spread my nets and in they go,
> And all men know me as a friend
> Throughout the land, from end to end.
> But one thing still I'd like to get:
> A dozen ladies in my net.
> Yes, I would think it very fine,
> If twelve young maidens could be mine.

He pipes.

> If twelve young maidens could be mine
> I'd build a cage of fine design;
> I'd choose the one who loved me best,
> We'd hop inside and make our nest.
> And if she then would be my wife
> And kiss and comfort me through life
> She'd sleep beside me, snug and warm,
> And I would keep her safe from harm.

He pipes and, when the aria is finished, goes toward the temple door.

TAMINO *(taking him by the hand)*

Hey there!

PAPAGENO

Who's that?

TAMINO

You're a lively fellow, my friend . . . who are you?

PAPAGENO
Who am I? *(to himself)* That's a silly question— *(aloud)* A man like you are. But who are you anyway?

TAMINO
Well, to begin with, I'm a Prince of royal blood.

PAPAGENO
Royal blood? Prince? You must speak more plainly if I'm to understand you.

TAMINO
My father is a king who rules over many countries and many people. That's why I'm called Prince.

PAPAGENO
Lands? People? Prince?

TAMINO
That's why I ask you—

PAPAGENO
Slowly! Let me ask the questions! Do you mean to say that beyond these mountains there are other countries and other people?

TAMINO
Yes! Many thousands.

PAPAGENO
What a market for my parakeets.

TAMINO
Now tell me, in what country are we?

PAPAGENO
In what country? *(looking around)* Between valleys and mountains.

TAMINO
That's right enough. And now you must tell me who rules this country?

PAPAGENO
How would I know? You might as well ask me how I came to be born.

TAMINO *(laughing)*
Don't you even know who your parents were?

PAPAGENO
Not a thing! I only know that an old but merry man brought me up and fed me.

TAMINO
He was your father no doubt!

PAPAGENO
I don't know.

TAMINO
Did you never know your mother?

PAPAGENO
I never knew her. I have been sometimes told that my mother used to serve the starblazing Queen of the Night in that closed building there. But whether she is still alive or what has become of her, I do not know. All I do know is that not far from here is my straw hut which protects me from rain and cold.

TAMINO
But how do you live?

PAPAGENO
By eating and drinking, like any other man.

TAMINO
How do you obtain that?

PAPAGENO
From barter. I catch all sorts of birds for the starblazing Queen and her ladies; in exchange I receive daily food and drink from her.

TAMINO *(aside)*
Starblazing Queen? Supposing it should be the powerful Sovereign of the Night! *(aloud)* Tell me, my good friend, have you ever been so lucky as to see this goddess of the night?

PAPAGENO *(who has been playing his pipes occasionally)*
Your last question is so stupid that I can tell that you come from a different country.

TAMINO
Don't be cross, my good friend! I only wanted to say—

PAPAGENO
See her? See the starblazing Queen? If you ask me another such birdbrained question, as sure as my name is Papageno I shall pop you in my birdcage and sell you with my other birds to the Queen of the Night and her ladies. They could then choose, as far as I'm concerned, between boiling you or roasting you.

TAMINO *(aside)*
What a strange man!

PAPAGENO
See her? See the starblazing Queen? What mortal could boast of having seen her? What human sight could see through her veil woven from darkness?

TAMINO *(aside)*
Now it is clear! This must indeed be the Queen of the Night of whom my father so often spoke to me. But it is beyond my

comprehension how I can have wandered here. This man is no ordinary man. Perhaps he is one of her attendant spirits.

PAPAGENO *(aside)*

How he stares at me! I am almost afraid of him. *(aloud)* Why are you staring at me so suspiciously?

TAMINO

Because—because I doubt whether you're human.

PAPAGENO

What was that?

TAMINO

Judging by your feathers, you might almost be some kind of bird— *(goes toward him)*

PAPAGENO

I'm no bird! You keep your distance! I'll have you know I've got the strength of a giant. *(aside)* If I don't succeed in frightening him, I'll make a hasty exit.

TAMINO

The strength of a giant? *(He looks at the serpent.)* Was it you who rescued me from this serpent?

PAPAGENO

Serpent? *(He looks around and shrinks back a few steps.)* What's that? Is it dead or alive?

TAMINO

You are trying to avoid my thanks with your modest questions. Thank you for saving my life, I'll always be grateful to you.

PAPAGENO

Think nothing of it—let's just be thankful it's dead.

TAMINO

But how did you kill this monster? You have no weapons.

PAPAGENO

I don't need them—brute strength.

TAMINO

You strangled it?

PAPAGENO

Strangled! *(aside)* I've never felt so strong in my life as I do today!

Scene 3

Enter the Three Ladies.

THE THREE LADIES *(calling threateningly)*

Papageno!

PAPAGENO
That'll be for me. Look behind you, friend!

TAMINO
Who are these ladies?

PAPAGENO
I don't exactly know who they are, but every day I hand over my birds to them, and they give me wine, sugar cakes, and sweet figs in return.

TAMINO
They must be very beautiful.

PAPAGENO
I shouldn't think so, or they wouldn't hide their faces.

THE THREE LADIES *(menacingly)*
Papageno!

PAPAGENO
Be quiet! Hear how angrily they call me! Are they beautiful, did you say? I've never seen three such beautiful veiled ladies in my life. That ought to please them.

THE THREE LADIES *(menacingly)*
Papageno!

PAPAGENO
What have I done to make them so angry? Look, my beauties, here are the birds for your breakfast.

FIRST LADY *(handing him a jug of water)*
And in return the Queen sends you clear, cold water instead of wine.

SECOND LADY
And instead of sugar cake she has ordered me to give you this stone. I hope it does you good.

PAPAGENO
What! Must I eat stones?

THIRD LADY
And instead of ripe figs I have the pleasure of closing your mouth with this golden lock.
She padlocks his mouth. Papageno protests vigorously.

FIRST LADY
Do you want to know why the Queen has punished you today?
Papageno nods.

SECOND LADY
So that in future you will not tell lies to strangers.

THIRD LADY
And so that you will never again boast of heroic deeds which were really performed by others.

FIRST LADY
>Tell me, did you kill this serpent?
>*Papageno shakes his head.*

SECOND LADY
>Who did then?
>*Papageno signals that he doesn't know.*

THIRD LADY
>It was we three who came to your rescue, young man, but do not be amazed. Joy and delight await you. Our sovereign lady the Queen sends you this picture of her daughter Pamina. If you find that you are not unmoved by the beauty of this portrait, then fortune, honor, and glory will be yours. Farewell, Prince. *(exits)*

SECOND LADY
>Adieu, Monsieur Papageno! *(exits)*

THIRD LADY
>Don't get indigestion! *(exits, laughing)*
>*Papageno does not stop gesticulating dumbly. Since he received the portrait, Tamino has gazed at it intently. Deaf to everything he feels his love growing.*

Scene 4

TAMINO
>No finer picture, I am sure,
>Was ever seen by man before!
>It moves me, and her pure young face
>Enchants my heart and makes it race.
>This strange and unfamiliar yearning,
>This fierce and ardent pleasure burning—
>What is this sweet and piercing flame?
>I know! It must be love alone.
>Oh, how I long to see her glory,
>I'd tell her—tell her—pure and kind—
>What would I say? Upon my heart would I press her,
>Within these loving arms caress her,
>And then I know she would be mine.
>*He begins to go.*

Scene 5

The Three Ladies return.

FIRST LADY
>Noble youth, you must summon up courage! Our royal lady—

SECOND LADY
Has ordered me to tell you—
THIRD LADY
That your future happiness is certain. She has—
FIRST LADY
Heard every word you said. She has—
SECOND LADY
Read the expression in your face. Her loving mother's heart—
THIRD LADY
Has decided to make you really happy. If this youth, she said, is as brave as he is tender-hearted, then my daughter is as good as rescued.
TAMINO
Rescued! What do you mean? Oh, endless darkness! The girl in the portrait—
FIRST LADY
Has been carried off by a powerful and malicious demon.
TAMINO
Carried off? O ye gods! Tell me how this happened.
FIRST LADY
One beautiful May morning she was sitting all alone in her favorite cypress grove when the villain sneaked in unnoticed—
SECOND LADY
Spied her and—
THIRD LADY
He has, besides an evil heart, the power to change into any imaginable shape; in this way, Pamina was—
FIRST LADY
Pamina is the name of the Queen's daughter, the one whom you adore.
TAMINO
O Pamina! You have been torn away from me—you are in the power of a wicked voluptuary! You are perhaps at this moment—horrible thought—
THE THREE LADIES
Silence, youth!
FIRST LADY
Do not slander the virtue of beauty so gracious. Innocence bears all patiently, defiant to torture. Neither force nor flattery could ever lead her into the ways of vice.

TAMINO
Tell me, maidens, tell me where this tyrant lives?

SECOND LADY
He lives very near to our mountains, in an enticing and delightful valley. His magnificent castle is closely guarded.

TAMINO
Come, maidens, show me the way! I will rescue Pamina and destroy the villain. I swear it by my love, by heart. *(At once a thunderous chord is heard.)* O gods! What is that?

THE THREE LADIES
Be brave!

FIRST LADY
It heralds the arrival of our Queen.
(thunder)

THE THREE LADIES
She comes! *(thunder)* She comes! *(thunder)* She comes!

Transformation

The mountains part, and the stage is transformed into a magnificent chamber.

Scene 6

The Queen is seated on a throne which gleams with sparkling stars.

QUEEN
You need not fear, my dearest son,
For you are blameless, noble, strong.
A young man like yourself can best imagine
The grief a mother feels, and show compassion.
I die a thousand deaths each moment
Without my daughter by my side,
And all my joy is turned to torment.
An evil man took her away.
I still see her terror
When held by her captors,
I saw her implore them
And tremble before them.
I saw the horror all too plainly.

"Oh, help," I heard her feebly cry.
Alas, I tried but could not save her,
For all my pow'r was far too weak.
You I choose now to be her savior,
You are the man to set her free.
And when you do succeed to save her
I give my word she'll be your bride.

Exeunt the Queen and the Three Ladies. The scene changes
back to what it was before.

Scene 7

TAMINO *(after a pause)*
Was that a vision I saw? Or are my senses confused? O ye gods!
Do not deceive me, or I shall fail your test. Strengthen my arm,
uphold my courage, and Tamino's heart will give you eternal
thanks.

He begins to leave but Papageno intercepts him.

PAPAGENO *(pointing sadly at the padlock on his mouth)*
Hm, hm, hm!

TAMINO
The poor young man has come to rue it.
A golden lock has sealed his tongue.

PAPAGENO
Hm, hm, hm!

TAMINO
I'd like to help but can't undo it.
The magic power is far too strong.

PAPAGENO
Hm, hm, hm!

Scene 8

The Three Ladies return.

FIRST LADY *(to Papageno)*
If you will promise you'll repent
(taking the lock from Papageno's mouth)
The Queen will end your punishment.

PAPAGENO
Now hear how Papageno chatters.

SECOND LADY

> But lying is a different matter.

PAPAGENO

> I'll never tell a lie again!

THE THREE LADIES

> This lock will be your warning then.

PAPAGENO

> The lock shall be my warning then.

ALL

> If ev'ry liar were made to wander
> With such a lock for his own good,
> Then hate, destruction, and vile slander
> Would yield to love and brotherhood.

FIRST LADY *(giving Tamino a golden flute)*

> O Prince, now take this magic flute.
> It's given by our Queen's command.
> Its pow'r protects through ev'ry danger,
> In all misfortune it will aid you.

THE THREE LADIES

> You'll rule mankind in godlike fashion,
> It gives power over human passion.
> It frees the soul of grief and pain,
> And hardened hearts know love again.

ALL

> Oh, this holy present is worth far more than crowns of
>   gold,
> For its power brings human hearts peace and joy
>   throughout the world.

PAPAGENO

> Now, you proud and lovely bevy,
> May I take my leave of you?

THE THREE LADIES

> Papageno, wait a moment.
> Hear the orders of the Queen.
> Take the Prince, your task is simple,
> To Sarastro's secret temple.

PAPAGENO

> No, I'm damned if I will go!
> You yourselves have let me know
> That he's fiercer than a foe,

And, I'm certain, without mercy
That Sarastro would ill-use me—
Chop me, chew me, rip me, pierce me,
Then he'd feed me to his dogs.

THE THREE LADIES
Then trust the Prince, he'll keep you safe
If you will be his willing slave.

PAPAGENO *(aside)*
To trust the Prince would be plain silly!
My life is all I've got;
I know he'd run off, willy-nilly,
And he'd leave me to rot.

FIRST LADY *(giving Papageno the magic bells in a little box)*
Now take this present, do not hide.

PAPAGENO
Ay, ay! I wonder what's inside?

THE THREE LADIES
You'll find a chime of bells a-ringing.

PAPAGENO
And may I also set them swinging?

THE THREE LADIES
Oh, yes, of course, of course you may!
Bells' enchantment, flute's perfection,
They shall be your sure protection.
Fare you well! You cannot stay,
So farewell! No more delay!

TAMINO AND PAPAGENO
Bells' enchantment, flute's perfection,
They shall be our sure protection.
Fare you well! We cannot stay,
So farewell! No more delay!

They all begin to go.

TAMINO
But lovely ladies, good and wise—

PAPAGENO
Tell us which way the temple lies.

THE THREE LADIES
Three spirits, young but old in wisdom,
Will take you to Sarastro's kingdom.
They'll be your guide in time of need.
Take their advice, go where they lead.

TAMINO AND PAPAGENO

> Three spirits, young, but old in wisdom
> Will take us to Sarastro's kingdom.

ALL

> So fare you well! The way is plain,
> Farewell, farewell! We'll meet again!

Exeunt.

Transformation

Scene 9

As soon as the scene has changed into a chamber richly furnished in the Egyptian style, two slaves bring on beautiful cushions and an ornate Turkish table; they roll out carpets. Enter the third slave.

THIRD SLAVE

Ha, ha, ha!

FIRST SLAVE

Pst! Pst!

SECOND SLAVE

What are you laughing about?

THIRD SLAVE

Our tormentor, the Moor who overhears all, will certainly be hanged or beheaded tomorrow. Pamina! Ha, ha, ha!

FIRST SLAVE

Well?

THIRD SLAVE

The delectable maiden! Ha, ha, ha!

SECOND SLAVE

Well?

THIRD SLAVE

Has escaped.

FIRST AND SECOND SLAVES

Escaped?

FIRST SLAVE

And she got away?

THIRD SLAVE

Certainly. That at least is my dearest wish.

SECOND SLAVE

O gods, I thank you! You have heard my prayer.

FIRST SLAVE
Haven't I always told you that the day of our revenge would come and black Monostatos will be punished?

SECOND SLAVE
What does the Moor say about this?

FIRST SLAVE
Has he heard about it yet?

THIRD SLAVE
Of course! She escaped right under his nose. According to some of our men, who were working in the garden and saw and heard everything from a distance, the Moor will not be saved even if Pamina is caught by Sarastro's attendants.

FOURTH SLAVE
Why not?

THIRD SLAVE
You know that tub of lard and his ways; but the maiden was more clever than I imagined. At the moment he imagined she was his, she called out the name of Sarastro. That startled the Moor, and he stood as if paralyzed. So Pamina ran away to the canal and escaped in a gondola toward the palm grove.

FIRST SLAVE
Oh, may this timid doe in mortal terror reach the palace of her beloved mother.

Scene 10

Monostatos calls from within.

MONOSTATOS
Hey, slaves!

FIRST SLAVE
Monostatos's voice.

MONOSTATOS
Hey, slaves, bring me chains and fetters!

ALL THREE SLAVES
Chains?

FIRST SLAVE *(running to the side door)*
Not for Pamina? O ye gods! Look, brothers, the girl has been recaptured.

SECOND AND THIRD SLAVE
Pamina? Oh, wretched sight!

FIRST SLAVE
  The pitiless devil is dragging her back with him—I cannot bear it. *(exits on the opposite side)*
SECOND SLAVE
  Nor I. *(exits)*
THIRD SLAVE
  To have to see this is a hellish torture. *(exits)*

Scene 11

Monostatos enters. Slaves drag in Pamina.
MONOSTATOS *(very quickly)*
          You won't escape, do what you can!
PAMINA
          You are heartless, evil man!
MONOSTATOS
          If life is dear, don't taunt me!
PAMINA
          But death itself can't daunt me!
          Thoughts of my mother pain me,
          So her grieving heart will break I know.
MONOSTATOS
          You slaves, now bind and fetter her.
          I'll teach you to disdain me.
  The slaves fetter her.
PAMINA
          I'd rather you had slain me
          Than lie here helpless in your power.
She sinks unconscious onto a couch.
MONOSTATOS
          Now go! Leave me alone with her.
  Exeunt slaves.

Scene 12

Papageno appears at the window, at first without being noticed.
PAPAGENO
          Where has he gone? I'm on my own?
          Aha! There's someone sleeping!
          Ah, well, I'll go inside.
          (enters)

Dear lady, like a bride
You lie there white as powder.

*Papageno notices Monostatos, and both are terrified at the
sight of each other.*

MONOSTATOS AND PAPAGENO
Oo! That must—be Lu—cifer—himself!
Have pity—and pardon me!
Oo! Oo! Oo!

Both run away.

Scene 13

PAMINA *(speaking as if in a dream)*
Mother! Mother! Mother! *(She recovers and looks around.)*
Am I still alive? Is my heart still beating? Not yet destroyed?
Have I woken to new torments? Oh, this is cruel, very cruel—
more bitter than death.

Enter Papageno.

Scene 14

PAPAGENO
Wasn't I a fool to be so frightened? There are black birds in the
world, so why shouldn't there be black men? Ah, look here!
The pretty young thing is still here. Greetings, daughter of the
Queen of Night!

PAMINA
Queen of the Night? Who are you?

PAPAGENO
A messenger from the starblazing Queen.

PAMINA *(joyfully)*
From my mother? Oh, joy! What's your name?

PAPAGENO
Papageno.

PAMINA
Papageno? Papageno? I remember hearing the name often, but
I've never seen you.

PAPAGENO
I've never seen you before either.

PAMINA
So you know my kind and gentle mother?

PAPAGENO

If you're the daughter of the Nocturnal Monarch—yes!

PAMINA

Oh, it is me!

PAPAGENO

I'll just confirm it. *(taking the portrait given to Tamino which hangs on a ribbon around his neck)* Eyes black—very black; lips red—very red; hair blond—very blond. Everything correct except for the hands and feet. To judge by this picture, you shouldn't have any, for they're not shown here.

PAMINA

Let me see—yes, it's really me. But where did you get it?

PAPAGENO

That's too long a story to tell you. It passed from hand to hand.

PAMINA

But how did it come into your hand?

PAPAGENO

In a very curious way. I caught it in a trap.

PAMINA

Caught it in a trap?

PAPAGENO

I had better tell you all the details. This morning, as usual, I arrived at your mother's palace to make my delivery—

PAMINA

Delivery?

PAPAGENO

Yes. For many years I have delivered to your mother and her ladies all the beautiful birds in the palace. This morning I was on my way to your mother's palace to hand over the birds as usual, when I came across a young man who calls himself Prince. This Prince so impressed your mother that she gave him this picture and ordered him to free you. He resolved to do so just as quickly as he fell in love with you.

PAMINA

Love? *(joyfully)* He fell in love with me? Oh, do say it again; I like to hear about love.

PAPAGENO

I can easily believe that—after all, you are a sweet young thing. Now where was I?

PAMINA

Talking about love.

PAPAGENO

Ah, yes, love. That's what I call a good memory. Well, to make a long story short, his great love for you spurred us on our way at top speed. Now we're here to tell you a thousand nice things, to clasp you in our arms, and to return to your mother's palace just as fast, if not faster.

PAMINA

That's very nicely said, but if this unknown youth or Prince, as he calls himself, is so in love with me, why is he taking so long to set me free?

PAPAGENO

That's just the problem. When we said goodbye to your mother's three ladies, they told us that three boys would guide us as to how to behave.

PAMINA

What did they say?

PAPAGENO

Nothing—we haven't been able to find them yet. So the Prince was thoughtful enough to send me on ahead to announce our arrival.

PAMINA

My friend, you've taken a great risk. If Sarastro should find you—

PAPAGENO

I wouldn't be making the return journey—I can imagine.

PAMINA

You would perish in endless torture.

PAPAGENO

To avoid that, let's leave soon!

PAMINA

What hour is it by the sun?

PAPAGENO

It's almost midday.

PAMINA

We haven't a moment to lose. This is the time when Sarastro usually returns from the hunt.

PAPAGENO

So Sarastro isn't even at home? Well! This should be easy as pie! Come, lovely young thing. Your eyes will pop out when you catch sight of this handsome youth.

PAMINA

All right, it's worth a try. *(As they are leaving, Pamina turns back.)* But supposing this is a trap and you're a malicious sprite sent by Sarastro? *(She looks at him suspiciously.)*

PAPAGENO

Me a malicious sprite? What are you thinking of, dear young lady? I'm the nicest sprite in the world.

PAMINA

It can't be. This picture convinces me that I am not being tricked; it comes from my good mother's hands.

PAPAGENO

Beautiful picture lady, should you have any further wicked doubts and suspect that I intend to deceive you, you have only to think hard about love and all your dark suspicions will vanish.

PAMINA

My friend, forgive me, forgive me if I offended you. You have a feeling heart, I can see that from everything about you.

PAPAGENO

Alas, I do have a feeling heart. But what's the use of that? I sometimes want to pluck out all my feathers one by one when I consider that Papageno has no Papagena.

PAMINA

Poor man, so you don't have a wife yet?

PAPAGENO

Not even a girlfriend, let alone a wife! Yes, it's depressing! For even we birdcatchers occasionally have some hours of cheer when it would be nice to enjoy socializing.

PAMINA

Patience, my friend. Heaven will send you a wife sooner than you expect.

PAPAGENO

If only it would send her quickly!

PAMINA

The gentle love of man and woman
Shows humans are a race apart.

PAPAGENO

It is a woman's tender duty
To give a man her loving heart.

BOTH

While love is ours, we'll freely give;
By love alone we breathe and live.

PAMINA

It's love that sweetens ev'ry sorrow
And blesses ev'ry waking hour.

PAPAGENO

> With love we need not fear the morrow,
> We feel its universal power.

BOTH

> We know the goal of human life—
> To live in love as man and wife.
> Wife and man, and man and wife,
> Live in love, for love is life.

Exeunt.

Transformation

The scene changes to a sacred grove. Right at the back is a beautiful temple with the inscription Temple of Wisdom. Two other temples are joined to this temple by colonnades: the one on the right is inscribed Temple of Reason; the one on the left, Temple of Nature.

Scene 15

The Three Boys lead Tamino in, each carrying a silver palm frond.
THE THREE BOYS

> The road you trod has led you here.
> Ask here, you'll find this goal you're seeking.
> But you must stand and show no fear.
> Be constant, patient, and be silent.

TAMINO

> But dear young spirits, tell me pray
> If my Pamina will be saved.

THE THREE BOYS

> We may not say: do what you can.
> Be constant, patient, and be silent.
> Remember this: you are a man,
> And you will reach the goal you're seeking.

TAMINO

> I'll heed their wisdom and I'll cherish
> Each word of truth until I perish.
> Where am I now? How can I tell?
> This seems a place for gods to dwell.
> It's written on portals and graven on pillars

That Wisdom, Endeavor, and Art here are rulers;
Where labor is honored and idleness shunned,
The hateful corruption of vice can't be found.
And so I'll walk through each open door.
My purpose is worthy and honest and fine.
So tremble, cruel sorcerer!
To save Pamina is my vow.

Tamino goes to the right-hand door and opens it, but when he begins to enter a voice is heard nearby.

VOICE

Go back!

TAMINO

Go back? I'll try here, come what may!

He approaches the left-hand door but hears a voice from within.

VOICE

Go back!

TAMINO

I'm turned away once more.

He looks around.

I see there's yet one more door.
Perhaps I'll find that way is clear.

He knocks, and an old Priest appears.

PRIEST

Intruder, tell me what you seek.
What makes you tread forbidden ground?

TAMINO

I go where truth and love are found.

PRIEST

Those words sound fine and brave, I know!
But say, how do you hope to find them?
For neither love nor truth is found
By men whose hate and vengeance blind them.

TAMINO

I only hate the wicked man.

PRIEST

You will not find such men within here.

TAMINO

Sarastro rules and is your leader.

PRIEST

Oh, yes! Sarastro rules us here!

TAMINO
> But not in wisdom's sacred home?

PRIEST
> He rules in wisdom's sacred home!

TAMINO *(about to leave)*
> Then it is all deceit and lies!

PRIEST
> So now you wish to go?

TAMINO
> Yes, I shall go, proud and free,
> Far from these temple walls.

PRIEST
> Explain your words to me.
> I say you are deceived.

TAMINO
> Sarastro is your Lord.
> You cannot be believed.

PRIEST
> If you still love your life,
> I charge you, stay a while.
> You hate Sarastro so?

TAMINO
> I hate his very name!

PRIEST
> At least explain your meaning.

TAMINO
> He is inhuman, not a man.

PRIEST
> And have you proof of all you're saying?

TAMINO
> There's proof in that unhappy woman
> Whose life is filled with bitter tears.

PRIEST
> You take a woman's tears as truth?
> Young man, learn wisdom: woman's sighs
> Are seldom felt and often lies.
> Oh, if you knew Sarastro well
> You'd know that ill was not his wish.

TAMINO
> His wishes are as clear as day.
> Did he not steal, without compassion,
> Pamina from her mother's arms?

PRIEST
>
> Young man, what you have said is true.

TAMINO
>
> Where is she—she he stole away?
> Oh, has her sacrifice begun?

PRIEST
>
> I cannot tell you now, my son,
> As yet I'm not allowed to say.

TAMINO
>
> Explain this myst'ry; help me now.

PRIEST
>
> An oath of silence is my vow.

TAMINO
>
> When shall this secrecy be broken?

PRIEST
>
> When friendship offers you its hand
> And bids you join our holy band. *(exits)*

TAMINO *(alone)*
>
> Oh, endless night, eternal darkness,
> When will the light dispel my blindness?

SOME VOICES
>
> Soon, stranger, you shall see!

TAMINO
>
> Soon, say if it may be!
> Mysterious voices, answer me,
> Does my Pamina live?

THE VOICES
>
> Pamina, yes, she lives!

TAMINO *(joyfully)*
>
> She lives!
> I need not ask for more.

He takes out his flute.
>
> Oh, could I find the joyful phrases,
> Almighty ones, I'd sing your praises.
> This flute shall speak my grateful thanks
> In music; and from here—here it speaks!

Tamino points to his heart. Then he plays on the flute, and animals of all sorts come forward to listen to him. He stops, and they flee. The birds accompany him.
>
> Ah, now I see your powerful spell, O magic flute.
> It is just as strong as I was told
> Since curious birds and animals come thronging.

Ah, but Pamina does not come.
He plays.
        Pamina, hear me.
He plays.
                In vain!
        Where? How can I make you hear?
He plays, and the sound of his flute is answered by Papageno's pipe.
        Ah! That is Papageno's pipe.
He plays, and Papageno again replies.
        Perhaps he's found Pamina there,
        Perhaps he's bringing her to me,
        Perhaps that means my love is near.
He hastens off.

Scene 16

Enter Papageno and Pamina, without chains.
BOTH
        Walk on tip-toe, courage high.
        We'll be safe now, you and I.
        But I hope Tamino's near
        Or they'll capture us, I fear.
PAMINA
        Oh, Tamino!
PAPAGENO
        Softly, softly, I can lure him.
He pipes, and Tamino's flute is heard in reply.
BOTH
        Oh, what joy it is to hear him.
        That's Tamino's flute, I know.
        Where the flute calls, we must go.
        Here's an end to care and worry.
        Only hurry, only hurry, only hurry!

Scene 17

Monostatos enters.
MONOSTATOS *(mocking them)*
        Only hurry, only hurry, only hurry!
        Ha! Now I have caught you both!

I shall clap you both in irons.
Then I'll feed you to the lions.
So you thought that you could cheat me.
It takes more than you to beat me!
Hey, you slaves, now bring the ropes.

Slaves bring chains.

PAMINA AND PAPAGENO

Ah! The end of all our hopes!

PAPAGENO

Do or die, nothing venture, nothing gain!
Now, you bells, our need is plain!
Let me hear your jingle ringle,
Set their arms and legs a-tingle.

He strikes his instrument.

MONOSTATOS AND SLAVES

That music enchanting, that music so pure!
Larala larala!
I never heard music so fine I am sure.
Larala, larala!

They exit dancing.

PAMINA AND PAPAGENO

How I wish that ev'ry man
Could set bells a-ringing,
Then he'd find that kindness can
Turn all strife to singing.
And throughout his life he'd see
Man can live in harmony.
Only love and singing,
Gentle and forgiving,
Only peace and harmony
Make this life worth living!

A vigorous march with trumpets and drums commences.

CHORUS *(from within)*

All honor Sarastro! Sarastro, hail him!

PAPAGENO

Now what's all this shouting? I'm shiv'ring, I'm quailing!

PAMINA

My friend, all hope is lost I fear!
That sound means that Sarastro's near.

PAPAGENO

Oh, if I were a mouse,

I'd vanish down a mousehole!
Or if I were a tortoise,
I'd curl up in my house.
O gods, deliver us from evil.

PAMINA

The truth will! The truth will,
Truth can shame the devil.

Scene 18

*A procession precedes Sarastro, who rides a triumphal chariot
pulled by six lions.*

CHORUS

All honor, Sarastro! Sarastro, our leader!
He rules us with kindness, his service is freedom!
Long may he reign over and govern our lives
With truth and with justice, all powerful, all wise.

The chorus continues until Sarastro steps down from his chariot.

PAMINA *(kneeling)*

Sir, it is true, I fled from you,
And this you well may call a crime.
But hear, the guilt is not all mine—
That wicked Moor tried to seduce me
And called it love. I had to flee.

SARASTRO

Arise and fear no more, my dear one.
For here we need no inquisition.
I know your heart is true and pure;
You love another, that is sure.
I need not curb this true emotion,
Though I can't grant your freedom yet.

PAMINA

But there's a voice I can't forget:
It is my mother's—

SARASTRO

Whom I shall destroy.
Believe me, she would kill your joy
If I should yield and hand you over.

PAMINA

But yet, I still must love my mother
For she is—

SARASTRO

> She is in my pow'r.
> But now a man must guide and teach you.
> For only he turns womankind
> From paths of pride to ways of virtue.

Scene 19

Monostatos leads in Tamino.

MONOSTATOS

> Now, proud young stranger, come this way;
> Hear what Sarastro has to say.

PAMINA

> Tamino!

TAMINO

> Pamina!

PAMINA

> I know it's him.

TAMINO

> Pamina!

PAMINA

> Tamino!

TAMINO

> It must be true.

PAMINA

> I'll fold you in my arms, my dear.

TAMINO

> I'll fold you in my arms, my dear.

BOTH

> And though death come I'll know no fear!

They embrace.

ALL

> What's this intrusion?

MONOSTATOS

> What an impertinence!
> Release each other! You go too far!

He separates them and kneels.

> O sir, pronounce your fearful sentence.
> I bring a sinner to repentance!
> Now look upon the evildoer.
> He used this curious birdman's lure

To steal Pamina from your palace.
He tried but I have foiled his malice.
You know me, know my watchful eyes—

SARASTRO

You've earned the just reward of spies,
So for your service I award—

MONOSTATOS

Your kindness overwhelms me, Lord!

SARASTRO

Just give him seventy-seven strokes.

MONOSTATOS

O Lord, I don't know what to say!

SARASTRO

No more—what you have earned, I'll pay!

Monostatos is taken away.

ALL

We honor Sarastro, and all men revere him!
He'll punish or pardon; we love him and fear him.

SARASTRO

Now lead these two young strangers in,
And through our temple be their guide;
But first ensure their heads are veiled
For they must now be purified.

*The Speaker and the Second Priest each bring a sort of sack
which they place over the heads of the two strangers.*

FINAL CHORUS

When justice and integrity
Fill ev'ry heart with charity,
When friendship and when brotherhood
Teach ev'ry heart to love the good,
Then ev'ry man shall scorn to lie,
The truth shall live, and death shall die.

ACT 2

*The scene is laid in a palm grove. The trees have silvery trunks
and golden leaves. There are eighteen seats made of palm
leaves, and on each are a pyramid and a large, black horn
bound with gold. In the center are the largest pyramid and the
tallest palm trees.*

Scene 1

Sarastro and the other priests enter solemnly; each holds a palm frond in his hand. A march for wind instruments accompanies their procession.

SARASTRO *(after a pause)*
Initiates of the Temple of Wisdom in the service the great gods Isis and Osiris! With a pure soul I declare that today's assembly is one of the most important of our time. Tamino, a king's son, twenty years of age, is waiting outside the northern gate of our temple. With a virtuous heart he longs to achieve the object which we can only reach through effort and diligence. He wishes to tear off his nocturnal veil and gaze into the sanctuary of supreme light. Today let it be one of our most pressing duties to watch over this virtuous man and to offer him the hand of friendship.

FIRST PRIEST *(rising)*
Is this man virtuous?

SARASTRO
He is.

SECOND PRIEST
Can he keep silent?

SARASTRO
He can.

THIRD PRIEST
Is he charitable?

SARASTRO
He is.—If you consider him worthy, then follow my example. *(They blow the horns three times.)* Touched by the unanimous support of your hearts, Sarastro thanks you in the name of humanity. Prejudice may always censure us, the Initiates, but wisdom and reason will sweep away prejudice like a spiderweb. They will never shake the pillars of our temple. Evil prejudice will vanish once Tamino himself fully grasps the grandeur of our demanding art.—The gods have destined Pamina, the gentle, virtuous maiden, for Tamino; and this is the reason why I took her away from her proud mother. That woman thinks herself powerful. Through deceit and superstition, she hopes to win the people's support and seeks to destroy our temple. But she shall not do so. Tamino, the noble youth, shall help us to defend it, as an Initiate, rewarding virtue and punishing vice.

The Threefold Chord is repeated by all.

SPEAKER *(rising)*

Great Sarastro, we well know and admire the wisdom of your words; but will Tamino endure the heavy trials which await him? Forgive me for speaking freely and expressing my doubts! I am afraid for the young man—that he may, depressed by grief, lose his spirit and fall in the difficult fight. He is a Prince.

SARASTRO

More than that, he is a man!

SPEAKER

What if he should perish in the attempt?

SARASTRO

Then he is given to join Isis and Osiris, and will share the happiness of the gods before we do. *(The Threefold Chord is repeated.)* Let Tamino and his companion be led into the forecourt of the temple. And you, friends, perform your sacred office and teach them their duty as men. *(to the Speaker, who kneels before him)* And you, my friend, whom the gods have chosen through us as the defender of truth, carry out your sacred duties and use your wisdom to instruct the two in the duties of man, and teach them the power of the gods. *(The Speaker exits with one of the Priests. The Priests assemble with their palm fronds.)*

O Isis and Osiris, hear us;
We pray that you will guide this pair!
Oh, grant them strength through all temptation,
Help them endure all dangers there.

CHORUS

Help them endure all dangers there!

SARASTRO

Should they be worthy then acclaim them;
But if they fail and death should claim them,
Then for these mortals life shall cease;
Take them to your abode of peace.

CHORUS

Take them to your abode of peace.

Exit Sarastro, followed by the others.

Transformation

It is night. Thunder from afar. The scene is a small forecourt of the temple, where the remains of sunken columns and pyramids

are visible amongst thorn bushes. On both sides stand service-
able, high doors in the Egyptian style which represent further
buildings at the sides.

Scene 2

Tamino and Papageno enter, led by the Speaker and the Second
Priest, who remove the sacks from their heads and leave them.

TAMINO

What a fearful night! Papageno, are you still there?

PAPAGENO

Yes, more's the pity.

TAMINO

Where do you think we are?

PAPAGENO

If it weren't so dark I could see to tell you—but now— *(thunder)* oh!

TAMINO

What's the matter now?

PAPAGENO

This whole thing is making me uneasy!

TAMINO

It sounds like you're afraid.

PAPAGENO

I'm not exactly afraid. It's just that I feel a chill running up and
down my spine. *(clap of thunder)* Oh, dear!

TAMINO

What's happening?

PAPAGENO

I think I must be coming down with a fever.

TAMINO

Nonsense, Papageno! Be a man!

PAPAGENO

I would rather be a girl! *(violent thunder clap)* Oh, woe! My
last hour has come!

Scene 3

Enter the Speaker and Second Priest with torches.

SPEAKER

Strangers, what do you seek here? What brings you within our
walls?

TAMINO
Friendship and love.

SPEAKER
Are you ready to fight for them with your life?

TAMINO
Yes!

SPEAKER
Even if death would be your lot?

TAMINO
Yes!

SPEAKER
Prince! There is still time to withdraw—one more step, and it will be too late.

TAMINO
May knowledge of wisdom be my achievement and Pamina, the lovely maiden, my reward!

SPEAKER
You are willing to undergo every trial?

TAMINO
I am.

SPEAKER
Your hand! *(They clasp hands.)* There!

SECOND PRIEST
Before you continue, allow me a few words with this stranger. *(to Papageno)* And are you ready to fight for the love of wisdom?

PAPAGENO
Fighting's not my business. I don't really ask for any wisdom. I'm a natural man who's satisfied with sleep, food, and drink; but if I could one day catch myself a pretty wife—

SECOND PRIEST
You'll never find her if you don't undergo our trials.

PAPAGENO
But what are these trials?

SECOND PRIEST
To submit to all our laws, even if you die in the attempt.

PAPAGENO
I'll stay single.

SECOND PRIEST
Even if you could win yourself a virtuous and beautiful girl?

PAPAGENO
I'll stay single.

SECOND PRIEST
But what if Sarastro has a girl waiting for you, just like you in form and feature?
PAPAGENO
Like me? Is she young?
SECOND PRIEST
Young and beautiful.
PAPAGENO
What's her name?
SECOND PRIEST
Papagena.
PAPAGENO
What?— Pa—?
SECOND PRIEST
Papagena.
PAPAGENO
Papagena? I wouldn't mind seeing her just out of curiosity.
SECOND PRIEST
See her you may!
PAPAGENO
But after I've seen her, then must I die? *(Second Priest shrugs his shoulders.)* I'll stay single.
SECOND PRIEST
You can see her, but you mustn't speak a word to her until the appointed time. Do you think you have enough resolve to hold your tongue?
PAPAGENO
Oh, yes!
SECOND PRIEST
Your hand. You shall see her.
SPEAKER
On you too, Prince, the gods impose a salutary silence; otherwise you will both perish. You will see Pamina but may not speak to her. This is first of your trials.
SPEAKER AND SECOND PRIEST
Be on your guard for woman's humors:
That is the rule we follow here.
For often man believes her rumors,
She tricks him, and it costs him dear.
She promises she'll never hurt him
But mocks his heart that's true and brave!

At last she'll spurn him and deceive him—
Death and despair was all she gave.
Exeunt both Priests.

Scene 4

PAPAGENO

Hey, bring some lights here! Lights here! It's odd. Every time
these gentlemen leave, the lights go out as well!

TAMINO

Be patient and mindful that it's the gods' will.

Scene 5

The Three Ladies suddenly appear from a trapdoor.

THE THREE LADIES

So! So! So!
You are in Sarastro's court?
Woe! Woe! Woe!
All your hopes will come to naught!
Tamino, you shall die, you're perjured!
You, Papageno, shall be murdered!

PAPAGENO

No, no, no, I'll die of fright!

TAMINO

Papageno, do be quiet!
A promise made cannot be broken,
But you'll break it once you've spoken.

PAPAGENO

You heard that we are both to die.

TAMINO

Just be patient, do be quiet!

PAPAGENO

Do be quiet and still, be quiet!

THE THREE LADIES

The Queen of Night is now nearby!
She found a secret way in here.

PAPAGENO

She's what? You say the Queen is near?

TAMINO

Still, be silent, quiet I say!

Must you always chatter,
Or do promises not matter?

THE THREE LADIES

Tamino, you are lost forever,
Because you disobey our Queen!
We hear a lot of evil stories
About this awful place of sin.

TAMINO *(aside)*

The wise man thinks and never fears
The evil rumors that he hears.

THE THREE LADIES

They say that once you join their band,
The devil drags you down to hell.

PAPAGENO

Now what the devil, are we damned?
Tell me, Tamino, me as well?

TAMINO

They're only lies old wives repeat,
Thought up by those who lie and cheat.

PAPAGENO

They say the Queen is warning you.

TAMINO

She's but a fickle woman, too.
Be still, you must believe I'm right.
Just be a man, and don't take fright.

THE THREE LADIES *(to Tamino)*

Now why do you behave so rudely?
Tamino humbly indicates that he must not speak.
You, Papageno, too—so cruelly?

PAPAGENO

I'd like to answer that—

TAMINO

Hush!

PAPAGENO *(quietly)*

You see I've got to keep—

TAMINO

Hush!
You find it hard to keep so silent,
But if you talk you'll get the blame!

PAPAGENO

It's really hard to keep so silent,

But if I talk I'll get the blame!

THE THREE LADIES

And now we see they're both defiant;
We'll have to leave them, full of shame!
Man is silent and he's strong;
He knows the time to hold his tongue.

TAMINO AND PAPAGENO

And now they see we're both defiant
They'll have to leave us, full of shame!
For man is silent and he's strong;
He knows the time to hold his tongue.

As the Three Ladies begin to exit, the Initiates call from within.

PRIESTS

The veil of our silence is broken!
Now banish the women who've spoken!

A frightening chord resounds: all the instruments, rolls and claps of thunder and lightning; two claps of thunder at once.

THE THREE LADIES

Away! Away! Away!

They disappear through a trapdoor.

PAPAGENO *(falling to the ground in fear; sings when the music is silent)*

Oh, dear! Oh, dear! Oh, dear!

The Threefold Chord sounds.

Scene 6

Enter the Speaker and Second Priest with torches.

SPEAKER

Young man, we salute you! Your resolute, manly behavior has passed the test. You still have many a rough and dangerous path to follow, but with the gods' help you will succeed. Let us go forward with a pure heart on our journey. *(He places the sack over Tamino's head.)* Follow me!

Exeunt.

SECOND PRIEST

What's this! Stand up, my friend! How are you feeling?

PAPAGENO

I've passed out.

SECOND PRIEST

Stand up! Pull yourself together and be a man!

PAPAGENO *(standing up)*
But tell me, my lords, why must I go through all this suffering and all these frights? If the gods have already destined Papagena for me, why do I have to go through so much danger to win her?
SECOND PRIEST
Your own reason should tell you the answer. Come! It's my duty to lead you onwards. *(He places the sack over his head.)*
PAPAGENO
After so much exercise a man could lose his appetite for love altogether.
Exeunt.

Transformation

The scene changes to a pleasant garden. Trees planted in a horseshoe pattern; in the center stands a bower of flowers and roses, where Pamina is asleep. The moon shines on her face. In front is a lawn seat.

Scene 7

Enter Monostatos, who pauses, then sits down.
MONOSTATOS
Ha, there she is, the coy beauty! And it is on account of this insignificant creature that they wanted to shred the soles of my feet! I can thank my lucky stars that I escaped with any skin left on them to tread on the ground. Hm! What was my offense anyway? That I was charmed by this exotic flower, transplanted here from some foreign soil? And what man could look at her and remain cool and collected, even if he came from a more temperate climate than I do? By all the stars above, this girl will drive me mad! The fire smoldering inside me will flare up and consume me. *(He looks around in all directions.)* If I could be sure I was alone, I'd risk it again. *(He fans himself with both hands.)* What a damnably foolish thing is love! A little kiss ought to be forgiven.

All enjoy the beds of passion,
Cling, caress, and stroke and kiss;
Why should I be out of fashion?
Only I'm denied the bliss.
I am black, that's why I'm hated!

I can love girls just as well.
Life for me without a woman
Is an ever-burning hell!
I'll deny myself no longer
All the secret joys of love!
Fear is strong, but lust is stronger;
Now the hawk desires the dove.
She lies there! And I am lusting;
Now I'll relish fierce desires!
If you find my love disgusting,
You can shut your stupid eyes.

He creeps slowly and quietly toward Pamina.

Scene 8

The Queen of the Night appears, with a thunder clap, from the central trapdoor, so she stands just in front of Pamina.

QUEEN
　Back!

PAMINA *(awaking)*
　O gods!

MONOSTATOS *(recoiling)*
　Oh, woe! That is, if I am not mistaken, the goddess of the night. *(He stands quite still.)*

PAMINA
　Mother! Mother! Mother! *(She falls into her arms.)*

MONOSTATOS
　Mother? Hm! I must hear as much as I can of this. *(He creeps aside.)*

QUEEN
　Be thankful that you were torn away from me by force; otherwise I would no longer call myself your mother. Where is the youth I sent after you?

PAMINA
　Oh, mother, he has withdrawn from the world and people eternally. He has gone to join the Initiates.

QUEEN
　The Initiates? Unhappy daughter! Now you are lost to me forever.

PAMINA
　Lost? Oh, let us escape together, dear mother! Under your protection I'll brave any danger.

QUEEN

Protection? Dear child, your mother can protect you no longer. With your father's death, all my power was buried.

PAMINA

My father—

QUEEN

Gave the sevenfold Circle of the Sun voluntarily to the Initiates. That powerful Circle of the Sun Sarastro now wears on his breast. When I tried to persuade him to change his mind, he replied with a wrinkled brow, "Woman, my last hour is upon me—all my treasure is for you and your daughter." "The all-consuming Circle of the Sun—" said I, interrupting him hurriedly. "Is destined for the Initiates," he answered. "Sarastro will control it as manfully as I have until now. And now no more; do not try to understand things which are inconceivable to a woman's mind. It is your duty to give yourself and your daughter to the authority of wise men."

PAMINA

Dear mother, to judge from all this, the young man must also be lost to me forever?

QUEEN

Lost—unless, before the sun's rays warm the earth once again, you can persuade him to escape with you by these underground chambers. The first light of day will decide whether he is completely given over to you or to the Initiates.

PAMINA

Dear mother, couldn't I love this young man when he is an Initiate as tenderly as I do now? My father himself associated with these wise men. He always spoke of them with joy, extolling their goodness, their understanding, their virtue. Sarastro is no less virtuous.

QUEEN

What do I hear? You, my own daughter, are capable of defending the ignominious principles of these barbarians? You could love a man who, in alliance with my mortal enemy, could at any moment prepare my downfall? Do you see this dagger? It was sharpened for Sarastro. You shall kill him and deliver the mighty Circle of the Sun to me.

PAMINA

But dearest mother!

QUEEN

Silence!

I feel my heart aflame with hate and murder.
Death and destruction blaze around my throne!
Should you not kill Sarastro as I order,
You are no longer any child of mine.
And you shall be neither daughter nor my child,
I'll break our ties forever, renouncing you forever,
Abandoning forever any mother love or care,
If you won't kill Sarastro as I order!
Hear, gods of vengeance! Hear a mother's vow!
She disappears.

Scene 9

PAMINA *(the dagger in her hand)*
Commit murder! O gods! I cannot—I cannot. *(She stands in thought.)*

Scene 10

Monostatos approaches fast, furtively, and very gleefully.
MONOSTATOS
So Sarastro's Circle of the Sun has its uses? And to obtain it, the lovely girl must murder him. That serves my purpose well.
PAMINA
Didn't my mother swear by all the gods that she would forsake me if I did not use this dagger against Sarastro? O gods! What should I do?
MOMOSTATOS
Trust in me! *(He takes the dagger from her. Frightened, Pamina screams.)* Why do you tremble? Because I am black, or because of your criminal intent?
PAMINA *(timidly)*
So you know!
MONOSTATOS
Everything. I know that your life and that of your mother also are in my hands. I have only to say a single word to Sarastro, and your mother would be drowned in that vault of water where the Initiates are, so they say, purified. She will never emerge unharmed from these caverns, unless I so decide. So there is only one way open to you to save yourself and your mother.

PAMINA
And that is?
MONOSTATOS
To love me!
PAMINA *(trembling; aside)*
O gods!
MONOSTATOS *(joyfully)*
The storm bends the little sapling toward me. Well, maiden, yes or no?
PAMINA *(firmly)*
No!
MONOSTATOS *(angrily)*
No? And the reason? Because I am the color of a black phantom? No! Ha! Then you will die! *(He seizes her by the hand.)*
PAMINA
Monostatos, see me here on my knees—spare me!
MONOSTATOS
Love or death! Speak! Your life is at the point of this blade!
PAMINA
I have offered my heart to the Prince.
MONOSTATOS
What do I care for your "offer"? Speak!
PAMINA *(firmly)*
Never!

Scene 11

Sarastro enters.
MONOSTATOS
So, die! *(Sarastro hurls him away.)* Sir, my intention is blameless. I am innocent! They swore to kill you, and I wanted to avenge you.
SARASTRO
I know all too much—know that your soul is as black as your face. And I would punish you with utmost severity for this black conspiracy if I did not know that it was a woman, as evil as her daughter is virtuous, who forged the dagger for the murder. Thanks to the wickedness of this woman's machinations, I will let you go unpunished. Leave!
MONOSTATOS *(while departing)*
Since I can't have the daughter, I'll go to her mother! *(exits)*

Scene 12

PAMINA
Sir, do not punish my mother. Her grief at my absence—
SARASTRO
I know everything—know that she is wandering in the vaults beneath the temple, plotting revenge on me and all humanity. But you will see how I am avenged on your mother. May heaven give the pleasing young man courage and constancy in his purpose, so that you may share his good fortune. Then your mother will have to retire in disgrace to her palace.

> To rule by hate and vengeance
> Is not our practice here,
> And if a man's repentant,
> He's saved by love, not fear.
> If he is lost, a loving hand
> Shows him with joy our happy land.
>
> Here peace and mercy govern,
> By love alone we live;
> Though tyrants rage and threaten,
> We love them and forgive.
> If man can't learn what love can do
> His days on earth are surely few.

Exeunt.

Transformation

The scene changes to a great hall, in which the flying machine can turn. The flying machine has a door and is decorated with roses and flowers. In the foreground are two lawn seats.

Scene 13

Tamino and Papageno, their heads uncovered, are led in by the two Priests.
SPEAKER
We shall leave you both alone here. When the trombone sounds, you must continue in that direction. Farewell, Prince! We shall see each other again just before you reach your goal. And once again, don't forget: silence! *(exits)*

SECOND PRIEST
Papageno, whoever breaks silence in this place will be punished by the gods with thunder and lightning! Farewell. *(exits)*

Scene 14

Tamino sits on a lawn seat.
PAPAGENO *(after a pause)*
Tamino!
TAMINO *(reprovingly)*
Sh!
PAPAGENO
Oh, this is a fine sort of life! Back in my straw hut or in the woods I could at least hear the birds chirping.
TAMINO *(reprovingly)*
Sh!
PAPAGENO
Surely I can talk to myself if I want to? And we two can talk together—after all, we're men.
TAMINO *(reprovingly)*
Sh!
PAPAGENO *(singing)*
Lalala—lalala! They don't even offer you a drop of water in this place, let alone anything stronger!

Scene 15

An ugly Old Woman enters with a large cup of water on a plate.
PAPAGENO *(looking at her for a long time)*
Is that for me?
WOMAN
Yes, my angel!
PAPAGENO *(looks at her again and drinks)*
No more and no less than water. Tell me, mysterious beauty, do you entertain all strangers like this?
WOMAN
Certainly, my angel.
PAPAGENO
I see! In that case, I don't suppose you see many visitors?
WOMAN
Very few!

PAPAGENO
> I can believe that. Come on, old lady, come and talk to me. I'm
> bored out of my feathers. Tell me, how old are you?

WOMAN
> How old am I?

PAPAGENO
> Yes!

WOMAN
> Eighteen years and two minutes.

PAPAGENO
> Eighteen years and two minutes?

WOMAN
> Yes!

PAPAGENO
> Ha, ha, ha! Is that so, my little angel? And have you got a
> boyfriend?

WOMAN
> Certainly!

PAPAGENO
> Is he as young as you are?

WOMAN
> Not quite. He is ten years older.

PAPAGENO
> Ten years older than you? That must be a fiery passion. What's
> your boyfriend called?

WOMAN
> Papageno!

PAPAGENO *(startled; a pause)*
> Papageno? Where is he, this Papageno?

WOMAN
> Sitting right here, my angel.

PAPAGENO
> You mean that I'm your boyfriend?

WOMAN
> Of course, my angel!

PAPAGENO
> *(quickly taking the water and splashing her face with it)*
> Then, tell me, what's your name?

WOMAN
> My name is—
> *A violent thunder clap. The old woman limps hurriedly away.*

PAPAGENO
> Oh, woe! *(Tamino stands up and rebukes him with his finger.)*
> Now I won't say another word as long as I live!

Scene 16

The Three Boys enter in a rose-bedecked flying machine. In its center is a beautifully laid table. One of the boys carries the flute; another the box with the bells.

THE THREE BOYS
> Twice now we've gladly come to meet you,
> Seeking you where Sarastro dwells.
> He bade us find you and, in greeting,
> Sends you the flute and magic bells.
> Now you have suffered thirst and fasting,
> He bids you eat and drink your fill.
> We shall return a third and last time,
> Joy shall reward your steadfast will!
> You must be brave and fear no ill.
> You, Papageno, silence still!
While singing, they put the table onto the stage and fly off.

Scene 17

PAPAGENO
> Tamino, aren't we going to eat anything? *(Tamino plays the flute.)* Oh, you whistle on your flute, and I'll wet my whistle. *(He drinks.)* Ah, this wine is fit for the gods. Now let me see whether Lord Sarastro's kitchen is as well-appointed as his wine cellar. Mm—I don't mind keeping quiet when my mouth is full.
Tamino stops playing the flute.

Scene 18

Enter Pamina.
PAMINA *(joyfully)*
> You're here? I thank the gracious gods for leading me this way! I heard the sound of your flute and ran fast as an arrow toward the sound. You look sad? You won't speak a syllable with your Pamina?

TAMINO *(sighing)*
  Ah!
  He gestures her to go away.
PAMINA
  What's this? Must you shun me? Don't you love me any more?
TAMINO *(sighing)*
  Ah!
  Again he gestures her away.
PAMINA
  I should flee without knowing why? Handsome youth! Have I offended you? Don't hurt my heart even more. I look for comfort and help from you—and would you make my loving heart suffer still more? Do you no longer love me? *(Tamino sighs.)* Papageno, can you tell me what has happened to my friend?
PAPAGENO
  Hm! Hm! Hm!
  His mouth full and holding food in both hands, Papageno waves her away.
PAMINA
  What? You, too? At least explain your silence to me.
PAPAGENO
  Sh!
  He gestures her away.
PAMINA
  Oh, this is worse than suffering, worse than death. *(pause)*
           Beloved, my only Tamino!
           Ah, I know that all is ended.
           Gone forever the joy of love!
           Never will those hours of beauty
           Come again to fill my heart!
           See, Tamino, see my weeping tears
           That flow for you alone.
           Just one word to say you love me,
           Or I'll find rest in death alone!
  Exit Pamina.

Scene 19

PAPAGENO *(eating hastily)*
  There, you see, Tamino, I can keep quiet too when it suits me! Yes, when it comes to important things, I'm a man! *(He drinks.)* I drink to the health of the head cook and the wine steward! *(Threefold*

Chord; Tamino indicates to Papageno to come along.) You go on ahead, I'll catch up. *(Tamino tries to lead him away forcibly.)* The stronger man stays here! *(Tamino threatens him and exits to the right.)* Now I can enjoy my supper in peace. Why should I rush off just when my taste buds are tingling? I'll let it go. I wouldn't leave now, even if Lord Sarastro hitched his six lions to me. *(The lions appear; Papageno is frightened.)* O gods, have pity on me! Tamino, save me! The Lord Lions intend to make a meal of me. *(Tamino returns hurriedly and plays his flute. The lions go away; he makes a sign to Papageno.)* I'm coming! Call me a rascal if I don't follow you everywhere. *(Threefold Chord)* That's for us. We're coming, we're coming! But listen, Tamino, what will become of us? *(Tamino points to the heavens.)* Must I ask the gods? *(Tamino nods.)* Ah, yes! The gods could obviously tell us more than we know! *(Threefold Chord; Tamino tears Papageno away forcibly.)* What's the hurry? We will only arrive in good time to be broiled. *Exeunt.*

Transformation

The scene changes into the vault of a pyramid. The Speaker and other Priests. Two Priests carry an illuminated pyramid on their shoulders; the other Priests hold transparent pyramids of the size of a lantern in their hands.

Scene 20

Eighteen Priests stand in a triangle, six to each side.
CHORUS OF PRIESTS
> O Isis and Osiris, gods resplendent!
> The darkness fades; the blazing sun's transcendent.
> Soon now this brave young man will find a new life:
> Soon too within these walls he'll find all we love.
> His heart is chaste, his soul is pure.
> Soon he will join us, cleansed and pure.

Scene 21

Tamino is brought before the assembly.
SARASTRO
> Prince, so far you have borne yourself with manly composure, but you still have two more dangerous paths to follow. If your

heart still beats so warmly for Pamina, and you wish to rule as
a wise sovereign, may the gods continue to accompany you.—
Your hand! Bring in Pamina!

*Silence falls upon the Priests. Pamina is brought in, wearing the
sack reserved for the Initiates. Sarastro unties the thongs which
hold on the sack.*

PAMINA
Where am I? What a dreadful silence! Tell me, where is my Tamino?
SARASTRO
He is waiting for you to bid a last farewell.
PAMINA
A last farewell? Oh, where is he? Lead me to him.
SARASTRO
Here.
PAMINA
Tamino!
TAMINO
Stay there!
PAMINA
My only joy, ah, must we part?
SARASTRO
You need not fear, but trust his heart!
PAMINA
I fear the dangers that may harm you!
TAMINO
I trust the truth to guard and arm me!
PAMINA
I fear the dangers that may harm you!
SARASTRO
Now trust the truth to guard and arm him!
TAMINO
I trust the truth to guard and arm me!
PAMINA
I hear a dreadful voice of warning
That makes me long for you to stay.
SARASTRO
I serve the lovely gods of morning—
Where they command, he must obey!
TAMINO
I serve the lovely gods of morning—
Where they command, I must obey!

PAMINA

> Oh, if you knew true love's devotion,
> You could not stay so firm and calm.

SARASTRO

> Trust me, he feels the same emotion,
> And know that love need fear no harm.

TAMINO

> Trust me, I feel the same emotion,
> And know that love need fear no harm.

SARASTRO

> The hour has struck, his trials are starting!

PAMINA AND TAMINO

> How grievous are the pangs of parting!

SARASTRO

> Tamino now must take his leave.

TAMINO

> Pamina, I must really leave!

PAMINA

> Tamino, must you really leave?

SARASTRO

> Now he must leave!

TAMINO

> Now I must leave!

PAMINA

> So you must leave!

TAMINO

> Pamina, fare you well!

PAMINA

> Tamino, fare you well!

SARASTRO

> So leave her now
> And keep your vow.
> The hour is come, for you must leave now!

TAMINO AND PAMINA

> Ah, peace of spirit, gone forever!
> Fare you well, fare you well!

SARASTRO

> But not forever!

Exeunt.

Scene 22

PAPAGENO *(off-stage)*
Tamino! Tamino! Do you want to desert me completely? *(He enters searching for Tamino.)* If only I knew where I was.— Tamino!—Tamino!—As long as I live I won't leave you again! Just this once, don't abandon your poor traveling companion.
He goes up to the door through which Tamino was led away.

A VOICE
Go back!
Then, with a clap of thunder, a flame bursts from the door, and there is a loud chord.

PAPAGENO
Merciful gods! Where can I turn? If only I knew where I came in.
He goes to the door through which he entered.

THE VOICE
Go back! *(a thunderclap, flames, and chord as before)*

PAPAGENO
Now they won't let me go forwards or backwards. *(crying)* I suppose they want me to die of starvation. I knew I was wrong to come on this trip.

Scene 23

Enter the Speaker carrying his pyramid.

SPEAKER
Papageno, you deserve to go wandering in the bowels of the earth forever; but the gracious gods release you from punishment. Yet now you will never know the heavenly pleasure of the Initiates.

PAPAGENO
Oh, well, there lots of other folk like me. Right now a good glass of wine would be the greatest pleasure.

SPEAKER
You have no other wish in this world?

PAPAGENO
Not so far.

SPEAKER
You will be served.
Exit the Speaker. At once a large goblet of red wine comes from the ground.

PAPAGENO

Now that's what I call service! *(Drinks)* Marvelous! Heavenly!—
Divine!—Ha! I feel so cheerful I could soar right up to the sun if
only I had wings. Ha! There's such a strange tugging at my heart!
I want—I wish—what might it be? *(While singing, he plays his
magic bells.)*

> I'd like a wife to hug me
> And keep me warm at night!
> A girl who'd really love me
> Is Papageno's right!
> Then living would give me such pleasure
> That princes would envy my treasure,
> I'd know the we meaning of life
> If Heaven would find me a wife.

> I'd like a wife to hug me
> And keep me warm at night!
> A girl who'd really love me
> Is Papageno's right!
> Oh, am I then really so ugly
> That no pretty girl wants to love me?
> Unless a young girl shares my bed,
> I'd really be better off dead.

> I'd like a wife to hug me
> And keep me warm at night!
> A girl who'd really love me
> Is Papageno's right!
> If all you young ladies still spurn me,
> The fire of my passion will burn me.
> But if one will give me a kiss,
> My heartache will turn into bliss.

Scene 24

The Old Woman enters dancing and leaning on her stick.

WOMAN

Here I am, my angel.

PAPAGENO

So you've decided to take pity on me?

WOMAN
Yes, my angel!

PAPAGENO
Just my luck!

WOMAN
And if you promise to be eternally true to me, you'll see how tenderly your mate will love you.

PAPAGENO
Oh, you sweet, foolish thing!

WOMAN
Oh, how I'll embrace you and fondle you and press you to my heart.

PAPAGENO
And press me to your heart?

WOMAN
Now give me your hand to seal our bargain.

PAPAGENO
Not so fast, my dearest. A decision like that needs some thought.

WOMAN
Papageno, I advise you not to hesitate. Give me your hand, or you'll be locked up here forever.

PAPAGENO
Locked up?

WOMAN
Bread and water will be your only food. You'll live friendless, and you'll have to abandon the world forever.

PAPAGENO
Only water to drink? Abandon the world? No, better an old woman than none at all. Well, here's my hand then, with the assurance that I will always be true to you, *(aside)* as long as I don't find anyone prettier.

WOMAN
You swear it?

PAPAGENO
Yes, I swear it! *(The Woman turns into a young woman, dressed just like Papageno.)* Pa—Pa—Papagena! *(He goes to embrace her.)*

Scene 25

SPEAKER *(taking her hastily by the hand)*
Away with you, young woman! He is not yet worthy of you! Back, I say, or pay the consequences!

He drags her inside; Papageno seeks to follow them.

PAPAGENO
Before I withdraw, the earth will have to swallow me up. *(He sinks down.)* O ye gods!

Transformation

The scene changes to a little garden.

Scene 26

THE THREE BOYS
    The sun arises like a vision
    And brings a brighter morn.
    It ends the reign of superstition;
    The day of truth will dawn.
    Let no dark evil now affright men;
    Let truth now shine here and delight them.
    Then every man shall scorn to lie;
    Then truth shall live, and death shall die.

FIRST BOY
    But see, some sorrow grieves Pamina!

SECOND AND THIRD BOYS
    What troubles her?

FIRST BOY
                She seems tormented.

THE THREE BOYS
    It's love that makes her feel this torture.
    Let's try to help and reassure her!
    Pamina's pain is our pain too,
    Though we but guess what love can do.
    She comes; let's wait in hiding here
    Until her purpose is more clear.

They move aside.

Scene 27

Enter Pamina, half-crazed and with a dagger in her hand.

PAMINA *(to the dagger)*
    And so a knife must wed me now?
    Embracing you, I keep my vow.

THE BOYS *(aside)*
>What were those fearful words she said?
>I fear her love has made her mad.

PAMINA
>Ah, see, my love, I'll be your bride;
>Our wedding knot will soon be tied.

THE BOYS
>Madness leads her to destruction;
>Suicide's her sure intention!
>*(to Pamina)*
>Sweet young lady, see us here!

PAMINA
>I will die now, since Tamino,
>Who said he'd always love me,
>Means to break the vow he gave me.
>*(pointing to the dagger)*
>See, my mother gave this knife.

THE BOYS
>Don't forget, God gave you life.

PAMINA
>Better far to end this anguish
>Than to live alone and languish.
>Mother, mother! Your curse makes me wild,
>And your knife destroys your child.

THE BOYS
>Wait, though! Wait and come with us!

PAMINA
>Ah, my cup of grief is full!
>False Tamino, fare you well!
>See, Pamina will not lie:
>Love's forsworn, I swear I'll die.
>*She swings out the dagger to stab herself.*

THE BOYS *(holding her arm)*
>Wait, unhappy girl, oh, wait!
>If you kill yourself through sorrow
>Then your love will die tomorrow,
>For his grief will be so great.

PAMINA *(recovering herself)*
>What? You say that he adores me,
>Though he scorns me and ignores me,
>And pretends he has not heard?

Why then can't he speak a word?

THE BOYS

We can't tell you, but believe us,
And we'll gladly take you with us!
You will see we don't deceive,
For your lover still is true;
He will dare to die for you.

PAMINA

Lead me there, I long to see him.

THE BOYS

Come with us and do not grieve.

ALL FOUR

Two loving hearts that beat together
Are safe from earthly woes forever.
They need not fear the fires of hell;
The gods themselves will guard them well.

Exeunt.

Transformation

Scene 28

*Two large mountains; in one a waterfall, from which the rushing
and roaring are heard; the other spits out fire. Each mountain
has a grille through which the fire and water can be seen; where
the fire burns, the horizon should be bright red, while a black
mist covers the water. Each of the mountains has a rock face
with an iron door. Tamino is lightly clothed, without sandals.
Two men in black armor lead in Tamino. Fire burns on their hel-
mets. They read aloud to him the words inscribed on a pyramid
rising high up in the center, near the grilles.*

THE TWO MEN IN ARMOR

Man that is born of woman walks through life in shadow,
Yet light and truth may pierce through pain and sorrow.
Man must brave death, the dread that haunts him from
    his birth;
Then he shall find his heaven here on earth.
Enlightened, man will see truth pure and whole,
And, finding truth, he shall find his immortal soul.

TAMINO

I'll not fear death, no man is braver;
In seeking truth, I'll never waver.

So fling the gates of terror wide;
I'll gladly bear the trials inside.

PAMINA *(from within)*

Tamino, wait, oh, wait for me!

TAMINO

What was that? Pamina calling?

THE MEN IN ARMOR

Yes, yes, you heard Pamina calling.

TAMINO

Praise be, now she may go with me,
And so as one we'll meet our fate,
Though even death may lie in wait.

THE MEN IN ARMOR

Praise be, for she may go with you,
And so as one you'll meet your fate,
Though even death may lie in wait.

TAMINO

And now, am I allowed to greet her?

THE MEN IN ARMOR

Yes, now you are allowed to greet her!

TAMINO

What joy to see my love again.

THE MEN IN ARMOR

What joy to see your love again.
With her, you'll feel no other pain.
A girl who'll brave death by his side
May surely fill a man with pride.

TAMINO

With her, I'll feel no other pain.
A girl who'll brave death by my side
May surely fill a man with pride.

The door is opened; Tamino and Pamina embrace.

PAMINA

Tamino mine! Oh, what great joy!

TAMINO

Pamina mine! Oh, what great joy!
See here the dreaded doorway
Where pain and death may lie.

PAMINA

Our love will find a sure way;
With you I'll live or die.

> I'll stay here by your side,
> And love shall be our guide!

She takes him by the hand.

> Beside our road the wild thorn grows,
> But midst the thorn there is a rose.
> So take the magic flute and play;
> Its sound will guard us on our way.
> 'Twas carved by father, in an hour of enchantment
> In the deepest forests,
> From root and wood of ancient oak;
> While lightning carved it, storm clouds broke.
> So take the magic flute and play;
> Its sound will guard us on our way.

TAMINO AND PAMINA

> We'll walk unharmed with music's power
> Through deepest night and death's dark hour.

THE MEN IN ARMOR

> They'll walk unharmed with music's power
> Through deepest night and death's dark hour.

The doors are closed behind them. Tamino and Pamina can be seen advancing. The spitting of fire and howling of wind can be heard; at times also the muffled sound of thunder and the rushing of water. Tamino plays his flute. Drums softly sound. As soon as they emerge from the fire, they embrace and take up a position in the center of the stage.

BOTH

> We walked unharmed through flames of passion,
> The temper of our souls was true.
> O flute, now guard us in this fashion,
> Whatever floods of grief may do.

Tamino plays. They are seen to descend and shortly afterwards to come up again. At once a door opens, through which the entrance to a brilliantly lit temple can be seen. Solemn silence. This sight must be of the utmost splendor. The Chorus begins to sing, accompanied by trumpets and drums, but first Tamino and Pamina.

TAMINO AND PAMINA

> O gods! We see a blessed sight!
> Now man's dark world is filled with light.

CHORUS

> Rejoice! Rejoice! You noble pair!

Your hearts were true, your courage rare!
The prize of virtue now is yours!
Come, see the temple's open doors!

Exeunt.

Transformation

The scene changes to the garden again.

Scene 29

Enter Papageno.
PAPAGENO *(calling with his pipes)*
　　　Papagena! Papagena! Papagena!
　　　Sweetheart! Hear me! Are you hiding?
　　　It's useless! Ah, she's gone forever!
　　　I should have tried to be more clever.
　　　I had to talk—I'd not be taught;
　　　I must admit it was my fault.
　　　Since I first drank that lovely wine,
　　　Since I first saw that lovely girl,
　　　I cannot rest till she is mine;
　　　My heart's on fire, my head's awhirl.
　　　Papagena! I adore you!
　　　Papagena! I implore you!
　　　It's no use! She cannot hear me!
　　　Now my life is cold and dreary!
　　　Papageno, save your breath;
　　　Farewell, life, and welcome, death.
He takes the rope from his waist.
　　　I shall hang here on the gibbet
　　　With a rope around my gizzard.
　　　Tired of life and crossed in love,
　　　Farewell, world, I'm off above.
　　　While I lived, the girls ignored me;
　　　Once I'm martyred, they'll adore me.
　　　That's enough, I'm going to die;
　　　Lovely ladies, do not cry.—
　　　But if one of you will have me,
　　　Well, you've one more chance to save me,

Tell me quick, or else I'll go!
Don't be shy, say yes or no—
No one answers; what a silence!
(looking around)
No one, no one loves me?
Not a single lady loves me!
Papageno, give up hope!
You must dangle from a rope!
(looking around)
No, I'll wait a bit, maybe
Till I've counted: one, two, three.

He pipes.

One!
(looking around; piping)
   Two!
(looking around)
      Two is already gone.
(piping)
            Three!
(looking around)
Ah, well, that's the end of me!
Since I cannot find my love,
Cruel world, I'm off above!
(prepares to hang himself)

THE THREE BOYS *(descending from above)*
Oh, wait, O Papageno, that's no way;
You've only one life, live it while you may.

PAPAGENO
That's very true and nicely spoken,
But don't you see my heart is broken?
One day you, too, will want a wife.

THE THREE BOYS
Well, why not ring the bells you carry?
They'll bring the girl you want to marry.

PAPAGENO
I'm such a fool to be so tragic!
Come on, you bells, let's hear your magic!
I long to see my girl again.
Now, bells, let your music
Bring my sweetheart here!

Sweet bells, sound your music!
Make my loved one hear!
As he strikes the bells, the Three Boys run to their flying machine
and bring out the woman.

THE THREE BOYS

Now, Papageno, turn around!
Papageno looks around. During the ritornello, each plays a comic
routine.

PAPAGENO

Pa—Pa—Pa—Pa—Pa—Pa—Papagena!

WOMAN

Pa—Pa—Pa—Pa—Pa—Pa—Papageno!

PAPAGENO

Ah, now shall we live together?

WOMAN

Yes, we'll always live together!

PAPAGENO

Then you'll be my wife forever?

WOMAN

Yes, I'll share your life forever!

BOTH

We'll live together, in love forever!
Oh, what happiness and joy
If the kindly gods will maybe
Bless our marriage with a baby,
A little girl or little boy!

PAPAGENO

First, send a little Papageno!

WOMAN

Then, send a little Papagena!

PAPAGENO

We'll have another Papageno!

WOMAN

Then have another Papagena!

BOTH

Papagena! Papageno! Papagena!
It is the sweetest human pleasure
To have a dear young Pa—Pa—Pa—Pa—pageno
Pa—Pa—Pa—Pa—pagena
To comfort their old parents' lives.

Exeunt both.

Transformation

Scene 30

Monostatos, the Queen, and the Three Ladies enter from two trapdoors, carrying black torches.

MONOSTATOS

> We must be silent, silent, silent!
> We're near the inner temple now.

QUEEN AND THE THREE LADIES

> We must be silent, silent, silent!
> We're near the inner temple now.

MONOSTATOS

> But, Highness, keep your word! You promised—
> I'd have your daughter as my wife.

QUEEN

> I'll keep my word; as I have promised,
> You'll have my daughter as your wife.

THE THREE LADIES

> Her child shall be your wife.

The sounds of muffled thunder and rushing water are heard.

MONOSTATOS

> But now I hear a fearful thunder
> Of roaring flames and surging waves.

QUEEN AND THE THREE LADIES

> Yes, sound of wind and crashing thunder;
> How it re-echoes through these caves!

MONOSTATOS

> Now they are met in solemn counsel.

ALL

> Then it is there we'll fall upon them—
> And while they worship their false lord
> We'll rise and put them to the sword.

THE THREE LADIES AND MONOSTATOS

> Thou, blazing Queen who rules in might,
> Now see us take the vengeance of night.

Transformation

The most violent chord, thunder, and lightning are heard. At once the scene changes so that the whole stage represents a sun.

Sarastro stands on high; Tamino and Pamina are both in priestly robes. On either side of them are the Egyptian Priests. The Three Boys hold flowers in their hands.

MONOSTATOS, QUEEN, AND THE THREE LADIES
>Ah, gods, we're cast down and our glory departs,
>The bright light of truth drives its sword through our
>hearts.

They sink into the ground.

SARASTRO
>The grandeur and glory of truth sheds its light,
>Destroyed are the sinful, destroyed is the night.

CHORUS OF PRIESTS
>Hail the two who triumphed!
>You dared all for truth!
>Praise the god of wisdom,
>See the truth shining bright!
>For truth is all-powerful,
>And love is his lord,
>And beauty and wisdom
>Shall earn their reward!

*Translated by Michael Geliot (lyrics)
and by Anthony Besch (dialogue);
adapted by James Steakley*

FIDELIO
An Opera in Two Acts

Libretto from the French of Jean-Nicolas Bouilly
by Joseph Sonnleithner, Stephan von Breuning,
and Georg Friedrich Treitschke

Ludwig van Beethoven

CHARACTERS

DON FERNANDO, *Minister of State*	Baritone
DON PIZARRO, *Governor of a state prison*	Baritone
FLORESTAN, *a prisoner*	Tenor
LEONORE, *his wife, under the name "Fidelio"*	Soprano
ROCCO, *the prison master*	Bass
MARZELLINE, *his daughter*	Soprano
JAQUINO, *keeper*	Tenor
FIRST PRISONER	Tenor
SECOND PRISONER	Bass
CAPTAIN OF THE GUARD, OFFICERS, SOLDIERS, PRISONERS OF STATE, AND PEOPLE	

Place: a Spanish state prison, some miles distant from Seville.
Time: the eighteenth century.

ACT 1

The courtyard of the state prison. In the background, the main gate and a high protective wall overhung with trees. Set into the closed gate itself is a small entrance which can be opened for individual visitors on foot. Near the gate is the gatekeeper's lodge. The stage set to the viewers' left depicts the chambers of the prisoners; all the windows are barred, and the numbered doors are iron-studded and secured with strong crossbars. Forwardmost is the door to the prison master's house. On the right stand trees enclosed in iron railings, which with a garden gate mark the entrance to the castle garden.

Scene 1

Marzelline is pressing laundry in front of her door; beside her is a coal brazier on which she heats the iron. Jaquino is standing near his lodge; he opens the door to several people who give him parcels that he puts in his lodge.

JAQUINO *(amorously, and rubbing his hands)*
   My treasure, at last we're alone
   To talk by ourselves without worry.

MARZELLINE *(continuing her work)*
   That talk we will have to postpone;
   There's work to be done—I must hurry.

JAQUINO
   You obstinate girl, just a word!

MARZELLINE
   Then say it, you're sure to be heard.

JAQUINO
   If you turn away, so disdaining,
   No words am I able to say.

MARZELLINE
   If you don't stop your complaining,
   I'll stop up my ears right away.

JAQUINO
   If you'll only listen to me
   One moment, then I'll let you be.

MARZELLINE
   I see he will not let me be!
   What is it then, tell it to me!

JAQUINO

You are the wife I selected,
You know that?

MARZELLINE

It seems very clear.

JAQUINO

And if I were not rejected,
You'd say then?

MARZELLINE

We'd be a pair.

JAQUINO

We could in a few weeks endeavor—

MARZELLINE

The day now, indeed, you decree!
Knocking is heard.

JAQUINO

The devil, they knock here forever!

MARZELLINE

At last he must go, I am free!

JAQUINO

And just when my vict'ry seemed near;
She never will say something clear!

MARZELLINE

His love makes me nervous, and it fills me with fear;
How endless the time is, whenever he's near!
*Jaquino opens the door, takes a parcel, and deposits it in his
quarters; meanwhile Marzelline continues.*
I know that the poor man must suffer,
It pains me to see his sad plight!
Fidelio I've chosen as lover,
And loving him brings me delight.

JAQUINO *(returning)*

Where was I? She will not attend!

MARZELLINE

He's back now, beginning again!

JAQUINO

When will your official consent be?
Today, won't you please let me know!

MARZELLINE *(aside)*

Oh, why does he have to torment me?
(to him) Today, then, tomorrow, and always and ever,
no, no!

JAQUINO

> Your heart is as cold as the snow!
> For all of my longing and begging no mercy you show!

MARZELLINE *(aside)*

> I have to be hard so he'll go;
> He'll hope if one smile I bestow.

JAQUINO

> So you mean I must ever, ever be sighing?
> You mean it?

MARZELLINE

> Now do go away!

JAQUINO

> What? To look at you, you are denying?
> That also?

MARZELLINE

> All right, you may stay.

JAQUINO

> You promised me that we'd be together—

MARZELLINE

> I promised? No, that could not be!

Knocking is heard.

JAQUINO

> The devil! They knock here forever!

MARZELLINE *(aside)*

> At last he must go, I am free!

JAQUINO *(aside)*

> She trembled and nearly agreed;
> Who knows, more time and I'll succeed.

MARZELLINE

> That knocking is welcome indeed;
> I'm worried from hearing him plead!

Another package is delivered.

JAQUINO

If I haven't opened this door at least two hundred times today, my name isn't Kaspar Eustach Jaquino. *(to Marzelline)* At last I can have another word with you. *(Someone knocks.)* Good Lord, so soon again! *(He goes to open.)*

MARZELLINE *(downstage)*

How can I help it if I'm no longer as fond of him as I used to be?

JAQUINO
(to the person who knocked, while closing the door hastily) All right! I'll take care of it. *(coming forward to Marzelline)* So— now no one will disturb us, I hope.

ROCCO *(calling from the castle garden)*
Jaquino! Jaquino!

MARZELLINE
Do you hear? Father is calling!

JAQUINO
We can let him wait a little. Now, to return to our love—

MARZELLINE
Do go along. Father will be wanting news of Fidelio.

JAQUINO *(jealously)*
Oh, of course, then one can't be quick enough.

ROCCO *(calling again)*
Jaquino! Don't you hear?

JAQUINO *(shouting)*
I'm coming! *(to Marzelline)* Just wait here; in two minutes we'll be together again.

He exits into the garden, the gate of which remains open.

Scene 2

MARZELLINE
Poor Jaquino. I almost feel sorry for him. But can I change it? I used to be quite fond of him; then Fidelio came to live with us, and since that time everything in me and around me has changed. Ah! *(She sighs ashamedly.)* My pity for Jaquino makes me realize how very much I care for Fidelio. I think he is fond of me, too, and if I only knew father's views, perhaps my happiness soon would be complete.

> Ah, how I long to be thy wife,
> With heart and hand committed!
> A maiden longs for love and life,
> Yet never dares admit it.
> But when no blush need cross my face,
> To share a loving, warm embrace,
> *(sighing and laying a hand on her breast)*
> When naught can separate us—
> My heart with hope is burning bright

That soon I'll know that sweet delight;
What joys untold await us!

In tranquil domesticity
I'll wake to meet the morrow;
We'll greet each other tenderly
And work to banish sorrow.
And when our daily chores are done,
Fair ev'ning dims the setting sun,
(sighing and laying a hand on her breast)
We'll rest in well-earned leisure.
My heart with hope is burning bright
That soon I'll know that sweet delight,
A life of untold pleasure!

Scene 3

Rocco enters from the garden. Jaquino follows him carrying garden tools and goes with them into Rocco's house.

ROCCO
Good day, Marzelline! Hasn't Fidelio come back yet?

MARZELLINE
No, father.

ROCCO
The hour is approaching for me to send the dispatches to the Governor, and Fidelio was to pick them up. I'm waiting for him impatiently.
During the last words, someone knocks at the gate.

JAQUINO *(coming out of Rocco's house)*
Coming, coming!
He runs with a show of zeal to open the gate.

MARZELLINE
He must have had to wait so long at the blacksmith's. *(Leonore has entered meanwhile; excitedly:)* Here he is! Here he is!

Scene 4

Leonore is clad in a dark doublet, red waistcoat, dark knee-breeches, short boots, a broad belt of black leather with a copper buckle; her hair is put up in a net cap. On her back she carries a basket with provisions and in her arms chains, which she puts down upon entering at the gatekeeper's lodge; at her side hangs a tin box on a cord.

MARZELLINE *(hastening to Leonore)*

How he's laden down! Dear God! Sweat is pouring from his brow.

She takes her handkerchief and dries Leonore's face.

ROCCO

Wait! Wait!

With Marzelline he helps her lay down the basket; it is set down left by the archway.

JAQUINO *(in the foreground, aside)*

To think I hurried to open up, just to let that fellow in!

He goes into his lodge but soon comes out again, bustling about busily while actually observing Marzelline, Leonore, and Rocco.

ROCCO *(to Leonore)*

Poor Fidelio, this time you've burdened yourself too much.

LEONORE *(coming forward, drying her face)*

I must admit, I am a little tired. The blacksmith took so long mending the chains, I thought he would never finish.

ROCCO

Are they all fixed now?

LEONORE

Certainly, good and strong. None of the prisoners will be able to break them.

ROCCO

How much did it cost, all together?

LEONORE

About twelve piasters. Here is the exact bill.

ROCCO *(looking over the bill)*

Good, well done! By heaven, there are things here on which we can earn at least double! You are a clever lad! I simply can't understand how you do your reckoning. You buy everything more cheaply than I do. In the six months since I turned the buying of provisions over to you, you've saved more than I did before in a whole year. *(aside)* The rascal's obviously going to all this effort for the sake of my Marzelline.

LEONORE

I'm just trying to do whatever I can.

ROCCO

Yes, yes, you're a good lad. No one could be more diligent, more sensible. You please me more with every passing day, and—you

may be sure—your reward will not be long in coming.
*During these last words he casts glances at Leonore and
Marzelline alternately.*
LEONORE *(embarrassed)*
  Please don't think I'm doing my duty just for reward—
ROCCO
  Hush! *(with glances as before)* Do you think I cannot read your
  heart?
  *He appears to enjoy Leonore's growing embarrassment and
  then goes to the side to examine the chains.*
MARZELLINE
  *(who, while Rocco was praising Leonore, showed the greatest
  feeling and gazed at her lovingly with growing emotion; aside)*
      What joy when he is near!
      My heart will burst in me!
      He loves me, it is clear;
      Ah, soon how happy I shall be.
LEONORE *(aside)*
      The danger is severe;
      And hope is hard to see.
      She loves me, it is clear;
      What pain the Fates decree!
ROCCO *(who meanwhile has returned downstage; aside)*
      She loves him, it is clear!
      Yes, daughter, I'll agree;
      A couple without peer,
      A happy pair they'll be!
JAQUINO
  *(watching them and moving closer and closer to the side, a little
  behind the others; aside)*
      What dreadful signs appear!
      Her father will agree!
      My heart will break, I fear;
      There's nothing left for me.
  Jaquino returns to his lodge.
ROCCO
  Listen, Fidelio! Even though I don't know how or where you
  came into the world, and even if you had no father at all, I
  know what I'm going to do; I—I'll make you my son-in-law.
MARZELLINE *(hastily)*
  Will you do it soon, father dear?

ROCCO *(laughing)*

My, my, what a hurry! *(more seriously)* Once the Governor has departed for Seville, we shall have more time. You know he goes once a month without fail to render an account of everything that has happened here in the state prison. In a few days he must go again, and the day after he leaves I'll let you two marry. You may count on that!

MARZELLINE

The day after he leaves! That does seem quite reasonable, father dear!

LEONORE *(very disconcerted beforehand, but now pretending joy)*

The day after he leaves? *(aside)* Oh, what a new predicament!

ROCCO

Well, my children, you're quite in love, aren't you? But that's not all it takes to make a good, contented household; one also needs— *(gestures as if counting money)*

> If one has no gold for spending,
> Happiness can never last;
> Life creeps sadly to its ending;
> Many troubles must be passed.
> But when you have pockets that jingle with gold,
> You'll find that your life is enchanted;
> Since love and power for money are sold,
> Your slightest desire will be granted.
> Good fortune is your slave to hold,
> If you possess that lovely thing called gold!
>
> With a naught, a naught combining
> Will remain a tiny sum;
> If on love alone you're dining,
> Hunger soon or late will come.
> With smiles and delight, may the future unfold,
> To guide and bless all your wishes;
> Your loved one to hold you, your purse full of gold,
> And life that is long and auspicious.
> Good fortune is your slave to hold,
> If you possess that mighty thing called gold!

LEONORE

That's easy for you to say, Master Rocco, but as for me, I assert that the union of two hearts that are in harmony is the source of true wedded bliss. *(warmly)* Oh, that bliss must be the greatest treasure on earth. *(catching and moderating herself)* But there is something else which I would cherish no less, though I'm sad to see that I shall not win it, despite all my efforts.

ROCCO
And what might that be?

LEONORE
Your trust! Forgive me this slight reproach, but I often see you coming back from this castle's subterranean vaults quite out of breath and exhausted. Why don't you allow me to accompany you there? I would be so glad if I could help you with your work and share your toil.

ROCCO
But you know I have the strictest orders to allow no one, whoever it may be, down to the prisoners of state.

MARZELLINE
But there are far too many of them in this fortress. You're working yourself to death, dear father.

LEONORE
She's right, Master Rocco. To be sure, one should do one's duty. *(tenderly)* But we are also allowed to consider now and then how we can spare ourselves a little for those near and dear.
She presses one of his hands into hers.

MARZELLINE *(pressing Rocco's other hand to her breast)*
A man ought to take good care of himself for the sake of his children.

ROCCO *(looking at them both with emotion)*
Yes, you're right, in time this hard work would be too much for me. The Governor is quite strict, but he must allow me to take you along to the secret dungeons. *(Leonore makes an impetuous gesture of joy.)* Yet there is one vault into which I'll never be able to lead you, even though I can trust you implicitly.

MARZELLINE
You must mean the one confining that prisoner of whom you have spoken a few times, father?

ROCCO
You've guessed it.

LEONORE *(tentatively)*
I suppose he's been imprisoned here a long time?

ROCCO
It's over two years now.

LEONORE *(vehemently)*
Two years, you say? *(regaining composure)* He must be a terrible criminal.

ROCCO
Or he must have terrible enemies; it amounts to much the same thing.
MARZELLINE
So no one has ever been able to find out where he comes from or what his name is?
ROCCO
Oh, how often he's wanted to speak with to me about all that!
LEONORE
And?
ROCCO
For people of our station, it's best to know as few secrets as possible; and so I've never listened to him. I might have revealed something at the wrong moment, and besides, it wouldn't have helped him anyway. *(confidentially)* Well, he won't be troubling me very long. He can't last much longer now.
LEONORE *(aside)*
Great God!
MARZELLINE
Good heavens, how did he earn such severe punishment?
ROCCO *(even more confidentially)*
For one month now, at Pizarro's command, I've had to reduce his ration. Now he gets no more than two ounces of black bread and a half-measure of water every twenty-four hours; no light but the shine of a lamp, no more straw, nothing—nothing!!
MARZELLINE
O dear father, don't take Fidelio to him; he couldn't bear the sight!
LEONORE
But why not? I'm courageous and strong.
ROCCO *(clapping her shoulder)*
Good, my son, good. If I could tell you how I had to struggle with myself at first in my profession! And I was quite a different sort than you, with your fine skin and your soft hands!

> My son, you're right;
> Who conquers fright,
> Can face all opposition.
> Be brave and strong,
> Though all goes wrong,
> And fear no apparition.

LEONORE *(with energy)*
> My eyes are clear,
> I have no fear;
> I shall be bold and daring.

For such a prize
Shall love arise
To suffer pain beyond all bearing.

MARZELLINE *(tenderly)*

Your tears will flow
As you, below,
To duty are attending.
But when you're done,
True love is won
And happiness unending.

ROCCO

Great fortune you shall be achieving.

LEONORE

In God and right I am believing.

MARZELLINE

Look also in my eyes,
Perceiving the pow'r of love is also great.
Ah, yes, what joys for us await.

LEONORE

Ah, yes, what joys may yet await.

ROCCO

Ah, yes, what joys for you await.
I shall request today the Governor's permission
That in my labors you may share.

LEONORE

If you delay your requisition
Another day, I shall despair.

MARZELLINE

Dear father, ask before tomorrow,
So shortly we shall be a pair.

ROCCO

I'm living now on time I borrow;
I need some help, I am aware.

LEONORE *(aside)*

How long have I been prey to sorrow!
Come, hope, with strength and comfort there!

MARZELLINE *(tenderly to Rocco)*

O father dearest, what would you say?
To guide and cheer us, you have to stay!

ROCCO

You must prepare, then you will share

The joys of which you're dreaming.
Now give your hand to seal the bond,
While tears of joy flow streaming.

LEONORE

Your kindly care will help me dare
To soon fulfill my dreaming.
(aside) I gave my hand in that sweet bond,
Now bitter tears are streaming.

MARZELLINE

My love, beware! How much I care,
What longings fill my dreaming!
A lasting bond with heart and hand,
What joyous tears are streaming.

ROCCO

But now it is time for me to take the dispatches to the Governor. *(march music)* Ah! Here he comes himself! *(to Leonore)* Give them here, Fidelio, and then off with you both! *Leonore takes off the tin box, gives it to Rocco, and goes with Marzelline into the house.*

During the foregoing march, the main gate is opened from outside by sentries, and officers enter with a detachment of soldiers. Then Pizarro enters, and the gate is closed again.

Scene 5

PIZARRO *(to the officers)*

Three sentries to the rampart! Six men day and night at the drawbridge, and as many on the garden side. Anyone approaching the moat of the fortress is to be brought before me at once! *(to Rocco)* Any developments?

ROCCO

No, sir!

PIZARRO

Where are the dispatches?

ROCCO *(taking the letters out of the tin box)*

Here they are.

PIZARRO *(opening the papers and looking through them)*

Always recommendations or reproofs. If I were to pay attention to all this, there would be no end to it. *(stops at one letter)* What's this? I think I recognize this handwriting. Let's see. *(He opens the letter and walks forward, while Rocco and the guards withdraw. Pizarro reads:)* "Let me inform you that the Minister has found out that the state prisons under your supervision hold several victims by arbitrary force. He is leaving tomorrow to surprise you with an investigation. Be on the alert, and secure yourself as best you may." *(disconcerted)* God! If he should discover that I'm holding this man Florestan here in chains, whom he imagines died long ago, the man who so often goaded me to vengeance— and if he should unmask me before the Minister and cause me to lose his favor! Yet there is one remedy! *(quickly)* One bold deed can dispel all my worries.

> I'll make the moment mine!
> To my revenge proceeding
> Fulfill destiny's design!
> To see him torn and bleeding;
> Oh, wonder, joy divine!
> I once was low in station,
> A prey to degradation,
> Just a beast to mock and flout!
> Now destiny is willing,
> The prey shall do the killing;
> And as his blood is flowing
> His dying breath is going,
> Then in his ear I'll shout:
> I've won the final bout!

CHORUS OF SENTRIES *(sotto voce to each other)*
> He speaks of wounds and dying;
> Sharp on your rounds be spying!
> Grave matters are about!

PIZARRO

I have not a moment to lose to ready everything for my scheme. The Minister is to arrive today. Only the utmost precaution and speed can save me. *(to the officer)* Captain, listen! *(He leads him forward and speaks quietly to him.)* Go at once to the top of the tower with a trumpeter. Keep the strictest watch on the road from Seville. As soon as you see a coach accompanied by cavalry approaching, have the trumpeter give a signal instantly. You understand: instantly! I expect utmost punctuality, and you are answerable for it with your head. *(The captain leaves; to the sentries:)* Away, to your posts! *(The sentries leave; to Rocco:)* Old man!

ROCCO
  Sir!

PIZARRO *(examining him attentively; aside)*
  I must try to win him over. Without his help I cannot carry it out.
  (aloud) Come closer!

      Now, old one, help me and hurry;
      And you shall not be sorry;
      You'll be a wealthy man;
      (throwing him a purse)
      Take that, to start my plan.

ROCCO

      Command me, in a hurry,
      I'll help you if I can.

PIZARRO

      Your head is calm, collected;
      Your courage is respected;
      Your post for years you've been fulfilling.

ROCCO

      Your wishes? Tell me!

PIZARRO

                Killing!

ROCCO *(terrified)*
      What!

PIZARRO

      Listen to the plan!
      You shake? Are you a man?
      We dare delay no longer;
      The danger to the state
      From him below is great
      And daily growing stronger.

ROCCO

      O sir!

PIZARRO

      You still would wait?
      (aside) His life must now be ending,
      Or all is lost to me.
      Pizarro is unbending.
      'Tis you shall fall to me.

ROCCO *(aside)*
      My knees, I feel, are bending;
      But how can I agree?

No life shall I be taking,
Whatever is to be.
(to Pizarro)
Sir, no! To do a killing
Is not my duty here.

PIZARRO

Then I myself am willing,
If you have so much fear.
Now hurry, quickly go
Where the prisoner below,
You know—

ROCCO

Who nearly dies,
And like a shadow lies?

PIZARRO *(fiercely)*

To him! Go to the knave.
I'll wait a little distant
While you enlarge the cistern
To make a grave.

ROCCO

And then?

PIZARRO

Then in disguise I'll come
Into his prison stealing.
He shows the dagger.
One blow—and he'll be dumb!

ROCCO *(aside)*

In chains, with nought to feed him,
How long have been his pains;
His death will bring him freedom,
The sword will cut his chains.

PIZARRO *(aside)*

His chains to death will lead him;
Too short has been his pain!
His death will be my freedom,
And peace I shall regain.
(to Rocco) Now, old one! We must hurry!
Did you understand me?
You give a signal,
Then, in disguise, I'll come
Into his prison stealing—

One blow—and he'll be dumb!
Pizarro exits to the garden, Rocco following him.

Scene 6

Leonore enters, in a state of extreme inner turmoil, from the opposite side and watches the two departing with increasing agitation.
LEONORE

O monstrous one, what is your quest?
What evil is your rage concealing?
Does mercy's voice or human feeling
Arouse no more your savage breast?
And yet, if angry waves are swirling,
Raging in his embittered heart,
For me a rainbow is unfurling
To force the threat'ning clouds to part.
Its tranquil light is softly falling,
The golden days of old recalling,
To calm my mind till fears depart.
Come, Hope, and let the final star
Of suff'ring shine unwaning!
And light my goal, though it be far,
The goal that my love shall be attaining.

I follow faith unswerving;
I shall not fail,
Love shall prevail
In wifely duty serving!
O thou for whom I've suffered so,
Could I but join your station,
Where malice chained you there below,
And bring sweet consolation!
She exits into the garden.

Scene 7

Marzelline comes out of the house, followed by Jaquino.
JAQUINO
But, Marzelline—
MARZELLINE
Not a word, not one syllable! I'll hear no more of your silly love-sighs, and that is final.

JAQUINO
Who could have foretold all this when I decided to go ahead and fall in love with you? Back then I was your good, dear Jaquino at every turn; you had me heat the iron, fold the laundry, take packages to the prisoners, in short, do everything a respectable girl can allow a respectable bachelor to do. But since this Fidelio—

MARZELLINE *(quickly interrupting him)*
I don't deny it, I liked you; but look, I'll be frank, it wasn't love. Fidelio appeals to me much more; between him and me I feel a much deeper understanding.

JAQUINO
What? Understanding with such a vagrant boy, who comes from God knows where, whom your father took in at the gate there out of pure pity, who—who—

MARZELLINE *(angrily)*
Who is poor and abandoned, and whom I will marry despite all that!

JAQUINO
Do you suppose I'll just put up with that? You'd best be sure it doesn't happen in my presence: I might play quite a trick on you two!

Scene 8

Rocco and Leonore enter from the garden.

ROCCO
What are you two quarreling about now?

MARZELLINE
Oh, father, he's after me all the time.

ROCCO
What for?

MARZELLINE *(running to Leonore)*
He wants me to love him, to marry him.

JAQUINO
Yes, yes, she ought to love me, she ought at least to marry me; and I—

ROCCO
What? So you're convinced that I took such good care of my one and only daughter, *(he strokes Marzelline's chin)* making such an effort to raise her to her sixteenth year, and all for this gentleman here! *(He looks laughingly at Jaquino.)* No, Jaquino, marriage with you is out of the question now; I'm occupied with other, wiser plans.

MARZELLINE
I understand, father. *(softly and tenderly)* Fidelio!

LEONORE
Let's change the subject.—Rocco, I've requested you a few times now to let the poor prisoners confined above ground here into our fortress garden. You've always promised it and postponed it. Today the weather is so beautiful, and the Governor doesn't come here at this time of day.

MARZELLINE
Oh, yes! I join in his entreaty!

ROCCO
Children, without the Governor's permission?

MARZELLINE
But he was talking with you for such a long time. Perhaps you're supposed to do him a favor, and then he won't be so exacting.

ROCCO
A favor? You're right, Marzelline. I can risk it because of that. All right, Jaquino and Fidelio, open the less secure prison cells. But I will go to Pizarro and keep him away while *(to Marzelline)* speaking on your behalf.

MARZELLINE *(pressing his hand)*
That's splendid, father.

Rocco exits into the garden. Leonore and Jaquino unlock the well-secured cell doors, then withdraw with Marzelline into the background, and observe with sympathy the prisoners, who gradually emerge.

Scene 9

During the ritornello, the prisoners gradually issue from the cell doors.

CHORUS OF PRISONERS
      Oh, what delight to draw a breath
      Where freedom's air refreshes!
      'Tis life, here life is precious;
      The prison is like death.

FIRST PRISONER
      We'll trust in God, depending
      On help of Heaven's sending!
      The voice of Hope still speaks to me,
      We shall find peace, we shall be free.

ALL OTHERS

> O Heaven! Rescue! How we yearn!
> O Freedom! Will you return?

Here a sentry appears on the ramparts and goes away again after brief observation.

SECOND PRISONER

> Speak softly and restrain your sighs!
> For all around are ears and eyes.—

ALL

> Speak softly and restrain your sighs!
> For all around are ears and eyes.
> Oh, what delight to draw a breath
> Where freedom's air refreshes!
> 'Tis life, here life is precious.
> Speak softly and restrain your sighs!
> For all around are ears and eyes.

Before the chorus is completely ended, Rocco appears in the background and speaks urgently with Leonore. The prisoners withdraw into the garden; Rocco and Leonore advance forward.

Scene 10

LEONORE

> Tell me, what news?

ROCCO

> It all is fine!
> With all the courage that is mine,
> I told him my request; can you envision
> What he replied to my plea?
> Your marriage and help in my work have his permission;
> From now on, on my rounds I'll take you down with me.

LEONORE *(impulsively)*

> From now on? From now on?
> Oh, what delight! Oh, what good fortune!

ROCCO

> I'm glad to see your pleasure,
> And now the time is right
> For us to go together—

LEONORE

> To where?

ROCCO

> To him who lies below,
> Whom, ev'ry time I feed him,
> Gets less to eat, and starves, I know.

LEONORE

> Ha! Will they give him freedom?

ROCCO

> Oh, no!

LEONORE

> Then what?

ROCCO

> Oh, no! Oh, no!
> *(mysteriously)*
> He shall be in a way set free;
> Before the hour is ended—
> In secret we'll attend it—
> Within his grave he'll be!

LEONORE

> So he is dead?

ROCCO

> Not still, not still!

LEONORE *(shrinking back)*

> Is it your duty then to kill?

ROCCO

> No, dear young fellow, fear no ill.
> Do murder Rocco never will.
> It is the Governor himself who'll meet us there;
> The grave is all that we'll prepare.

LEONORE *(aside)*

> My husband's grave to be preparing!
> Could one suffer more than I?

ROCCO

> I dare not help with food or caring;
> It would be better that he die.
> To work we now must be proceeding;
> You come and give what help I'm needing.
> Hard does the jailer earn his bread.

LEONORE

> I'll follow you unto the death.

ROCCO

> There is a well that needs repairing;

It will be easy, digging there.
Think not I like the job we're sharing;
It makes you shudder, I'm aware.

LEONORE

I'm not accustomed to it yet.

ROCCO

I share the burden with regret,
But I'm too weak alone, I fear,
To serve a master so severe.

LEONORE *(aside)*

Oh, what distress!

ROCCO *(aside)*

He seems to weep now.
(aloud) No, no, you stay here; I'll go alone now.
I'll go alone.

LEONORE *(clinging to him fervently)*

Oh, no, oh, no!
I still must fly to him who lies there,
Though it be I myself who dies there.

ROCCO, LEONORE

So let us no more linger here;
The call of duty is severe!

Scene 11

Jaquino and Marzelline burst in breathlessly.

MARZELLINE

Ah, father, run away!

ROCCO

What have you heard?

JAQUINO

Do not delay!

ROCCO

What has occurred?

MARZELLINE

Pizarro follows raging, wild,
And threatens you!

ROCCO

Steady, steady!

LEONORE

All quickly go!

ROCCO

One question, though:
Say, does he know?

JAQUINO

He already knows!

MARZELLINE

It was a guard who told
Him the pris'ners were out,
And you had freed them.

ROCCO

Into their cells now quickly lead them!
Jaquino exits into the garden.

MARZELLINE

You know his awful rages;
His anger knows no bounds.
She hastens after Jaquino.

LEONORE

My blood within me rages!
My heart so wildly pounds!

ROCCO

Compassion is courageous;
I fear no tyrant's frowns.

Scene 12

Enter Pizarro.

PIZARRO

Presumptuous idiot! For what reason
Dare you to flout the law's decree?
You, who are paid to guard the prison
Bars, let the prisoners go free?

ROCCO *(abashed)*

O sir!

PIZARRO

So then!

ROCCO *(seeking an excuse)*

The springtime breezes,
The sun was warm, the air was clear.
(growing bolder)
Then—if my action still displeases,
Another reason you should hear.

(doffing his cap)
This is the name-day of our ruler;
'Tis so the prison celebrates.
(aside to Pizarro)
Down there, he'll die—let these then wander
Still, happily walk here and yonder;
Reserve your rage for him who waits.

PIZARRO *(quietly)*
Go down, then; dig his grave, and hurry;
Here let me find surcease from worry.
Lock in their cells once more the men,
And do not be so bold again!

THE PRISONERS *(returning from the garden)*
Farewell, O warm and sunlit day,
Too soon your light is ending.
The night is now descending;
For us will come no dawning ray.

MARZELLINE *(gazing at the prisoners)*
How fast they came to greet the day;
How slowly they're descending.
(aside) Their murmurs rise, heart-rending;
Here can no joy, no pleasure stay.

LEONROE *(to the prisoners)*
You heard his words, so don't delay,
Down to the cells descending.
(aside) Fear with my hope is blending!
Is there no justice to gainsay?

JAQUINO *(to the prisoners)*
You heard his words, so don't delay,
Down to the cells descending.
(aside, observing Rocco and Leonore)
What can they be intending?
Could I but hear the words they say.

PIZARRO
Now, Rocco, you must not delay,
Down to his cell descending.
(aside) You shall not be ascending
Until my justice has its way.

ROCCO
No, sir, I shall no more delay,

At once I'll start descending.
(aside) My trembling knees are bending!
What dreadful orders I obey!
*The prisoners return to their cells, which Leonore and Jaquino
lock up.*

ACT 2

*A dark, subterranean dungeon. To the left is a cistern covered
with stones and rubble. In the background are several openings
in the wall, covered with grilles through which can be seen the
steps of a stairway leading down from the heights; on the right
are the final steps and the door to the cell. A lamp is burning.*

Scene 1

*Florestan, alone, is seated on a stone; around his body is a long
chain, the end of which is fastened to the wall.*

FLORESTAN

Lord, how dark it is! By silence I'm tormented!
Here in the black abyss, nought, of life there is no sign.
Oh, dreadful trial! Yet 'tis right if God has sent it!
I'll not complain, the worst of suff'ring has been Thine.

With my life in spring still youthful,
All my hopes I sacrifice;
And for daring to be truthful,
Here in chains I pay the price.
I'll endure all castigation,
End my life in pain and shame;
In my heart is consolation:
I have fought in honor's name.
(in a nearly mad, yet peaceful exaltation)
Am I not by breezes caressingly kissed,
And does not a light shine to guide me?
I see how an angel in rose-colored mist
Appears now consoling, consoling beside me:
An angel, Leonore, Leonore, my angel of love;
She leads me to freedom in heaven above.
*Exhausted from the last burst of emotion, he sinks down on the
stone seat, his hands covering his face.*

Scene 2

Through the grilles, Rocco and Leonore are seen descending the steps by the light of a lantern, carrying a jug and tools for digging. The door at back opens, and the scene is half-illuminated.

LEONORE *(in an undertone)*
How cold it is in this underground vault!

ROCCO
That's natural, it's so deep.

LEONORE *(looking all around anxiously)*
I thought we'd never find the entrance.

ROCCO *(turning toward Florestan)*
There he is.

LEONORE *(with a broken voice, while seeking to recognize the prisoner)*
He seems quite motionless.

ROCCO
Perhaps he's dead.

LEONORE *(shuddering)*
You think so?
Florestan makes a movement.

ROCCO
No, no, he's asleep. We must take advantage of that and set to work immediately; we have no time to lose.

LEONORE *(aside)*
It's impossible to make out his features. God help me if it's him!

ROCCO *(sets his lantern on the rubble)*
Here, under this rubble, is the cistern I told you about. We don't have to dig far to reach the opening; give me a pickaxe, and you stand here. *(He climbs into the hole up to his waist, placing the jug and a bunch of keys nearby. Leonore is standing at the edge and hands him the pickaxe.)* You're trembling; are you afraid?

LEONORE *(with a forced tone of firmness)*
Oh, no, it's just so cold.

ROCCO *(quickly)*
Get to work then; that's sure to warm you up.
As the ritornello begins, Rocco begins to work; meanwhile Leonore uses the moments when Rocco bends down to observe the prisoner. The entire duet is sung sotto voce.

ROCCO *(sotto voce, as he works)*
　　　　Now come and dig, for we must hurry;
　　　　Ere long, he has to go inside.

LEONORE *(likewise working)*
>In me you'll have no cause to worry,
>To please you I have ever tried.

ROCCO *(lifting a large stone)*
>Come, help, come, help, this boulder must be shifted.
>Take care, take care! The weight is great!

LEONORE *(helping to lift)*
>I'll give you aid, only wait,
>With all my strength I'll try to lift it.

ROCCO
>A little more!

LEONORE
>I'll try!

ROCCO
>'Tis done!

LEONORE
>A little now!

ROCCO
>It weighs a ton!

LEONORE
>A little more!

They let the stone roll over the rubble and catch their breath.

ROCCO *(resuming work)*
>Now come and dig, for we must hurry,
>Ere long, he has to go inside.

LEONORE
>I'll gather strength, sir, do not worry;
>The ending now is well in sight.

She tries to look at the prisoner; aside.
>Whoever you may be, I'll save you;
>By God, no victim shall you be.
>Indeed, the chains the villain gave you,
>Poor man, I'll break and set you free.

ROCCO *(suddenly straightening up)*
>Are you reluctant now to work?

LEONORE *(she begins working again)*
>My father, no, I do not shirk!

ROCCO
>Now come and dig, for we must hurry,
>Ere long, he'll come inside.

LEONORE
>
> In me you'll have no cause to worry,
> I'll gather strength, sir, do not worry,
> And by our work I shall abide.

Rocco drinks; Florestan is recovering and raises his head, without turning toward Leonore.

LEONORE
He's waking!

ROCCO *(abruptly stops drinking)*
He's waking up, you say?

LEONORE *(in greatest agitation, gazing fixedly at Florestan)*
Yes, he just raised his head.

ROCCO
No doubt he'll be asking me a thousand questions again. I must speak with him alone. Well, soon it will be over for him. *(He climbs out of the pit.)* Climb down in my place and clear away enough so that we can open the cistern.

LEONORE *(descends a few steps, trembling)*
What's going on inside me is indescribable.

ROCCO *(pauses briefly, then to Florestan)*
So you've been resting again for a few moments?

FLORESTAN
Resting? How could I find rest?

LEONORE *(aside)*
That voice!—If only I could see his face for an instant.

FLORESTAN
Will you always be deaf to my grievances, you cruel man?
With his last words, he turns his face toward Leonore.

LEONORE *(aside)*
God! It's he!
She faints at the edge of the pit.

ROCCO
What would you have me do? I carry out the orders I receive; that is my task, my duty.

FLORESTAN
Just tell me this: who is the Governor of this prison?

ROCCO *(aside)*
Now at least I can satisfy him without danger. *(to Florestan)* The Governor of this prison is Don Pizarro.

FLORESTAN
Pizarro!

LEONORE *(gradually recovering; aside)*
O barbarian! Your cruelty restores my strength.

FLORESTAN
Oh, send a messenger to Seville as soon as possible, ask for Leonore Florestan—

LEONORE *(aside)*
God! He little imagines that she's now digging his grave.

FLORESTAN
Tell her that I am lying here in chains.

ROCCO
It's impossible, I tell you. I would doom myself without having helped you.

FLORESTAN
If I am indeed condemned to end my life here, don't make me waste away slowly.

LEONORE *(jumps up and supports herself on the wall; aside)*
O God! Who can bear this?

FLORESTAN
Out of charity, give me just one drop of water; that's so little to ask.

ROCCO *(aside)*
Against my will, it touches my heart.

LEONORE *(aside)*
He seems to be softening.

FLORESTAN
You give me no answer?

ROCCO
I can't give you what you request. All that I can offer you is what remains of the wine that I have in my jug. Fidelio!

LEONORE *(bringing him the jug in greatest haste)*
Here it is! Here it is!

FLORESTAN *(looking at Leonore)*
Who is this?

ROCCO
My keeper, and in a few days my son-in-law. *(He gives the jug to Florestan.)* It's only a little wine, but I give it to you gladly. *(to Leonore)* You are deeply moved, aren't you?

LEONORE *(in greatest confusion)*
Who would not be? You yourself, Master Rocco—

ROCCO
That's true; the man has such a voice. . . .

LEONORE
  Indeed, it penetrates the depths of my heart.
FLORESTAN
          I hope some better world repays you;
          So Heaven has answered my pray'r.
          My thanks! You save me from despair,
          I have no proper means to praise you.
ROCCO *(quietly to Leonore, whom he draws aside)*
          I gladly give what help I can,
          For now the end is near, poor man.
LEONORE *(aside)*
          My blood is pounding in my veins,
          To beat in joy and bitter pains.
FLORESTAN *(aside)*
          I sense emotion in the youth,
          The man compassion also shows.
          O God, Thou sendest Hope in truth,
          I still may win them to my cause!
LEONORE
          The fatal hour is drawing nigh,
          When I shall save his life or die.
ROCCO
          I follow where my duty leads,
          But I abhor these cruel deeds.
LEONORE
  (quietly to Rocco, taking a morsel of bread from her pocket)
          This piece of bread—I meant to save it
          And put it here two days ago.
ROCCO
          I wish I could, but you must know
          That goes too far. I dare not brave it.
LEONORE *(coaxingly)*
          Ah! You gladly helped him in his plight.
ROCCO
          I have no right, I have no right.
LEONORE *(as before)*
          His time on earth is now so slight.
          He has so little time to live.
ROCCO
          So be it, it shall be; I'll let you brave it.

LEONORE *(in utmost agitation, giving the bread to Florestan)*
> Then take the bread, unhappy man.

FLORESTAN *(grasping Leonore's hand and pressing it to himself)*
> Accept my thanks! My thanks, my thanks!
> Oh, I hope a better world repays you.
> 'Tis Heaven's answer to my pray'r.
> My thanks! Heaven sent you here to me.
> Thank you for giving me sweet refreshment!

LEONORE
> May Heaven only set you free,
> Then shall my highest hopes be repaid.

ROCCO
> Your pain aroused my heart in me,
> Forbidden 'twas to give you aid.
> *(aside)* I'd gladly help him if I can,
> For now the end is near, poor man.

LEONORE
> Endure so much, no woman can.

FLORESTAN
> I'd thank you more than now I can.

He eats the bread ravenously.

ROCCO *(after momentary silence, to Leonore)*
Everything is ready. I'll go to give the signal.
He goes into the background.

LEONORE
O God, give me courage and strength!

FLORESTAN *(to Leonore, as Rocco goes to open to the door)*
Where is he going? *(Rocco opens the doors and gives a signal with a sharp whistle.)* Does that portend my death?

LEONORE *(with utmost emotion)*
No, no! Calm yourself, dear prisoner.

FLORESTAN
O my Leonore! So I shall never see you again?

LEONORE *(feeling drawn to Florestan and trying to suppress this impulse)*
My whole heart pulls me to him! *(to Florestan)* Be calm, I tell you! Whatever you may hear and see, do not forget that Providence rules over everything. Yes, yes, there is a Providence! *She withdraws and goes toward the cistern.*

Scene 3

Pizarro enters, concealed in a cloak.
PIZARRO *(to Rocco, disguising his voice)*
Is everything ready?
ROCCO
Yes, the cistern need only be opened.
PIZARRO
Good; have the boy leave now.
ROCCO *(to Leonore)*
Go; leave us!
LEONORE *(in greatest confusion)*
Who?—Me?—And you?
ROCCO
Don't I have to remove the prisoner's shackles? Go, go!
Leonore withdraws into the background and in the shadows grad-
ually approaches Florestan again, keeping her eyes on Pizarro.
PIZARRO *(aside, casting a glance at Rocco and Leonore)*
I'll have to get rid of those two today, so that nothing may ever
come to light.
ROCCO *(to Pizarro)*
Should I remove his chains?
PIZARRO
No, but unchain him from the stone. *(aside)* Time is pressing.
He draws his dagger.
> He'll perish! First he'll be enlightened
> Whose hand will tear his heart in two.
> Now vengeance's shadows be brightened;
> See here! All shall be clear to you!
He flings open his cloak.
> Pizarro, whom you wished to tumble,
> Pizarro, who will make you humble,
> He stands in vengeance here!
FLORESTAN *(calmly)*
> A murderer appears.
PIZARRO
> Once more I'd make it clear,
> I now repay the score;
> You have a moment more,
> Before my blade—

He is about to stab Florestan. Leonore plunges forward with a piercing cry and shields Florestan with her own body.

LEONORE

                Go back!

FLORESTAN

      O God!

ROCCO

           What's this?

LEONORE

                Imbed it
In my heart first, you must;
The curse of death be dreaded
Upon your murder-lust.

PIZARRO *(hurling her aside)*
      Insanity!

ROCCO *(to Leonore)*
           Say no more!

PIZARRO

      Insanity! This I shall not ignore!

LEONORE *(once again shielding her husband)*
      Kill first his wife!

PIZARRO AND ROCCO

             His wife?

FLORESTAN

             My wife?

LEONORE *(to Florestan)*
      Yes, here is Leonore!

FLORESTAN

             Leonore?

LEONORE *(to the others)*
      I am his wife, who's sworn to his
      Good in life, to bring you down!

PIZARRO *(to Leonore)*
      So much, a wife would dare!

FLORESTAN *(to Leonore)*
      What joy beyond compare!

ROCCO

      I shiver in despair!

LEONORE *(aside)*
      His anger I can bear.

PIZARRO
> By woman am I made faint-hearted?

LEONORE
> The curse of death be dreaded.

PIZARRO
> My anger shall to both apply!

He again sets upon Leonore and Florestan.

LEONORE
> Imbed it in my heart first, you must!

PIZARRO
> From him in life you'd not be parted;
> Therefore, with him you now shall die!

LEONORE *(quickly pointing a pistol at him)*
> Another word—and you are dead!

The trumpet sounds from the tower.

LEONORE *(falls on Florestan's neck)*
> Ah, 'tis your salvation! Lord above!

FLORESTAN
> Ah, 'tis my salvation! Lord above!

PIZARRO *(dazed)*
> Ha, ha! Don Fernando! Hell and death!

ROCCO *(dazed)*
> Oh, what is that? Good Lord above!

The trumpet sounds more loudly.

Scene 4

Bearing torches, Jaquino and soldiers appear at the uppermost grille of the stairway.

JAQUINO
Father Rocco! The Minister is arriving. His entourage is already at the castle gate.

ROCCO *(joyful and surprised; aside)*
Praised be God! *(to Jaquino, very loudly)* We're coming—yes, we'll come at once. And these people with torches should come down and escort the Governor up.

The soldiers descend to the door; Jaquino exits.

LEONORE / FLORESTAN
> The vengeful hour has sounded,
> When blessed freedom reigns.
> On courage love is founded,
> So love will break your / my chains.

PIZARRO

    The cursed hour has sounded!
    I'm mocked for all my pains.
    By desperation bounded
    My vengeance lies in chains!

ROCCO

    The fearful hour has sounded!
    For me, Lord, what remains?
    No more will I be bounded
    By what his rage ordains!

Pizarro rushes off. While leaving, Rocco gestures reassuringly to Leonore. Soldiers with torches lead the way.

Scene 5

FLORESTAN

My Leonore! Beloved wife! Angel, sent by God like a miracle to save me, let me press you to my heart. *(embrace)* But can we still hope?

LEONORE

We can! The arrival of the Minister, whom we know, Pizarro's confusion, and above all Father Rocco's comforting signs are all reasons for me to believe that our suffering may have run its course and the time of our happiness is beginning.

FLORESTAN

Speak, how did you get here?

LEONORE *(quickly)*

I left Seville and came here on foot, in men's clothing; the prison master took me into his service—your persecutor himself made me a keeper.

FLORESTAN

Faithful wife! Woman beyond compare! What have you endured for me?

LEONORE

Nothing, my Florestan! My soul was with you; how could my body not have felt strong while fighting for its better self?

FLORESTAN

    Oh, overwhelming pleasure!
    On Leonore's breast!

LEONORE

    Oh, overwhelming pleasure!
    My husband on my breast!

BOTH
> From torment none can measure,
> In ecstasy to rest!

LEONORE
> Once more in tenderness caressing!

FLORESTAN
> Lord! how merciful Thy blessing!

LEONORE / FLORESTAN
> We thank Thee, Lord, for this Thy grace!
> My husband / wife here in my embrace.
> Oh, overwhelming pleasure!

FLORESTAN
> 'Tis you!

LEONORE
> > 'Tis I!

FLORESTAN
> Oh, heavenly enchantment!
> Leonore!

LEONORE
> > Florestan!

BOTH
> Oh, wondrous, overwhelming pleasure,
> From torment none can measure
> In ecstasy to rest!

Scene 6

ROCCO *(rushing in)*
> Good tidings, you poor sufferers. The Minister brought a list of all
> the prisoners; all are to be brought before him. Jaquino is opening
> the upper prisons. You alone *(to Florestan)* are not mentioned; your
> detention here is an unauthorized act on the part of the Governor.
> Come, follow me upstairs! You, too, gracious lady! And if God
> empowers my words, and if He rewards the heroic deed of this most
> noble wife, you will be free and your happiness will be my work.

FLORESTAN
> Leonore!

LEONORE
> By what miracles?

ROCCO
> Away, don't delay. Upstairs you will learn everything. And keep
> these chains on. May God grant that they plead compassion for

you and will be put on the cruel man who caused you so much suffering.
Exeunt.

Transformation

Parade grounds of the castle, with a statue of the king.

Scene 7

The castle sentries march in and form an open square. Then from one side the Minister Don Fernando appears, accompanied by Pizarro and officers. The people hasten in. From the other side, led by Jaquino and Marzelline, the prisoners of state enter and kneel before Fernando.

CHORUS OF THE PEOPLE AND PRISONERS

> Hail to the day, hail to the hour!
> So long we hoped despite our fears,
> When mercy, joining righteous power,
> Before our prison door appears!

FERNANDO

> The best of kings gave me the mission,
> To visit you, who've suffered long,
> To seek the truth of your condition,
> Clearing the clouds of doubt and wrong.
> No, no man should grovel to another;
> *(the prisoners stand up)*
> The days of tyranny shall end.
> Let ev'ry man seek out his brother,
> And offer help as friend to friend.

CHORUS OF THE PEOPLE AND PRISONERS

> Hail to the day, hail to the hour!

FERNANDO

> Let ev'ry man seek out his brother,
> And offer help as friend to friend.

Scene 8

Rocco pushes through the sentries, Leonore and Florestan behind him.

ROCCO

> Then help them, free them from oppression!

PIZARRO
>> Who is it? Ha!

ROCCO *(to Pizarro)*
>>> It troubles you?

PIZARRO *(to Rocco)*
>> Go back!

FERNANDO *(to Rocco)*
>> Speak freely!

ROCCO
>>> Great compassion
>> Should be bestowed upon these two!
>> *(leading Florestan forward)*
>> Don Florestan—

FERNANDO *(astounded)*
>>>> Whom we thought perished,
>> Who nobly fought for truth and right?

ROCCO
>> And suffered torment and distress!

FERNANDO
>> My friend, whom I thought perished?
>> In fetters, pale, before me stands.

LEONORE AND ROCCO
>> Yes, Florestan, before your glance.

ROCCO *(presenting Leonore)*
>> And Leonore—

FERNANDO *(even more amazed)*
>>> Leonore?

ROCCO
>>> —the crown of womankind, his mate;
>> She journeyed here—

PIZARRO
>>>> Two words I'd tell you—

FERNANDO
>> Be silent! *(to Rocco)* She came—

ROCCO
>>>> —here, to my gate,
>> And asked for work here in my service,
>> And gave such brave and loyal service
>> That I gave her my child to wed.

MARZELLINE
>> Dear Heaven, help me! What is it he said!

ROCCO
> That monster had arranged and planned it,
> This hour Florestan should die.

PIZARRO *(in greatest fury)*
> Had planned with him!

ROCCO *(pointing to himself and Leonore)*
> We were commanded.
> *(to Fernando)*
> 'Twas your arrival held him back.

CHORUS OF THE PEOPLE AND PRISONERS *(very animatedly)*
> Dire punishment be his reward
> For innocence oppressed;
> Let justice wield a righteous sword
> Till wrongs are all redressed!

At a sign from Fernando, Pizarro is led away by the sentries.

FERNANDO *(to Rocco)*
> You opened up his tomblike cell;
> Now you shall loose his chains as well.
> But wait! You, noble wife, are she
> Whose right it is to set him free.

Leonore takes the key and, with profound emotion, removes the chains from Florestan; he sinks into her arms.

LEONORE
> O God! What a joy, at last!

FLORESTAN
> Oh, what a moment unsurpassed!

FERNANDO
> How just, O Lord, how righteous is Thy will!

MARZELLINE AND ROCCO
> He tries us, but He guides us still.

ALL
> O God! Oh, what a joy at last!
> Oh, what a moment unsurpassed!
> How just, O Lord, how just Thy will,
> To try us, yet to guide us still.

CHORUS OF THE PEOPLE AND PRISONERS
> Let him join our celebration
> Who has found a loyal wife.
> Give her the highest acclamation,
> She who saved her husband's life.

FLORESTAN

> Life for me your love provided,
> Evil flees from virtue's spear.

LEONORE

> By my love I have been guided,
> Who loves truly knows no fear.

CHORUS OF THE PEOPLE AND PRISONERS

> Praise with high joy at length
> Leonore's noble strength!

FLORESTAN *(advancing and indicating Leonore)*

> Let him join our celebration
> Who possesses such a wife.
> She deserves all acclamation,
> She who saved her husband's life.

LEONORE *(embracing him)*

> Loving gave me inspiration,
> Strength to free you through all strife.
> Loving, sing in exultation,
> Florestan is mine for life.

CHORUS OF THE PEOPLE AND PRISONERS

> Let him join our celebration,
> Who has found a loyal wife.
> She deserves all acclamation,
> She who saved her husband's life.

LEONORE

> Loving, sing in exultation,
> Florestan is mine for life!

ALL OTHERS

> She deserves all acclamation,
> She who saved her husband's life.

Lyrics translated by Paul Csonka and Ariane Theslöf
Dialogue translated by James Steakley

PARSIFAL
A Stage Dedication Festival Play
in Three Acts

Richard Wagner

CHARACTERS

AMFORTAS, *son of Titurel and ruler of the Kingdom of the Grail*	Bass-Baritone
TITUREL, *former ruler*	Bass
GURNEMANZ, *a veteran Knight of the Grail*	Bass
KLINGSOR, *a magician*	Bass
PARSIFAL	Tenor
KUNDRY	Soprano
FIRST AND SECOND KNIGHTS	Tenor and Bass
FOUR SQUIRES	Sopranos and Tenors
SIX OF KLINGSOR'S FLOWER MAIDENS	Sopranos
BROTHERHOOD OF THE KNIGHTS OF THE GRAIL, YOUTHS AND BOYS, FLOWER MAIDENS	

The scene is laid first in the domain and in the castle of the Grail's guardians, Monsalvat, where the country resembles the northern mountains of Gothic Spain; afterwards in Klingsor's magic castle on the southern slope of the same mountains which looks toward Moorish Spain. The costume of the Knights and

Squires resembles that of the Templars: a white tunic and man-
tle; instead of the red cross, however, there is a dove flying
upwards on scutcheon and mantle.

ACT 1

A forest, shadowy and impressive, but not gloomy. Rock-strewn
ground. A clearing in the middle. Left rises the way to the castle
of the Grail. The background slopes steeply down in the center to
a forest lake. Daybreak. Gurnemanz (elderly but still vigorous)
and two youthful Squires are lying asleep under a tree. From the
left, as if from the castle, sounds a solemn reveille on trombones.

GURNEMANZ *(waking and rousing the Squires)*
He! Ho! Wood guardians you?
Sleep guardians I call you:
awake at least with the morning.
The two Squires leap up.
Hear you the call? Give thanks to God
that He has chosen you to hear it!
He sinks to his knees with the Squires and joins them in silent
morning prayer: as the trombones cease, they slowly rise.
Now up, young pages! See to the bath;
time now for you to greet our master.
The sickbed of the King is near,
I see the heralds on their way!
Two Knights enter.
Hail there! How fares our King today?
He comes far earlier than usual:
the balsam that Gawain
with skill and daring boldly won,
I'm hopeful that it eased his pain.

SECOND KNIGHT
You still can hope, you who all things know?
His pain returned more keenly,
more grievous than before;
sleepless and racked with anguish,
he bade us swift prepare the bath.

GURNEMANZ *(sadly bowing his head)*
Fools we are, to seek for balm to ease him;
one single healing cures him!
We search for balsams, soothing potions,

search in vain far through the world:
there is but one thing,
only one man!
SECOND KNIGHT
Tell us his name!
GURNEMANZ *(evasively)*
See to the bath!
*The two Squires, who have returned to the background, look
off right.*
SECOND SQUIRE
But look, who's wildly riding here!
FIRST SQUIRE
Hey! The mane of the devil's mare is streaming!
SECOND SQUIRE
Ha! Kundry's here!
FIRST SQUIRE
She brings some weighty tidings?
SECOND SQUIRE
Her mare is stumbling.
FIRST SQUIRE
Flew she through the air?
SECOND SQUIRE
She's falling upon the ground.
FIRST SQUIRE
With her mane she's wiping the grass.
They all eagerly look off right.
SECOND KNIGHT
The rider has flung herself off.
*Kundry rushes in, almost staggering. She is in wild garb, her
skirts tucked up by a snakeskin girdle with long hanging cords,
her black hair loose and dishevelled, her complexion deep
ruddy-brown, her eyes dark and piercing, sometimes flashing
wildly, more often strangely fixed and staring. She hurries to
Gurnemanz and presses on him a small crystal phial.*
KUNDRY
Here! Take it! Balsam . . .
GURNEMANZ
Tell me where it was found.
KUNDRY
From further off than your mind can reach:
if this balsam fails,

Arabia offers
naught else to soothe his pain.
Ask no further!
She throws herself on the ground.
I am weary.
A procession of Squires and Knights appears from the left, carrying and escorting the litter on which lies Amfortas. Gurnemanz has at once turned from Kundry to the approaching company.
GURNEMANZ *(as the procession reaches the stage)*
He nears; they bear him on the litter.
Ah woe! Can I thus bear to see him,
when in the pride of flowering manhood,
the proud king of a conquering race
is to his sickness made a slave!
(to the Squires)
Be careful! Hear, our master groans.
The Squires halt and set down the litter.
AMFORTAS *(raising himself a little)*
Good so! My thanks. A moment's rest!
An anguished painful night
now yields to morning's light.
The holy lake
will make my sufferings lighter:
it soothes my woe;
my night of pain grows brighter.
Gawain!
SECOND KNIGHT
Sire! Gawain is not here;
for when the healing herb
he strove so hard to bring you
proved to be of no avail,
upon another search at once he ventured.
AMFORTAS
Unbidden? May he not regret it,
to leave before the Grail commands!
Oh, woe to him, so boldly daring,
if he in Klingsor's snares should fall!
And so let none presume to help me!
I wait for one, the one appointed:
"Made wise through pity,"
was it not so?

GURNEMANZ
You told us it was so.

AMFORTAS
"The blameless fool."
I think that I can name him:
for soon as Death I'll claim him.

GURNEMANZ *(handing Kundry's phial to Amfortas)*
First, my lord, please see if this will help you.

AMFORTAS *(examining it)*
Whence came this strange, mysterious flask?

GURNEMANZ
For you from far Arabia it was brought.

AMFORTAS
And who has brought it?

GURNEMANZ
There lies the wild maid. Up, Kundry! Come!
Kundry refuses and remains on the ground.

AMFORTAS
You, Kundry? Again I have to thank you,
you shy and restless maid?
'Tis well, your balsam now I mean to try:
I give you thanks for your devotion.

KUNDRY *(writhing uneasily on the ground)*
Not thanks! Ha, ha! How can it help you?
Not thanks! Be off—your bath!
Amfortas gives the signal to move on. Gurnemanz, gazing sadly after it, and Kundry, still stretched on the ground, remain. Squires come and go.

THIRD SQUIRE *(a young man)*
Hey, you, there! Still lying there
like a savage beast?

KUNDRY
Are the creatures here not holy?

THIRD SQUIRE
Yes! But if you are holy,
of that we are not so sure.

FOURTH SQUIRE *(likewise a young man)*
And with her magic balm, maybe
she'll harm our master, even destroy him.

GURNEMANZ
Hm! Has she done harm to you?

When you are all perplexed,
and wonder how you can get news
to distant brothers fighting afar off
and hardly know where to send,
she, while you are still in debate,
comes and goes on wings of the wind,
to bear your tidings and bring reply.
You feed her not, you house her not,
she has nothing in common with you:
but when you're in need
she gives her aid,
with zeal she flies to do your will,
and never asks one word of thanks.
I ask you, is this harmful,
when nothing but good she brings you?

THIRD SQUIRE
She hates us though;
just look, see how her eyes are flashing hate!

FOURTH SQUIRE
She's a heathen maid,
a sorceress.

GURNEMANZ
Yes, under a curse she well may lie.
Now she lives here,
perhaps renewed,
to atone for guilt she may be driven,
some former guilt still unforgiven.
Though she may serve us but as a penance,
yet the noble band of knights is grateful:
good are her deeds,
from them we can tell:
she helps us . . .
herself as well.

THIRD SQUIRE
And so, perhaps, that guilt of hers
brought upon us our great distress?

GURNEMANZ *(recollecting)*
True, when so long she stayed away from us,
then cruel misfortune came to pass.
I long have known her well:
but Titurel knew her still longer.

(to the Squires)
He found her, when first he built our castle,
asleep among the bushes here,
benumbed, lifeless, as dead.
Thus I myself did find her lately,
when our misfortune came to pass,
when that foul schemer over the mountains
so shamefully assaulted us.
(to Kundry)
Hey! You! Hear me and say:
Where were you wandering on the day
when by our lord the Spear was lost?
Kundry is gloomily silent.
On that day why did you not help?

KUNDRY
I give no help.

FOURTH SQUIRE
She says it herself.

THIRD SQUIRE
If she's so true, and free of fear,
then send her off to fetch our missing Spear!

GURNEMANZ *(gloomily)*
That's for another . . .
That task we're denied.
(with deep emotion)
O wounding, wonderful, all-holiest Spear!
I saw you wielded by unholiest hand!
(absorbed in recollection)
Thus surely armed, Amfortas,
boldly daring,
what power could prevent you
from vanquishing the enchanter?
Beside the walls
virtue was snatched away . . .
a fearful beauteous woman
holds him in sway,
her warm embraces he is drinking,
the Spear from his hand is sinking.
A deathly cry!
To him I fly!
See mocking Klingsor standing there,

with impious hand grasping the Spear.
The King escaped,
I guarded his returning,
but he was wounded,
in his side the wound was burning:
a wound it is
that ne'er will close again.
The First and Second Squires return from the lake.
THIRD SQUIRE *(to Gurnemanz)*
So then you knew Klingsor?
GURNEMANZ *(to the two returning Squires)*
How fares our King now?
FIRST SQUIRE
He seems refreshed.
SECOND SQUIRE
The balsam eased his pain.
GURNEMANZ *(to himself)*
A wound it is that ne'er will close again!
*The Third and Fourth Squires have already sat down at Gur-
nemanz's feet; the other two join him under the great tree.*
THIRD SQUIRE
But Gurnemanz, say: we long to know:
you once knew Klingsor—how was that so?
GURNEMANZ
Titurel, our noble lord, he knew him well.
To him, when evil forces showed their might,
and he the realm of faith defended,
to him there came one holy solemn night
our blessed Savior's angels descending:
they brought the Cup used at the Last Supper,
the blessed Cup, that glorious holy relic,
which at the Cross received His sacred blood:
they brought the Spear as well, which shed that flood.
These tokens of God's love, of wondrous worth,
to Titurel they gave to guard on earth.
For them he built our mighty sanctuary.
And to its service you were bidden
by pathways from all sinners hidden;
you know that here no other
save pure in heart, as brother
may enter; to those who work the will of Heaven

the Grail's most wondrous might is given.
So, it was to him, of whom you ask, denied,
Klingsor, though eagerly and long he tried.
Yonder the valley where he made his dwelling;
beyond it lie luxuriant heathen lands.
I knew not what sin he there committed;
he sought atonement for it, yes, holy he would be!
Unable to kill the sinful, raging lust within him,
his hand upon himself he turned
to gain the Grail for which he yearned,
and by its guardian he with scorn was spurned.
Afire with rage, then Klingsor swiftly learned,
how his unholy, shameful deed
to evil, unholy craft could lead:
he mastered it!
The desert bloomed for him as magic garden,
where blossom devilish, lovely women;
there he now lies in wait to lure our brothers
to shameful joy and hell's defilement:
those whom he snares serve him as master:
and many fell in foul disaster.
When Titurel, bowed down with age and stricken,
to his son dominion had given,
Amfortas planned without delay
to end this plague: went on his way.
What happened you now understand:
the Spear is held in Klingsor's hand;
and now he uses it to wound our brothers.
The Grail he covets; he hopes soon to win it!
Kundry has been running back and forth in furious agitation.

FOURTH SQUIRE
Then first of all the Spear we must reclaim!

THIRD SQUIRE
Ha! Who does that wins lasting joy and fame!

GURNEMANZ
Before the ravished sanctuary
in fervent prayer lay Amfortas,
a sign of pardon he entreated:
the Grail was lighted by a mystic radiance;
a holy vision then appeared to him and spoke,
these words of mystic meaning shone before him:

"Made wise through pity,
the blameless fool,
wait for him,
the one I choose."
THE FOUR SQUIRES *(deeply moved)*
"Made wise through pity,
the blameless fool—"
*From the lake are heard shouts and cries from the Knights and
Squires. Gurnemanz and the four Squires start up and turn in
alarm.*
SQUIRES
Woe! Woe!
KNIGHTS
Hoho!
SQUIRES
Ah!
KNIGHTS
Who dared to do it?
A wild swan flutters unsteadily over the lake.
GURNEMANZ
What is it?
FOURTH SQUIRE
There!
THIRD SQUIRE
Here!
SECOND SQUIRE
A swan!
FOURTH SQUIRE
A forest swan!
THIRD SQUIRE
And it is wounded!
ALL KNIGHTS AND SQUIRES
Ha! Shameful! Shameful!
GURNEMANZ
Who shot the swan?
*The swan, after a labored flight, falls to the ground exhausted;
the Second Knight draws an arrow from its breast.*
FIRST KNIGHT
The King had hailed it as a happy omen
as o'er the lake circled the swan,
and then a shaft . . .

Knights and Squires lead in Parsifal.
KNIGHTS
  He it was!
SQUIRES
  He shot!
  See his bow there!
  (indicating Parsifal's bow)
SECOND KNIGHT *(producing the arrow)*
  And the arrow is just like his.
GURNEMANZ *(to Parsifal)*
  Did you deal to our swan his death-blow?
PARSIFAL
  Of course! I shoot at all things that fly!
GURNEMANZ
  You killed the swan?
  And feel no horror at the crime?
SQUIRES AND KNIGHTS
  Punish the culprit!
GURNEMANZ
  Shameful, cruel deed!
  So you can murder, here, within this forest,
  where quiet, holy peace should reign?
  The woodland creatures, are they not your friends?
  Are they not gentle and tame?
  From the branches the birds sang their songs to you.
  What harm did the faithful swan?
  His mate he was seeking, so they both
  might fly and circle over the lake,
  thus nobly consecrating the bath.
  Were you not amazed?
  No, all you did was loose a cruel shaft from your bow.
  He was our friend: what is he to you?
  Gurnemanz kneels down by the swan.
  Here, look here! 'Twas here you struck,
  his blood not yet dry, limp, drooping his wings now,
  his snowy plumage darkened and stained,
  and broken his eye; see how he looks!
  Parsifal has followed Gurnemanz with growing emotion; now
  he breaks his bow and hurls his arrows away.
  Do you regret an act so heartless?
  Parsifal passes his hand over his eyes.

Speak, boy, do you repent your cruel deed?
How could you commit this crime?

PARSIFAL

I did not know then.

GURNEMANZ

Where are you from?

PARSIFAL

I do not know.

GURNEMANZ

Who is your father?

PARSIFAL

I do not know.

GURNEMANZ

Who sent you to seek this forest?

PARSIFAL

I do not know.

GURNEMANZ

What name have you?

PARSIFAL

I once had many,
but now those names are all forgot.

GURNEMANZ

There's nothing that you know?
(aside)
Then one so dull I've never met—save Kundry here!
(to the Squires, who have assembled in increasing numbers)
Be off!
The King requires your attendance there!
Go!
The Squires reverently lift the dead swan onto a bier of fresh branches and move away with it toward the lake. At length only Gurnemanz, Parsifal, and—apart—Kundry remain behind. Gurnemanz turns back to Parsifal.
Now speak: you cannot answer my questions:
but tell what you can,
for something you must remember.

PARSIFAL

I have a mother, Herzeleide her name!
In woods and in lonely meadows we made our home.

GURNEMANZ

Who gave you your weapons?

PARSIFAL
   I made them myself
   to fright the savage eagles from the forest.
GURNEMANZ
   An eagle you seem yourself, and nobly born too;
   why did your mother not find you
   worthier weapons to handle?
   Parsifal is silent.
KUNDRY
   *(who during Gurnemanz's recital of the fate of Amfortas has been
   violently writhing in furious agitation, now, still lying in the undergrowth, eyes Parsifal keenly and, as he is silent, hoarsely calls)*
   All fatherless did his mother bear him,
   for in battle slain was Gamuret!
   To save her son from dying
   as his father perished, far from arms
   and people, as simple fool she raised him:
   more fool she.
   She laughs.
PARSIFAL *(who has listened to her with sudden attention)*
   Yes! And once I saw a glittering array
   of men on noble horses
   pass the edge of the forest;
   I wanted to be like them:
   but laughing they galloped away.
   So I pursued, but I could not overtake them;
   through savage places passing, over hill and dale;
   night followed day, day followed night:
   my bow and arrows defended me
   when the beasts or men attacked me . . .
   Kundry has risen and moved toward the men.
KUNDRY
   Yes! Robbers and giants fell to his might;
   the fearless boy soon taught them to fear him.
PARSIFAL
   Who fears me? Say!
KUNDRY
   The wicked!
PARSIFAL
   So those who fought me, were they wicked?
   Gurnemanz laughs.

Who is good?

GURNEMANZ *(serious again)*
Your dear mother, whom you deserted,
and who for you now must mourn and grieve.

KUNDRY
She grieves no more: for his mother is dead.

PARSIFAL *(in fearful alarm)*
Dead? My mother? Who says so?

KUNDRY
As I rode by I saw her dying:
and, fool, she sent you her greeting.
*Parsifal springs furiously at Kundry and seizes her by the
throat. Gurnemanz restrains him.*

GURNEMANZ
So wild and violent! Brutal again?
After Gurnemanz has freed Kundry, Parsifal stands as if dazed.
What harm has she done? She tells the truth,
for Kundry sees much and never lies.

PARSIFAL *(seized with violent trembling)*
I am fainting!
*Kundry, seeing Parsifal's condition, at once hastens to a spring
in the wood and now brings water in a horn, sprinkles Parsifal
with it, and then gives it to him to drink.*

GURNEMANZ
Right so! That is the Grail's compassion:
the evil ends when with good it's returned.

KUNDRY *(gloomily)*
Good I do never: for rest I'm yearning,
I'm yearning, ah! I'm weary.
*She turns away sadly and, while Gurnemanz tends Parsifal in a
fatherly way, she creeps, unobserved by them, toward a thicket
in the wood.*
Slumber! Oh, may I not be wakened!
(starting in fear)
No! Not slumber! Terrors seize me!
*She falls into a violent trembling, then lets her arms and head
drop wearily.*
Vain to resist! The time has come.
*By the lake there is movement, and at length in the background
the procession of Knights and Squires returning home with
Amfortas's litter.*

Slumber—slumber—I must!
She sinks down behind the bushes and is not seen further.

GURNEMANZ
But from the lake the King returns;
the sun is high now:
so to our celebration let me lead you.
If you are pure,
then now the Grail will comfort and refresh you.
*He has gently put Parsifal's arm round his neck, and supporting
him in this way he leads him with very slow steps. Very gradually, the scene begins to change.*

PARSIFAL
Who is the Grail?

GURNEMANZ
That can't be told;
but if to serve it you are bidden,
that knowledge long will not be hidden.
Behold! I think I know you now indeed:
no pathway to the Grail doth lead,
and none can venture to approach it
unless the Grail itself has called him.

PARSIFAL
I scarcely stir,
yet all things move apace.

GURNEMANZ
You see, my son,
here time is one with space.
*Gradually, while Gurnemanz and Parsifal appear to walk, the scene
changes more perceptibly: the woods disappear and in the rocky
walls a gateway opens, which closes behind them. The way has led
upwards through walls of rock, and the scene has entirely changed.
Gurnemanz and Parsifal now enter the mighty hall of the castle of the
Grail. Gurnemanz turns to Parsifal, who now stands as if bewitched.*
Now pay good heed and let me see:
if you're a fool and pure,
what wisdom your folly may secure.

Scene Two

*A pillared hall with a vaulted dome over the Feast-chamber. On
both sides at the far end the doors are opened; the Knights of*

the Grail enter from the right and range themselves by the Feast-tables.

KNIGHTS OF THE GRAIL

O Feast of Love undying,
from day to day renewed,
(a procession of Squires passes rapidly across the backstage)
draw near, as for the last time,
to taste this sacred food.
(a second procession of Squires crosses the hall)
Who revels in good deeds
this holy Feast still feeds:
he dares approach the shrine
to share this gift divine.

The assembled Knights station themselves at the tables. From the left door Amfortas is borne in on a litter by Squires and serving brothers; before him walk the four Squires bearing the covered shrine of the Grail. This procession moves to the center backstage, where there is a raised couch on which Amfortas is set down from the litter; before it is an oblong stone altar on which the Squires place the covered shrine of the Grail.

YOUTHS *(from halfway up the dome)*

For sins of the world
with thousand sorrows
His sacred blood He offered;
to the world's Redeemer
with joyful heart,
oh, how gladly my blood I proffer:
He died, for sin atoning thus,
He lives, by death He lives in us!

BOYS *(from the summit of the dome)*

In faith and love,
behold the dove,
the Savior's shining token:
take ye the wine,
His blood divine,
and bread of life here broken!

When all have taken their places, and after a complete silence, the voice of the aged Titurel is heard in the extreme background from a vaulted niche behind Amfortas's couch, as if from a tomb.

TITUREL

My son Amfortas, are you prepared?

(silence)
Shall I the Grail see once again and live still?
(silence)
Must I die then, without its light to guide me?
AMFORTAS *(in an outburst of painful desperation)*
Sorrow! Oh, eternal grief!
My father, oh! just once more
resume the sacred task!
Live, live and let me perish.
TITUREL
Entombed I live here by our Savior's grace;
too weak, however, now to serve Him.
You make atonement for your guilt!
Reveal the Grail!
AMFORTAS *(restraining the Squires)*
No! Leave it unrevealed! Oh!
May no one, no one know the burning pain
caused by the holy sight that gives you delight!
What is the Spear-wound, all its raging smart,
compared to the pain, the agony
of being condemned to serve this task!
Woeful my birthright, defiled by sinning;
I, only sinner, am the guardian
who holds the Grail for sinless others,
entreating its holy blessing on my brothers!
Chastisement! Merciless chastisement
from, ah! the offended God of mercy!
For Him, for His all-holy greeting,
my stricken heart is yearning;
in deepest innermost repentance,
for Him my soul is burning.
The time is near:
a light beam sinks upon the holiest shrine:
the covering falls.
The blood within that pure, holiest Cup
now glows and shines with tender light.
Transfixed by rapturous and joyful pain,
the fount of that holy blood,
I feel it flowing in my heart:
the furious surge of my own guilty blood,
my vile blood now defiled

by shame, recoils before it;
to the world of sin and lust
how wildly now it is gushing.
The wound has opened again,
my blood now is streaming forth,
here, through the spear-wound, a wound like His,
inflicted by the Spear that wounded Him,
the Spear that inflicted the sacred wound,
through which with bleeding tears
the Holy One wept for the sins of man,
in pity's holiest yearning.
And now here from me, in my sacred office,
the guardian of godliest treasure,
of redemption's balm the keeper,
my fevered sinful blood flows forth,
ever renewed by the tide of yearning
that, ah! no repentance ever stills!
Have mercy! Have mercy!
All-merciful! Ah, have mercy!
Take back my birth-right,
end my affliction,
that holy I perish—
pure, whole, and healed!
He sinks back as if unconscious.
BOYS AND YOUTHS *(from halfway up the dome)*
"Made wise through pity,
the blameless fool:
wait for him,
the one I choose."
THE KNIGHTS
So truly you were promised:
wait on in hope,
fulfill your task today!
TITUREL
Reveal now the Grail!
Amfortas raises himself slowly and with difficulty. The acolytes remove the cover from the golden shrine and take from it an antique crystal chalice, from which they also remove a covering, and place it before Amfortas.
YOUTHS' VOICES *(from on high)*
"Take my body and eat,

take and drink my blood,
in holy, loving token!"
While Amfortas bows devoutly in silent prayer before the chalice, a dusky glimmer envelops the hall.

BOYS *(from the summit)*
"Take and drink my blood,
take my body and eat,
as a remembrance of me."
Here a dazzling ray of light falls from above on the crystal cup, which now glows ever more intensely in a brilliant crimson, shedding a soft light on everything around. Amfortas, transfigured, raises the Grail aloft and waves it gently round to every side, consecrating the bread and wine. All are kneeling.

TITUREL
O holiest rapture!
How radiant God's greeting today!
Amfortas sets down the Grail again, and its glow gradually fades as the darkness lightens: at this the acolytes replace the vessel in the shrine and cover it as before. Daylight returns.

BOYS *(from the summit)*
Wine and bread of that Last Supper,
changed by Him, the Lord of mercy,
through the saving might of love
into blood, which He then shed,
into flesh, which men then broke!
Meanwhile, the four Squires, after closing the shrine, take from the altar table the two wine flagons and two baskets of bread, which Amfortas had previously blessed by passing the chalice of the Grail over them, distribute the bread among the Knights, and fill with wine the cups standing before them. The Knights seat themselves at the Feast, as does Gurnemanz, who has kept a place empty beside him and signals to Parsifal to come and partake of the meal. Parsifal, however, remains standing apart, motionless and silent, as if completely transported.

YOUTHS' VOICES *(from on high)*
Blood and body, gift of Heaven,
changed today for your salvation,
in our sacred Feast of Love,
to the wine filling your cup,
to the bread that now you eat.

THE KNIGHTS *(first group)*
　　Take ye the bread,
　　change it anew
　　to manly strength and valor,
　　brave unto death,
　　steadfast and true
　　to work here the highest will of Heaven!
THE KNIGHTS *(second group)*
　　Take ye the wine,
　　change it anew
　　to fiery blood in you burning,
　　banded as one,
　　brothers and true
　　to fight on with courage unfailing!
ALL KNIGHTS
　　Blessed in faith and in loving!
YOUTHS AND BOYS
　　Blessed in loving!
　　Blessed in faith!
　　*The Knights rise and walk from each side to the center, where
　　they solemnly embrace. Amfortas, who has taken no part in the
　　meal, has gradually sunk down from his state of inspired exalta-
　　tion; he bows his head and presses his hand to his wound. The
　　Squires approach him, and their movements show that the wound
　　has broken out afresh; they attend to it, and assist their master
　　back to the litter. Then, while all are preparing to leave, they bear
　　out Amfortas and the holy shrine in the order in which they came.
　　The Knights likewise fall into solemn procession and slowly leave
　　the hall. The procession with Amfortas disappears entirely. The
　　light diminishes. Squires pass quickly through the hall. The last
　　Knights and Squires have now left the hall, and the doors are
　　closed. Parsifal still stands stiff and motionless; on hearing
　　Amfortas's cry of agony, he had pressed his hand suddenly and
　　convulsively to his heart, remaining long in that position.*
GURNEMANZ
　　(coming up to Parsifal in an ill humor and shaking him by the arm)
　　You're still standing there?
　　Know you what you saw?
　　Parsifal presses his heart convulsively and shakes his head.
　　Gurnemanz is much irritated.
　　So you are nothing but a fool!

He opens a small side door.
Off with you, on your way again!
And hark to Gurnemanz:
henceforth leave our swans in peace
go seeking—you gander—for geese!
He pushes Parsifal out and bangs the door angrily upon him.
While he follows the Knights, upon the last bar the curtain closes.
AN ALTO VOICE *(from on high)*
"Made wise through pity,
the blameless fool."
VOICES *(from the mid-height and the summit)*
Blessed in loving!
Bells.

ACT 2

Klingsor's magic castle. In the inner keep of a tower which is open to the sky. Stone steps lead up to the battlements and down into the darkness below the stage which represents the rampart. Magical and necromantic apparatus. Klingsor on the offset of the tower to one side, sitting before a metal mirror.
KLINGSOR
The time is come.
The fool's attracted by my castle,
with childish laughter he's approaching me!
In deathly slumber held by curse she lies,
but by my spells I'll waken her.
Up then! To work!
He moves down toward the center and lights incense, which immediately fills the background with blue smoke. He then seats himself again before his magical instruments and calls with strange gestures into the depths below.
Arise! Arise! To me!
Your master calls you, nameless woman,
first she-devil! Rose of Hades!
Herodias were you, and what else?
Gundryggia then, Kundry here!
Come here! Come here now, Kundry!
Your master calls: arise!
In the blue light Kundry's figure rises up. She seems asleep. Finally she utters a terrible cry.

Awake now? Ha!
To my spell again
you surrender now, in time of need.
Kundry gives a loud wail of misery that sinks gradually into
low accents of fear.
Say, where have you been roaming again?
Fie! There with that rabble of knights
though like a beast they have treated you!
With me don't you fare much better?
And when for me you conquered their leader—
ha ha!—the Grail's most holy defender,
what drove you to seek them again?

KUNDRY *(hoarsely and brokenly, as though striving to regain speech)*
Ah!—Ah!
Deepest night . . .
Madness . . . Oh!—Rage . . .
Ah! Sorrow!
Sleep . . . sleep . . .
deepest sleep . . . death!

KLINGSOR
Has someone else aroused you? Hey?

KUNDRY *(as before)*
Yes . . . my curse.
Oh! Yearning . . . yearning!

KLINGSOR
Ha, ha! So for the knights you're yearning?

KUNDRY
There . . . I . . . served them.

KLINGSOR
Yes, yes, atoning for the evil
that you had maliciously wrought?
But they cannot help;
all can be purchased,
when I provide the price:
the strongest will fall,
sinking in your embraces,
and so he falls by the Spear
that from their king himself I have seized.
The most dangerous of all today must be met:
his folly shields him well.

KUNDRY
 I will not.—Oh . . . oh! . . .
KLINGSOR
 You'll do it, for you must.
KUNDRY
 You . . . cannot . . . compel me.
KLINGSOR
 But I can force you.
KUNDRY
 You? . . .
KLINGSOR
 Your master.
KUNDRY
 And by what power?
KLINGSOR
 Ha!—Because I'm immune
 from your power—I alone.
KUNDRY *(with a shrill laugh)*
 Ha, ha! Are you chaste?
KLINGSOR *(furiously)*
 Why ask me that, accursed witch?
 Fearful my fate!
 So I am derided now,
 because once to be holy I strove?
 Fearful my fate!
 Fiery longings and scorching pain,
 hellish desires and pangs of lust,
 which I once stifled at fearful cost,
 rise to mock me aloud
 through you, you devil's bride!
 Ha!—beware!
 One for his scorn and contempt pays dearly,
 that proud one, strong in holiness,
 who drove me from his side:
 his son has fallen;
 unredeemed
 shall that holiest guardian now languish,
 and soon, I'm certain,
 I shall possess the Grail.
 Ha ha!

Was he to your taste, Amfortas the brave,
whom I procured for your delight?

KUNDRY

Oh! Sorrow! Sorrow!
Weak even he—weak all men!
I'm accursed and I
bring all to ruin!
Oh, never-ending sleep,
only release,
how—how can I find it?

KLINGSOR

Ha! One who spurns you can set you free:
so try with the boy drawing near!

KUNDRY

I will not!

KLINGSOR *(hastily mounting the tower wall)*
See him, he's scaling the wall.

KUNDRY

Oh! Sorrow! Sorrow!
Is that why I wakened?
Must I? Ah!

KLINGSOR *(looking out)*
Ha! He is fair, he's handsome!

KUNDRY

Oh!—Oh!—Ah! What grief!
Klingsor, leaning out, blows a horn.

KLINGSOR

Ho! You watchmen! Ho! Warriors!
Heroes! Up! Foes are near!
Ha! How they rush to the ramparts,
my deluded band of warriors,
defending their beautiful witches!
So!—Courage! Courage!
Ha ha! But he's not afraid:
from bold Sir Ferris he's wrested a weapon,
and fights with it fiercely, braving them all.
Kundry falls into wild hysterical laughter, which ends in a woeful moan.
How feebly those dull ones resist his attack!
Some struck in the thigh, others in the shoulder!
Ha ha! They're yielding! They're fleeing!

*The blue light is extinguished and all is dark below, in contrast
to the bright blue sky over the walls.*
Sorely wounded they're running for home!
What pleasure that gives me!
Would that the whole
despised assembly of knights
thus might destroy one another!
Ha! How proudly he stands on the rampart!
He's laughing, and flushed with his victory,
with childish surprise
sees deserted the garden below!
He turns toward the back.
Hey! Kundry!
(not perceiving her)
Ha! At your work?
Ha ha! The magic spell I know
that always compels you to serve my designs!
(turning outwards again)
You there, childish and free,
though—your
mission was foretold,
so young and dull,
you'll fall right into my hands:
when pureness once has left you
then I will be your master.
*The whole tower rapidly sinks with him; in its place rises the
magic garden. The magic garden fills the whole stage with trop-
ical vegetation and a luxuriant growth of flowers. It rises in ter-
races to the extreme background, where it is bounded by the
battlements of the castle. On one side appear projections of the
palace building, in rich Moorish style. Upon the rampart stands
Parsifal, gazing in astonishment into the garden. From all sides
rush in the Flower-Maidens clad in light veil-like garments, first
singly, then in groups, forming a confused, many-colored
throng. They seem as though just startled out of sleep.*
ALL MAIDENS *(to one another)*
Here they were fighting!
Weapons! Wildly shouting!
Weapons! Who is the culprit?
Where is the culprit?
We'll have vengeance!

1ST MAIDEN 1ST GROUP
  My beloved is wounded!
1ST MAIDEN 2ND GROUP
  Oh, where can I find him?
2ND MAIDEN 1ST GROUP
  When I woke he had left me!
ALL MAIDENS
  Where have they fled to?
1ST MAIDEN 2ND GROUP
  Where is my beloved?
3RD MAIDEN 1ST GROUP
  Oh, where can I find him?
2ND MAIDEN 2ND GROUP
  When I woke he had left me!
1ST MAIDEN 1ST GROUP
  Oh, sorrow! Sorrow!
ALL MAIDENS *(to one another)*
  Where are our beloveds?
  Inside the castle!
  Where are our beloveds?
  We saw them go in there.
  We saw them all bleeding and wounded.
  Ah! My lover!
  Ah, come help me!
  And who is our foe?
  They perceive Parsifal and point him out.
  There—see him!
  There—see him! There—there!
  Where he stands, there he stands!
  Where? Ha! I saw!
1ST MAIDEN 1ST GROUP
  And my Ferris's sword in his hand!
2ND MAIDEN 1ST GROUP
  My beloved's blood red on the blade.
CHORUSES I AND II
  I saw! The castle he stormed!
3RD MAIDEN 2ND GROUP
  And I heard the master's horn.
3RD MAIDEN 1ST GROUP AND 2ND MAIDEN 2ND GROUP
  Yes, we all heard the horn.

CHORUSES I AND II
Yes, he!

1ST AND 3RD MAIDENS 1ST GROUP
My hero obeyed.

CHORUSES I AND II
They all obeyed the command.
but they fell to his sword!
Alas! Ah! He inflicted a wound!

2ND MAIDEN 1ST GROUP AND MAIDENS FROM CHORUS I
He wounded my lover.

1ST MAIDEN 1ST GROUP AND MAIDENS FROM THE CHORUSES
He struck at my friend.

2ND MAIDEN 2ND GROUP AND MAIDENS FROM THE CHORUSES
His sword is still bleeding!

1ST MAIDEN 2ND GROUP AND MAIDENS FROM THE CHORUSES
My beloved's foe.

ALL MAIDENS
Ah! You there! Alas!
Why inflict such a blow?
Accursed, accursed you must be!
Parsifal leaps somewhat farther into the garden. The maidens
hastily retreat. Now he pauses, full of wonder.
Ha! Bold one!

1ST MAIDEN 1ST GROUP, 1ST AND 2ND MAIDENS 2ND GROUP
Dare you approach us?

2ND AND 3RD MAIDENS 1ST GROUP, 3RD MAIDEN 2ND GROUP
Why did you wound our beloveds?

PARSIFAL
You lovely children, I was forced to smite them!
For they, you fair ones, they tried to keep me from you.

1ST MAIDEN 2ND GROUP
You knew we were here?

1ST MAIDEN 1ST GROUP
You'd seen us before?

PARSIFAL
I have never beheld a scene so bright:
if I said fair, would that seem right?

2ND MAIDEN 1ST GROUP
Then truly you will not harm us?

2ND MAIDEN 2ND GROUP
You will not harm us?

PARSIFAL
   I couldn't do that.
1ST MAIDEN
   And yet you injured us severely—
2ND AND 3RD MAIDENS 1ST AND 2ND GROUPS
   —grievously harmed us!
1ST MAIDENS 1ST AND 2ND GROUPS
   You wounded all our companions!
ALL MAIDENS
   Who'll play with us now?
PARSIFAL
   Gladly will I!
   The maidens, passing from wonder to enjoyment, break into a
   merry laugh. While Parsifal steps nearer to the excited throng, the
   maidens of the first group and first chorus slip away unperceived
   to complete their flower-adornment behind the flower-hedges.
CHORUS II
   If you are kind—
2ND GROUP
   Why stay so far?
CHORUS II
   —stay so far from us.?
1ST MAIDEN 2ND GROUP
   And if you do not chide us—
2ND MAIDEN 2ND GROUP
   —reward you have beside us:
2ND GROUP
   We do not play for gold.
1ST MAIDEN 2ND GROUP
   But only for love's reward.
2ND MAIDEN 2ND GROUP
   If you seek to console us—
1ST MAIDEN 2ND GROUP
   —Ah, then ties of love must hold us!
   The maidens of the first group and first chorus return adorned
   with flowers, appearing like the flowers themselves, and make a
   rush at Parsifal.
2ND FLOWER 1ST GROUP
   Leave him for me now!
1ST FLOWER 1ST GROUP
   He belongs to me!

3RD THEN 2ND FLOWER 1ST GROUP
No! No!
CHORUS I
No! Me!
CHORUS II AND 2ND GROUP
Ha! The sly ones! In secret decked
themselves!
*While the newcomers throng round Parsifal, the maidens of the
second group and second chorus hastily leave the stage to adorn
themselves also.*
CHORUS I AND 1ST GROUP
*During the following the maidens dance in a graceful childlike
manner about Parsifal, caressing him gently.*
Come! Come!
Handsome stranger!
For you I'll bloom now!
Come! To delight and please you,
that is all I long for!
1ST FLOWER 1ST GROUP
Come, handsome stranger!
2ND AND 3RD FLOWERS 1ST GROUP
Handsome stranger!
*The second group and the second chorus return, attired like the
first, and join in the play.*
ALL FLOWER MAIDENS
Come! Come!
Handsome stranger!
Ah! For you I'll blossom,
to delight and please you,
that is my labor of love!
PARSIFAL
(standing in the midst of the maidens in silent enjoyment)
How fragrant you are!
Are you then blossoms?
1ST FLOWER 1ST GROUP
The garden's joy—
1ST FLOWER 2ND GROUP
—its gentle fragrance—
1ST FLOWERS 1ST AND 2ND GROUPS
—in spring plucked by our master!—

2ND FLOWERS 1ST AND 2ND GROUPS
We flourish here—
1ST FLOWERS 1ST AND 2ND GROUPS
—in summer and sunlight—
1ST AND 2ND FLOWERS 1ST AND 2ND GROUPS
—for you we blossom in gladness.
3RD FLOWERS 1ST AND 2ND GROUPS AND CHORUS I
You must be kind and true!
2ND FLOWERS 1ST AND 2ND GROUPS AND CHORUS I
And give to the blossoms their due!
ALL FLOWER MAIDENS
If you cannot love us and cherish,
we'll wither and sadly we'll perish.
1ST FLOWER 2ND GROUP
Oh, hold me close to your heart!
ALL FLOWER MAIDENS
Come! Handsome stranger!
1ST FLOWER 1ST GROUP
Your brow, oh, let me cool it!
CHORUSES
Let me for you blossom!
2ND FLOWER 1ST GROUP
Soft cheeks, oh, let me stroke them!
2ND FLOWER 2ND GROUP
Soft mouth, let me kiss it!
1ST FLOWER 1ST GROUP
No! I! The fairest am I!
2ND FLOWER 1ST GROUP
No! I am the fairest!
CHORUSES I AND II
I am fairer!
1ST FLOWER 2ND GROUP
No! I am more fragrant!
ALL THE OTHERS
No! I! I! Yes, I!
PARSIFAL *(gently moving them back)*
You wild throng of blossoms enchanting,
if I am to play with you, some space you must grant me!
1ST FLOWER 2ND GROUP
Why do you scold?

PARSIFAL
  Because you quarrel.
1ST FLOWER 1ST GROUP, THEN 2ND FLOWER 2ND GROUP
  But only over you.
PARSIFAL
  Have done, then!
2ND FLOWER 1ST GROUP
  Let go of him: it's me he likes!
3RD FLOWER 1ST GROUP
  Me rather!
3RD FLOWER 2ND GROUP
  No, me!
2ND FLOWER 2ND GROUP
  No, no, it's me he likes!
1ST FLOWER 2ND GROUP
  You're pushing me away?
1ST FLOWER 1ST GROUP
  You drive me away?
2ND AND 3RD FLOWERS 1ST GROUP, 3RD FLOWER 2ND GROUP
  Avoiding me?
CHORUS II
  You're afraid of women?
ALL FLOWERS 2ND GROUP
  Can't you trust yourself then?
CHORUS II
  Can't you trust yourself then?
1ST FLOWER 1ST GROUP
  How sad you're so cold and prudish!
BOTH CHORUSES
  How sad! So shy?
1ST FLOWER 2ND GROUP
  How sad you're so cold and prudish!
CHORUS II
  So shy and cold!
1ST FLOWER 1ST GROUP
  Would you have the butterfly wooed by the flowers?
2ND AND 3RD FLOWERS 1ST GROUP
  So shy and cold!
2ND AND 3RD FLOWERS 2ND GROUP
  So shy and cold!

CHORUS I
  The fool won't awaken!
1ST AND 2ND GROUPS
  By us he is forsaken.
CHORUS II
  And so by us he's taken.
2ND GROUP
  No, he belongs to me!
ALL FLOWER MAIDENS
  No, he belongs to us!
  To us! Not you! To us, to us!
PARSIFAL *(half angrily, frightening the maidens off)*
  No more! I'll not be caught!
  He is about to escape, when, hearing Kundry's voice out of the
  flower-foliage, he stands still in surprise.
KUNDRY
  Parsifal!—Stay here!
PARSIFAL
  Parsifal . . . ?
  So named me, dreaming one day, my mother.
  At the sound of Kundry's voice, the maidens, terror-stricken,
  withdraw at once from Parsifal.
KUNDRY *(gradually coming into sight)*
  Here linger! Parsifal!
  To greet you, gladness and joy are here.
  You amorous children, leave him alone;
  fast-withering flowers,
  be off, he was not sent for your sport.
  Go home, tend to the wounded;
  lonely awaits you many a knight.
  The maidens, turning timidly and reluctantly away from
  Parsifal, withdraw to the palace.
1ST FLOWER THEN 3RD FLOWER, 2ND GROUP
  Must I leave you!
2ND FLOWER 2ND GROUP
  Must I lose you!
3RD FLOWER THEN 1ST FLOWER, 1ST GROUP
  Oh, what sorrow!
2ND FLOWER 1ST GROUP
  Oh, sorrow and pain!

BOTH CHORUSES
  Oh, sorrow!
ALL FLOWERS 1ST GROUP
  From all I'd gladly part forever—
1ST AND 2ND GROUPS
  —to be alone with you.
BOTH CHORUSES
  Farewell! Farewell!
  You fair one, you proud one,
  you—fool!
  Laughing, the maidens disappear into the palace.
PARSIFAL
  This garden—is it all a dream?
  He looks round timidly to the side whence the voice came.
  There appears through an opening of the flower-hedges a young
  and very beautiful woman—Kundry, in altered form—lying on
  a flowery couch, wearing a light veil-like robe of Arabian style.
  Did you call to me, the nameless?
KUNDRY
  I named you, foolish pure one,
  "Fal parsi"—
  so pure and foolish: "Parsifal."
  So cried, in far Arabian land where he died,
  your father Gamuret to you, his son,
  who in your mother's womb were stirring,
  yes, thus he named you as he perished;
  to tell these tidings I was waiting here:
  what drew you here if not the wish to know?
PARSIFAL
  Ne'er saw I, nor dreamed before, what now
  I see, and what has filled my heart with fear.
  Are you a flower grown in this lovely garden?
KUNDRY
  No, Parsifal, you foolish pure one!
  Far, far from here my homeland.
  For you to find me, I lingered here awhile;
  from far hence came I, many things I've seen.
  I saw the child upon his mother's breast,
  his early laughter lingers in my ear;
  her heart was grieving,

but laughter inspired Herzeleide,
when, through her sorrows,
on you, her son, her eyes she feasted.
On tender mosses you were cradled,
your sleep was lulled with soft caresses;
in anxious vigil,
your slumber was by your mother guarded;
and every morning
a mother's glowing tears would wake you.
Forever weeping, born of sorrow,
she mourned your father's love and death:
as holy duty she decided
to save you from a fate like his.
From clash of arms, from men in deadly conflict,
she ever strove to shield you and protect you.
So anxious was she, ah! and fearful:
no news of fighting arrived to disturb you.
Can you remember her anxious cry
when late and far you were roaming,
Can you remember how she laughed
in relief when you had returned;
and how she caught you in her embrace?
Oh, did you not fear her kisses then?
You were heedless of all her care,
of all her anguished grieving,
when one day you did not return
and left no trace behind you.
Long days and nights she waited,
until her cries grew silent,
when grief consumed all the pain;
for quiet death she yearned:
then sorrow broke her heart,
and Herzeleide died.

PARSIFAL
(in growing surprise and alarm sinks down at Kundry's feet,
overcome with distress)
Sorrow! Sorrow! What did I? Where was I?
Mother! Sweetest, dearest mother!
Your son, your son was then your murderer!
O fool! Blind and blundering fool!
I wandered away, I could forget you,

mother, I could forget you?
Truest, dearest mother!
KUNDRY
  Had you not felt such grief,
  then consolation's
  sweet relief you'd not know;
  let sorrow that you feel,
  let torment yield
  to the joy that love can reveal.
PARSIFAL *(sinking lower in his sadness)*
  My mother, my mother, could I forget her!
  Ha! What else did I also forget?
  Have I remembered anything?
  What else but folly lives in me?
  *Kundry, still reclining, bends over Parsifal's head, gently touches
  his forehead, and winds her arm confidingly round his neck.*
KUNDRY
  Acknowledge
  your fault and then it's ended;
  by knowledge
  your folly soon is mended.
  Of love now learn the rapture
  that Gamuret once learned,
  when Herzeleide's passion
  within him fiercely burned!
  For love that gave you
  life and being,
  must death and folly both remove,
  love sends
  you now
  a mother's blessing, greets a son
  with love's first kiss!
  *She has bent her head completely over his and now presses her
  lips to his mouth in a long kiss. Suddenly Parsifal starts up with
  a gesture of intense fear; his demeanor expresses some fearful
  change; he presses his hands tightly against his heart, as though
  to subdue a rending pain.*
PARSIFAL
  Amfortas!
  The Spear-wound!—The Spear-wound!—
  It burns here in my heart!

Oh! Torment! Torment!
Fearfullest torment,
the cry of anguish pierces my heart.
Oh!—Oh!—
Keen anguish!
Piteous sufferer!
The wound that I saw bleeding
is bleeding now in me!
Here—here!
No! No! Not the Spear-wound is it.
Freely the blood may stream from my side.
Here! Here, a flame in my heart!
The yearning, the wild fearful yearning
that fills my senses and holds them fast!
Oh!—pain of loving!
How all things tremble, quiver, and shake
in sinful, guilty yearning!
*While Kundry stares at him in fear and wonder, Parsifal
appears to fall wholly into a trace. He continues calmly.*
This gaze is fixed now on the holy Cup—
the sacred blood now glows:
redemption's rapture, sweet and mild,
to every heart brings all its healing;
but here—in this heart will the pain not lessen.
The Savior's cry is stealing through me,
lamenting, ah, lamenting
for the profaned sanctuary:
"Redeem me, rescue me
from hands defiled and guilty!"
Thus rang his lamentation,
fearful, loud, loud to my spirit.
And I, a fool, a coward,
to childish deeds of daring fled away!
He throws himself despairingly on his knees.
Redeemer! Savior! Lord of grace!
Can I my sinful crime efface?
*Kundry, whose astonishment has changed to sorrowful wonder,
seeks hesitatingly to approach Parsifal.*
KUNDRY
O noble knight! Cast off your fear!
Look up and find redemption here!

PARSIFAL
(still kneeling, gazes fixedly at Kundry, who during the following, bends over him with the caressing movements that he describes)
Yes! With these accents she called to him;
and with this look—I seem to know it well,
and this one, with its remorseless laughter,
these lips too, yes, they tempted him thus,
she bent her neck toward him,
thus boldly rose her head,
thus fluttered her tresses around him,
thus twined she her arms round his neck—
so tenderly his cheek caressing;
with all the powers of pain united,
his soul's salvation
these lips once kissed away!
Ha!—and her kiss!
Parsifal has gradually risen and pushes Kundry from him.
Destroyer!—Go from my side!
Ever, ever be gone!
KUNDRY *(very passionately)*
Cruel man!
If in your heart you feel
only others' sorrows,
now feel what sorrows are mine!
If you're a savior,
then what restrains you
from joining with me in my salvation?
Through endless ages you I awaited,
my savior, ah! so late!
Whom once I dared revile!
Oh!—
If you knew the curse
that holds through sleep and waking,
through death and living,
pain and laughter . . .
To new afflictions newly steeled . . .
endless torment racks my soul!
I saw Him—Him—
and mocked Him . . .
on me fell His look!

I seek Him now from world to world,
till once more I behold Him.
In deepest woe—
I feel that He must be near,
I see that look He gave.
Then once more my accursed laughter fills me:
a sinner sinks in my embraces!
I laugh then, laugh then,
I cannot weep,
but crying, raving,
storming, raging,
I sink again into shameful night,
from which, remorseful, scarce I wake.
One I desire with deathly yearning,
One whom I knew, though I despised Him:
let me upon His breast lie weeping,
for one brief hour with you united,
and then though God and world might scorn,
I'd be redeemed by you and reborn!

PARSIFAL

For evermore
you'd be condemned with me,
for that brief hour,
forgetful of my calling,
within your arms enfolded!
For your salvation I was sent,
if of your yearnings you repent.
The solace that can end your suffering
from purer fountains sweetly flows,
and grace will never be accorded
until the sinful fount you close.
Another grace, another, yes!
For which in sorrow once I saw
the brothers pine: what cares distressed them,
what fear tormented and oppressed them!
But who with soul unclouded knows
that fount whence truly healing flows?
Oh, anguish—putting hope to flight!
O night of worldly error:
in quest of true salvation's light,
we drink damnation's draught of terror!

KUNDRY *(in wild ecstasy)*
So it was my kiss
that made you see all these things clearly?
The full embrace of my loving
surely to godhead will raise you.
Redeem the world then, if that's your task:
become a god this moment,
let me be condemned for evermore,
my wound remain unclosed!

PARSIFAL
Redemption, sinful one, I offer you.

KUNDRY *(entreatingly)*
Then as a god let me love you,
redemption you would bring to me.

PARSIFAL
Love and redemption will be granted—
if the way
to Amfortas you now show.

KUNDRY *(breaking out in fury)*
No—you'll never find him!
He has fallen, so let him perish,
the unhallowed,
shame-welcomer,
whom I derided—laughing—laughing—
Ha ha! Who fell by his own good Spear!

PARSIFAL
Who dared then to wound him with the sacred Spear?

KUNDRY
He—he—
who once my laughter rebuked:
his curse—ha! it gives me strength;
'gainst you yourself I'll summon the Spear
if for that sinner you dare to plead!—
Ha, madness!
(beseechingly)
Mercy! Mercy on me!
And for one hour be mine!
For one brief hour be mine . . .
To Amfortas
then I shall lead the way!
She tries to embrace him. He thrusts her forcibly from him.

PARSIFAL
Begone, accursed woman!

KUNDRY
She recoils in wild raging fury and calls into the background.
Help me! Help me! To me!
Seize the intruder! Oh, help!
Bar him from leaving!
Guard every pathway!
(to Parsifal)
And though you should escape, and search through
every road in the world,
the path that you seek,
that path you'll never discover
each road and pathway
that leads from my presence,
I now curse them to you:
Wander! Wander!
Share in my fate!
Wander like me evermore!
*Klingsor appears on the rampart and prepares to throw the
Spear toward Parsifal.*

KLINGSOR
Halt there! I hold the weapon that will serve!
The holy fool will fall by his master's Spear!
He hurls the Spear, which remains hanging over Parsifal's head.

PARSIFAL *(seizing the Spear, which he holds over his head)*
So with this Spear I vanquish your enchantment:
and the wound shall be healed now
by the Spear that wounded.
To darkness and ruin
falls your deceiving display!
*He swings the Spear in the sign of the Cross; the castle falls as
by an earthquake. The garden withers to a desert; the ground is
scattered with faded flowers. Kundry sinks down with a cry.
Parsifal, hastening away, pauses on the top of the ruined wall,
and turns back to Kundry.*
You know
where once again you can find me when you choose!
*He hastens off. Kundry has raised herself a little and looks after
him.*

ACT 3

*The curtains open. Pleasant, open spring landscape in the
domain of the Grail. Flowering meadows rise gently toward the
background. The edge of the forest is seen in the foreground,
stretching away, right, to rising rocky ground. By the woodside
a spring; and opposite this, farther back, a hermit's hut, built
against a mass of rock. Very early morning. Gurnemanz, grown
very old and grey, and dressed as a hermit in the tunic of the
Grail Knights, steps out of the hut and listens.*

GURNEMANZ
From there I heard the groaning.
So woefully moans no beast,
least of all today—this blessed and holy morn.
A dull groaning is heard.
I think I recognize that call of grief.
*He walks purposefully toward a thorn thicket at the side, much
overgrown; he forces the undergrowth apart, then suddenly stops.*
Ha! She's back again.
By wintry brambles and thorns
she was concealed: how long now?
Up! Kundry! Up!
Now winter's fled, and spring is here!
Awaken! Awaken to spring!—
*He draws Kundry stiff and lifeless out of the bushes, and bears
her to a grassy mound nearby.*
Cold and stiff!
This time I truly fear she's dead:
and yet her groaning came to my ear?
*As Kundry lies before Gurnemanz, he rubs her hands and tem-
ples, and does his utmost to relax her stiffness. At last life seems
to awaken her. She is now fully awake, opens her eyes and
utters a cry. She wears the coarse robe of a penitent, as in the
first Act; her face is paler; the wildness has vanished from her
looks and behavior. She gazes long at Gurnemanz. Then, raising herself, she arranges her hair and dress, and moves away as
though a serving maid.*
How strange you are!
Have you no word for me?
Is this my thanks,

when from deathly slumber
I waken you once again?
Kundry slowly bares her head; at length she speaks, hoarsely and brokenly.
KUNDRY
  Serving . . . serving.
GURNEMANZ *(shaking his head)*
  Your task will be but light:
  for now no messengers we need;
  herbs and roots
  each of us finds for himself.
  From beasts of the forest we learned.
Kundry has meanwhile looked about her, sees the hut, and goes into it. Gurnemanz gazes after her, wondering.
  How different from what she was before!
  Can this holy day be the cause?
  O day of mercy past comparing!
  In truth, for her salvation
  I was allowed to wake
  this soul from deathly slumber.
Kundry returns from the hut; she carries a pitcher and goes with it to the spring. Here, glancing into the wood, she sees someone approaching in the distance, and turns to Gurnemanz to point this out to him. He looks into the wood.
  Who comes toward the sacred spring
  In gloomy war apparel?
  He is not one of our band!
During Parsifal's entry, Kundry fills her pitcher and moves slowly away into the hut, where she busies herself. Parsifal enters from the wood in a suit of black armor: with closed helm and lowered Spear he strides slowly forward, and moves with bowed head in dreamy uncertainty to the little grass mound beside the spring, where he seats himself. Gurnemanz, having gazed long at Parsifal in astonishment, now steps toward him.
  Hail there, my guest!
  Are you astray, and may I direct you?
Parsifal gently shakes his head.
  No word of greeting to your host?
Parsifal bends his head. Gurnemanz continues, disconcerted.
  Hey!—What!—
  Some vow perhaps

has constrained your lips to silence,
but mine are bound to speak,
to tell you plainly what is right.
This place you see is holy ground:
a man should bear no weapons here,
no visored helmet, shield, or spear;
and least today! Do you not know
what holy day this is?
Parsifal shakes his head.
No? From whence have you come?
Among what heathens have you dwelt,
that you know not there dawns
on us now the all-holy Good Friday morn?
Parsifal sinks his head yet lower.
Lay down your weapons!
Injure not the Lord, who this day,
bare of defiance, His holy blood
once shed to redeem the sinful world!
*Parsifal raises himself after a further silence, thrusts his Spear into
the ground before him, lays shield and sword beneath it, raises his
visor and, removing it from his head, lays it with the other arms,
and then kneels in silent prayer before the Spear. Gurnemanz
watches Parsifal in wonder and emotion. He beckons to Kundry,
who has just reappeared from the hut. Parsifal raises his eyes
devoutly to the Spear-head. Gurnemanz addresses Kundry softly.*
You know him now?
He it is who once the swan destroyed!
Kundry nods her head slightly.
In truth, 'tis he,
the fool, whom I roughly turned away.
Kundry gazes fixedly but calmly at Parsifal.
Ha! By what pathway came he?
The Spear—I know it now.
(with great solemnity)
O holiest day
to which my soul is wakening!
*Kundry has turned her face away. Parsifal rises slowly from
prayer, looks calmly about him, recognizes Gurnemanz, and
extends his hand to him in greeting.*
PARSIFAL
Praise God! Once again I have found you!

GURNEMANZ
    You still remember me?
    You still recall me,
    whom grief and care have deeply bowed?
    How came you here—and whence?

PARSIFAL
    Through error and through suffering's pathways came I;
    and can I rightly think I can escape them,
    now that the forest's murmurs
    once again I'm hearing,
    and, good old man, again I greet you? . . .
    Or—do I err still?
    For everything seems altered.

GURNEMANZ
    But say, who is it you are seeking?

PARSIFAL
    The man whose deepest anguish
    in foolish wonder once I heard—
    whom I can heal; I bring
    his ordained salvation, as foretold.
    But—ah!—
    the way of healing never finding,
    I wandered in error,
    by a fearful curse led astray;
    numberless dangers,
    battles, and duels
    forced me to leave the pathway,
    even when I thought it was found.
    Then I was seized with dread of failure,
    to keep the Spear unprofaned;
    so to defend it, and to guard it,
    I suffered many a wound on the way,
    the Spear itself
    could not be wielded in battle;
    unprofaned
    at my side then I bore it;
    and home I now restore it:
    you see it shining pure and clear—
    the Grail's most holy Spear.

GURNEMANZ *(in a transport of joy)*
    O glory! Boundless grace!

O wonder! Holy, highest wonder!
(to Parsifal, after somewhat composing himself)
O Lord! If it was a curse
that drove you from the chosen path,
be sure the spell is broken.
You're standing in the Grail's domain,
our noble knights await you here.
Ah, we have need of healing,
the healing that you bring!
Since that morning when you first were here,
the sorrow that you witnessed then,
the anguish grew to direst need.
Amfortas, maddened with the torment
he in soul and body suffered,
at last with raging defiance longed for death.
No pleas, no sorrow of the brethren
could move him to fulfill his sacred office.
The shrine lay shrouded, unrevealed the Grail:
its guardian, racked with sinful suffering,
who could not die so long
as he beheld its light,
thus hoped that he would perish,
and with his life thus end his cruel torment.
The food of Heaven we are now denied,
and common fare must now support us:
and so there faded all our heroes' might.
No suppliants seek us now;
no call to holy strife in distant countries:
pale, dejected, wandering
and lost, and leaderless our knightly band.
Here in the forest I have come to dwell
till death shall come to claim me,
as death my aged warrior-lord has claimed:
yes, Titurel, my holy King,
when once the Grail's refreshment was denied him,
he died—a man, like others!
PARSIFAL *(springing up in intense grief)*
    And I—I it is,
    who brought this woe on all!
    Ha! What transgression!
    With a load of sin

must this my foolish head
eternally be laden.
for no repentance, no atonement
my blinded eyes can lighten;
though chosen by God as a savior,
I lost myself in error;
salvation's only path has vanished!
*Parsifal seems about to fall senseless. Gurnemanz supports him
and lets him sink down onto the grassy mound. Kundry hastily
fetches a basin of water with which to sprinkle Parsifal.*

GURNEMANZ *(gently refusing Kundry)*
Not that!
The holy spring itself
must now refresh our pilgrim's brow.
I feel some holy work
he must today accomplish,
perhaps fulfill some sacred office:
let him be pure of stain,
the dust of doubtful ways
our sacred spring can wash away!
*They both gently move Parsifal to the edge of the spring.
During the following Kundry unbinds the greaves of his armor,
and Gurnemanz removes his breastplate.*

PARSIFAL *(gently and wearily)*
This day to Amfortas shall I be guided?

GURNEMANZ *(still busy)*
Most surely, for the lofty hall awaits:
the solemn funeral of my dearest lord
has summoned me today.
The Grail shall once more be to us revealed,
the long neglected office
shall once more be fulfilled,
to sanctify the noble father
who by his son's misdeed was slain;
the son would now atonement make:
this vow Amfortas swore.
*Parsifal gazes in quiet wonder at Kundry, who with eager humil-
ity is bathing his feet.*

PARSIFAL *(to Kundry)*
You washed my feet so humbly,
now bathe for me my brow, good friend!

Gurnemanz takes some water in his hand from the spring and sprinkles Parsifal's head.

GURNEMANZ

Be purified, you pure one, by this water!
It washes every guilt
and care away from you!
During this Kundry draws a golden phial from her bosom, pours its contents over Parsifal's feet, and dries them with her hair, which she has hastily unbound.

PARSIFAL

(gently taking the phial from her and passing it to Gurnemanz)
My feet you have anointed;
my head now, friend of Titurel, anoint;
this very day as King you shall acclaim me!

GURNEMANZ

(pouring the phial over Parsifal's head, upon which he lays his hand in blessing)
So truly it was promised;
my blessing on your head,
as King I now acclaim you.
O—pure one!
Pitying sufferer,
all-wise deliverer!
You have redeemed him, torments you have suffered,
now lift the load forever from his head!

PARSIFAL

Unnoticed, he has filled his hands with water from the spring, and he now bends forward to Kundry, who is still kneeling before him, and pours it over her head.
My first of tasks I thus perform:—
baptized be,
have faith in the Redeemer!
Kundry sinks her head to the earth; she seems to weep passionately. Parsifal, turning away, gazes in gentle ecstasy upon field and forest, which are glowing in the morning light.
Today the fields and meadows seem so fair!
Many a magic flower I've seen,
which wildly sought to twine itself around me;
but ne'er before so fair and mild
the meadow flowers blooming;
their scent recalls my childhood days
and tells of loving trust to me.

GURNEMANZ

It is Good Friday's magic, lord!

PARSIFAL

O sorrow, that day of agony!
When all creation, all that blooms,
that breathes, lives, and lives anew,
should only sigh and sorrow.

GURNEMANZ

You see, it is not so.
The sinner's tears of true repentance
today with holy dew
bedeck the flowery mead
and make them glow so brightly;
while all created things rejoice
to see the Savior's sign of grace,
and raise a prayer to praise Him.
Himself, the Savior crucified, they see not:
and so they raise their eyes to man redeemed,
the man set free from sin, set free from terror,
by God's most loving sacrifice made pure:
today each blade and bloom upon the meadow
knows well the foot of man will do no harm;
in truth, as God with heavenly loving care
endured for man and for him bled,
so man now will repay that love
and walk with gentle tread.
And grateful, all creation sings,
all things that bloom and pass away;
nature her innocence has won,
all is renewed once more this day.
*Kundry has slowly raised her head and gazes up with tearful
eyes, filled with calm and earnest entreaty, at Parsifal.*

PARSIFAL

I saw them withering when once they mocked me:
are they now for redemption yearning?
A dew of sorrow from your eyes is flowing:
you're weeping . . . look, they smile, the meadows!
*He kisses her gently on the forehead. A distant pealing of bells is
heard.*

GURNEMANZ
Midday:
the time has come.
Allow me, lord, as your squire to lead you!
From the hut Gurnemanz has fetched his Grail Knight's man-
tle, with which he and Kundry invest Parsifal.—Parsifal
solemnly takes up the Spear and with Kundry follows
Gurnemanz, who leads slowly. The scene changes very gradu-
ally, as in the first Act, but from right to left. After remaining
for a time visible, the three entirely disappear, while the forest
gradually vanishes, and in its place the rocks draw near.
Through the arched passages, the sound of bells swells ever
louder. The rock walls open, disclosing the lofty Grail Hall, as
in the first Act, but without the feast-tables. Dusky light.
From one side appear Knights bearing Titurel's coffin, from
the other side those escorting Amfortas in the litter, preceded
by the covered shrine of the Grail.

1ST PROCESSION OF KNIGHTS *(with Amfortas)*
While we with sacred awe, concealed in this shrine,
the Grail escort to the altar,
concealed there in gloomy shrine,
in mourning whom do you bear?

2ND PROCESSION OF KNIGHTS *(with Titurel's body)*
We bear a hero within this shrine,
it holds the heavenly might,
whom God Himself once chose as His guard:
Titurel hither we bear.

1ST PROCESSION OF KNIGHTS
By whom was he killed, who, in God's own guard,
God's self had in keeping?

2ND PROCESSION OF KNIGHTS
He fell by the hand of conquering age,
when the Grail's pure light was denied him.

1ST PROCESSION OF KNIGHTS
Who kept him the Grail's pure light from beholding?

2ND PROCESSION OF KNIGHTS
The man you're escorting, the Grail's sinful guardian.

1ST PROCESSION OF KNIGHTS
We escort him today because once more now,
and once more only

he'll fulfill his office.
Ah, the final time!
Amfortas is now placed on the couch behind the Grail altar; the coffin is set down in front. During the following, the Knights turn to Amfortas.

2ND PROCESSION OF KNIGHTS
Sorrow! Sorrow! Guardian of the Grail,
the final time
be your office performed!

AMFORTAS *(wearily raising himself a little)*
Yes—sorrow! Sorrow! Sorrow for me!
So cry I gladly with you:
gladder still if you would deal me death,
for sin like mine small atonement.
The coffin is opened. All, at the sight of Titurel's corpse, break into a cry of woe. Amfortas raises himself high on his couch and turns to Titurel's corpse.
My father!
Highly blessed among all heroes!
You pure one, to whom once angels descended:
attempting myself to die,
I dealt you your death!
Oh! You are now in glory on high
and behold the Savior's face.—
Entreat Him for me that His holiest blood,
if but once more now its blessing
the brothers here may quicken,
renewing life within them,
may bring me solace in death!
Death!—Dying!
Only mercy!
The wound and the poison, destroy their torment:
they gnaw my heart: so let it be stilled!
My father! Oh—hear me:
You must cry unto Him:
"Redeemer, grant to my son release!"

THE KNIGHTS *(pressing nearer to Amfortas)*
Reveal now the Grail!—
Do now your office!
Your father demands it:
You must!—You must!

Amfortas springs up in maddened despair and rushes among the Knights; they recoil.

AMFORTAS

No!—No more! Ha!
Dark shadows of death close around me,
and once more you would recall me to life?
Insane you are!
Who would compel me to live now,
when instant death you can grant me?
He tears open his robe.
Here am I, behold my open wound!
See here the poison, here flows my blood:
Unsheathe your weapons! Plunge every swordblade
deep—deep, in my heart!
Come! You heroes,
slay now the sinner and end his woe,
on you once more the Grail then will glow!
All have shrunk back in fear from Amfortas who now, in terrible ecstasy, stands alone. Parsifal, accompanied by Gurnemanz and Kundry, has appeared unobserved among the Knights, and, now advancing, he extends the Spear and touches with its point Amfortas's side.

PARSIFAL

One weapon only serves:
the Spear that smote
must heal you of your wound.
Amfortas's face shines with holy rapture; he staggers, as though overcome with awe and emotion; Gurnemanz supports him.
Be healed, forgiven, and atoned!
Now I shall undertake your task.
Oh, blessed be your suffering,
for pity's highest power
and purest wisdom's might
to this weak fool they brought!
Parsifal strides toward the center, the Spear raised high before him.
The sacred Spear
I bring you once again!
All gaze in highest rapture upon the upheld Spear, to the point of which Parsifal raises his eyes, as he continues ecstatically.
Oh! Wondrous miracle of joy!
This holy weapon that has healed you,

upon its point fresh blood is flowing
and yearning to join the kindred fountain,
that darkly in the Grail is glowing.
No more conceal that holy shrine:
reveal now the Grail, open the shrine!
*Parsifal ascends the altar steps, takes the Grail from the shrine
already opened by the Squires, and sinks to his knees in silent
prayer before it. The Grail softly shines. Increasing gloom
below and growing light from above.*

BOYS, YOUTHS, AND KNIGHTS
Highest holy wonder!
Redeemed the redeemer!
*The ray of light falls from above, and the Grail glows brightest.
From the dome a white dove descends and hovers over
Parsifal's head. Kundry, with her gaze uplifted to Parsifal, sinks
slowly lifeless to the ground. Amfortas and Gurnemanz kneel in
homage before Parsifal, who waves the Grail in blessing over
the worshipping Knights. The curtains slowly close.*

Translated by Andrew Porter

*The translation was made for,
and with admiration, affection, and gratitude
is dedicated to, Sir Reginald Goodall.*

THE ROSE CAVALIER
A Comedy for Music
by Hugo von Hofmannsthal

Richard Strauss

CHARACTERS

THE FELDMARSCHALLIN, *Princess von Werdenberg*	*Soprano*
BARON OCHS AUF LERCHENAU	*Bass*
OCTAVIAN, *called Quinquin, a young gentleman of noble family*	*Mezzo-Soprano*
HERR VON FANINAL, *a rich merchant, newly ennobled*	*High Baritone*
SOPHIE, *his daughter*	*High Soprano*
MARIANNE LEITMETZER, *the Duenna*	*High Soprano*
VALZACCHI, *an intriguer*	*Tenor*
ANNINA, *his partner*	*Contralto*
A COMMISSAR OF POLICE	*Bass*
MAJOR-DOMO TO THE PRINCESS	*Tenor*
MAJOR-DOMO TO FANINAL	*Tenor*
A NOTARY	*Bass*
LANDLORD	*Tenor*
A SINGER	*Tenor*
A SCHOLAR	
A FLUTE PLAYER	
A HAIRDRESSER	
HAIRDRESSER'S ASSISTANT	

A NOBLE WIDOW	*Mezzo-Soprano*
THREE NOBLE ORPHANS	*Soprano, Mezzo-Soprano,*
	Contralto
A MILLINER	*Soprano*
A VENDOR OF PETS	*Tenor*
FOUR FOOTMEN OF THE PRINCESS	*2 Tenors, 2 Basses*
FOUR WAITERS	*1 Tenor, 3 Basses*

A LITTLE BLACK PAGE, FOOTMEN,
COURIERS, COACHMEN, ALMONER,
NOTARY'S CLERK, MAIDSERVANTS,
HEIDUCKS, HEAD COOK AND
ASSISTANT, KITCHEN BOYS, GUESTS,
MUSICIANS, TWO CONSTABLES, FOUR
LITTLE CHILDREN, VARIOUS
PERSONAGES OF SUSPICIOUS APPEARANCE.

The action takes place in Vienna, during the first years of the reign of Maria Theresa.

ACT 1

The Marschallin's bedroom. In the alcove to the left the large, tent-shaped fourposter. Next to the bed a three-leaved Chinese screen, behind which some clothes are scattered. A small table, chairs, etc. On a little sofa to the left lies a sword in its sheath. To the right, great folding doors leading to the antechamber. In the center, scarcely visible, a small door in the wall. No other doors. Between the alcove and the small door, a dressing table and a few armchairs against the wall. The curtains of the bed are half-drawn. Through the half-open window the bright morning sun streams in. From the garden the song of birds can be heard.

    Octavian kneels on a footstool, half embracing the Princess who is reclining in bed. Her face is hidden; only her beautiful hand and arm, peeping from the sleeve of her lace nightgown, can be seen.

OCTAVIAN *(rapturously)*
  I alone! None but I
  know the treasures of your kindness!
MARSCHALLIN *(raises herself on her pillows)*
  Do you reproach me for that, Quinquin?
  Would you have all the world share them?

OCTAVIAN *(passionately)*
Angel! No! Blessed am I,
For it is I, I alone, who know their secrets.
All your secrets! All your treasures!
You, you, you!—Why speak of "you"? This "You and I"?
Do you know what they mean?
These are words, merely words—yes—you know.
All the same, though, there is something within them,
a feeling, a craving, a yearning, a striving,
a longing, a burning:
My hand reaches out to search for your hand,
and I must touch you, I want to hold you.
All I want is only you;
but then "I" am lost in that "you" . . .
I am your boy—but then when I am carried away in your arms—
then where is your boy?
MARSCHALLIN *(softly)*
You are my boy, you are my love.
(very tenderly)
I love you so.
They embrace.
OCTAVIAN *(starts up)*
Why is it day? It shall not be day.
What use is the day?
Then everyone sees you. Dark it shall be.
He rushes to the window, closes it, and draws the curtains.
The distant tinkling of a bell is heard. The Marschallin laughs
to herself.
Why do you laugh?
MARSCHALLIN
Why do I laugh?
OCTAVIAN
Angel!
MARSCHALLIN
Dearest, my sweetest love!
(again a discreet tinkling)
Hark!
OCTAVIAN
I will not!
MARSCHALLIN
Quiet, be still!

OCTAVIAN
I will not listen. What can it be?
The sound comes closer.
Is it footmen with letters and pretty verses?
From Saurau, from Hartig, or the Portuguese ambassador?
Here no one enters but I. I am master here!
The little door in the center opens, and a Little Black Page in yellow, hung with silver bells, trips across the room bearing a salver with chocolate. The door is closed behind him by unseen hands.
MARSCHALLIN
Quick, go and hide yourself, for breakfast comes.
Octavian steps behind the screen.
Take your sword, put it there behind the bed.
Octavian makes a dash for the sword and hides it. The Marschallin lies down again, after drawing the curtains. The Black Page places the salver on one of the small tables, moves it to the front of the stage, pulls up the sofa next to it, and bows to the Princess with his hands crossed over his breast. Then he dances daintily backwards, with his face always to the Marschallin; at the door he bows again and disappears. The Marschallin appears from behind the bed curtains. She has put on a light, fur-trimmed dressing gown. Octavian reappears from between the wall and the screen.
You scatterbrain! What were you thinking of?
Gentlemen do not leave their swords lying in the room of a lady
of fashion.
You should go to school again to learn your manners.
OCTAVIAN
But if my manners are not to your taste,
if it offends you that I've no experience in matters such as this,
why then, I have no notion how to please.
MARSCHALLIN *(tenderly, from the sofa)*
Now don't philosophize, my love, and come to me.
Now let's have breakfast. Everything in its own time.
Octavian seats himself beside her. They are very tender over breakfast. He puts his face in her lap. She strokes his hair. He looks up at her.
OCTAVIAN
Marie Thérèse!
MARSCHALLIN
Octavian!

OCTAVIAN
Bichette!
MARSCHALLIN
Quinquin!
OCTAVIAN
My heart!
MARSCHALLIN
My boy!
They continue breakfast.
OCTAVIAN *(merrily)*
The Feldmarschall stays in far Croatian woods, and hunts for
brown bear there and wild lynx,
and I, in the flower of my youth, stay here, hunting for what?
Ah, what joy! Ah, what joy!
MARSCHALLIN *(a shadow flitting over her face)*
Oh, leave the Feldmarschall in peace!
I dreamed of him last night.
OCTAVIAN
Last night? Last night you dreamed of him? Last night?
MARSCHALLIN
My dreams are not mine to command.
OCTAVIAN
Do you mean you really dreamed of him last night? The Prince?
MARSCHALLIN
Don't stare so, don't be angry. It's no fault of mine. My hus-
band was at home again.
OCTAVIAN
The Feldmarschall?
MARSCHALLIN
There was a noise without of horse and man—and he was here.
For fright I started up in haste—now look you,
now look you what a child I am—still I can hear it, all the noise
without.
'Tis ringing in my ears, do you not hear it?
OCTAVIAN
Yes, truly, sounds I hear: but why think it must be your husband?
Think but where he's a-hunting—far away,
at Esseg or a score of leagues beyond.
MARSCHALLIN
Is he so far, think you?

OCTAVIAN
Then something else it is we hear, and all is well.
You look so full of fear, Thérèse.

MARSCHALLIN
But see, Quinquin, though it be distant,
the Prince at times can travel wond'rous fast; for once—

OCTAVIAN
What did he, once? What did he, once? What did he, once?
Bichette, Bichette! What did he, once?

MARSCHALLIN
Oh, let him be—why should I tell you all things?

OCTAVIAN
See how she flouts my love!
(throws himself in despair on to the sofa)
Why will you drive me to despair?

MARSCHALLIN
Command yourself. 'Tis true. It is the Prince indeed.
For were a stranger here, the noise would surely be there in the
  antechamber.
It is my husband. I hear his footsteps in the closet.
In vain the lackeys bar his way. Quinquin, it is the Prince.
Octavian draws his sword and runs to the right.
Not there, there is the antechamber.
There, sure, a crowd with wares to offer, and a score of lackeys
  are in waiting.
There!
She points to the small door. Octavian runs in that direction.
Too late! I hear them in the closet now. There's but one chance.
Conceal yourself!
(after a brief pause of helplessness)
There!

OCTAVIAN
I will not let him pass: I stay with you!

MARSCHALLIN
There—by the bed—there in the curtains! And do not move!

OCTAVIAN *(hesitating)*
Should I be caught by him, what fate is yours, Thérèse?

MARSCHALLIN *(pleading)*
Conceal yourself, beloved.
She stamps her foot impatiently.

OCTAVIAN *(by the screen)*
  Thérèse—
MARSCHALLIN
  Quick now, be still!
  (with flashing eyes)
  Now let me see
  who dares to stir one inch toward the door while I am here.
  I'm no faint-hearted Italian brigadier. Where I stand, stand I.
  She walks energetically toward the little door and listens.
  They're worthy fellows, keeping guard without there, vowing
    they'll not make way for him,
  vowing I sleep—most worthy fellows!
  The noise in the anteroom grows louder.
  (listening)
  That voice!
  That is not, truly, no, 'tis not my husband's voice.
  'Tis Baron that they're calling him: 'tis a stranger!
  (gaily)
  Quinquin, it is someone else.
  She laughs.
  Soon escape will be quite easy.
  But in hiding remain
  so that the footmen do not see you.
  That loutish, foolish voice, surely it's familiar.
  Who can it be? My God, it's Ochs,
  it is my cousin of Lerchenau. It's Ochs of Lerchenau.
  What does he want? Heavens above us!
  She bursts into a laugh.
  Quinquin, listen. Quinquin, you cannot have forgot?
  She goes a few steps toward the left.
  One day a letter was brought—
  we were alone in my carriage,
  and someone came galloping up with a letter in his hand.
  That letter came from Ochs.
  And now I have entirely forgotten what it said.
  She laughs.
  And it is you who are guilty, Quinquin.
VOICE OF THE MAJOR-DOMO *(outside)*
  Herr Baron, will you be pleased to wait in the gallery.
  During the next speeches the small doors at the back are pulled

ajar several times and shut again, as if someone outside were try-ing to force his way in, and someone else were preventing him.

VOICE OF THE BARON *(without)*

Where did you learn such manners as these?

Herr Baron Lerchenau can't be kept waiting.

MARSCHALLIN

Quinquin, where are you now? Where have you gone?

OCTAVIAN

He comes out from behind the screen in a skirt and a bodice, his hair tied with a kerchief and ribbon to look like a cap, and makes a curtsey.

Your Ladyship's servant! I've not long been in Your Highness's household here.

MARSCHALLIN

You dear!

And only one kiss may I give you. That's for your wages.

She kisses him quickly. There is more noise outside.

He's hammering the door down, my dear cousin.

Now, as quickly as may be,

boldly march by all the footmen there.

It's sport for brazen rogues like you! And soon come back, my love,

but in men's clothing and through the main gate, if you please.

She sits down on the sofa to the left with her back to the door and begins to sip her chocolate. Octavian hurries toward the small door and tries to go out, but at that moment the door is flung open, and Baron Ochs enters, the Footmen trying in vain to keep him back. Octavian lowers his head and tries to escape quickly, but collides with him and backs up to the wall on the left in confusion. Three Footmen have entered with the Baron and stand at a loss.

BARON *(pompously to the Footmen)*

I'm quite certain Her Highness will receive me.

He comes forward, while the Footmen on his left try to bar his passage.

(to Octavian, with interest)

Pardon, my pretty child.

Octavian in confusion turns his face to the wall.

(with gracious condescension)

I said, "Pardon, my pretty child."

The Princess looks over her shoulder, rises, and goes to meet the Baron, who addresses Octavian gallantly.

I hope I did not really frighten you.

THE FOOTMEN *(nudging the Baron)*
  Her Most Excellent Highness!
  They take up their position in a tight row near the Marschallin,
  right in front of the small doors. The Baron bows in the French
  manner, with two repetitions.
MARSCHALLIN
  My dear cousin, you're looking well today.
BARON *(bows again, then to the Footmen)*
  See what I told you, she is simply delighted that I came.
  The Baron goes to the Princess with the bearing of a man of the
  world, giving her his hand and leading her forward.
  And why should Your Highness not be glad!
  The hour is unimportant when one's a person of rank.
  Have I not morning after morning
  visited our dear Princess Brioche, just to pay my respects to her,
  while in her bath she sat at ease,
  with nothing except a tiny silk screen between her and me?
  I am astounded
  (looking angrily around)
  that any lackey dare—
  Octavian would have liked to slip out in the meantime; the
  astonished glances of the Footmen force him to be extremely
  cautious, and with affected ease he makes his way along the wall
  to the alcove.
MARSCHALLIN
  Forgive them, please.
  My orders were given; they have obeyed them.
  I suffered this morning from a migraine.
  At a sign from the Marschallin, the Footmen have brought the two
  small sofas forward and retired. Octavian busies himself about the
  bed as inconspicuously as possible. The Marschallin seats herself
  on the sofa at the right after offering the Baron the sofa at the left.
BARON
  (trying to sit down, much distracted by the presence of the
  pretty maid; aside)
  A pretty wench! A tasty, saucy baggage!
  The Marschallin rises and ceremoniously again offers him a seat.
  The Baron seats himself with hesitation, trying not to turn his
  back completely on the pretty maid. In the ensuing dialogue he
  turns sometimes toward the Marschallin, on his left, and some-
  times to Octavian, on the right.

MARSCHALLIN
And even now I'm not quite well.
My dear Cousin, bearing that in mind, will have the kindness—
BARON
Why surely.
He turns to his right to look at Octavian.
MARSCHALLIN
It's my waiting woman, a young girl from the country.
I'm afraid, though, her manners may not please Your Lordship.
BARON
She's very sweet!
What? She does not please me! Me? The contrary!
He beckons to Octavian with his hand; then to the Marschallin.
But Your Highness perhaps was surprised to learn that I'm to
be a bridegroom—
(looking around)
but yet—meanwhile—
MARSCHALLIN
A bridegroom?
BARON
Yes, I wrote it all in the letter that I sent to Your Highness—
(to himself)
a rascal, very juicy, just a babe in arms!
MARSCHALLIN *(relieved)*
You wrote a letter. Why of course, and who's the lucky bride to be?
I have forgotten for the moment.
BARON
Eh?
(over his shoulder)
Fresh as paint! So clean! So healthy! What a wench!
MARSCHALLIN
But tell me who's the bride?
BARON
Sophie Faninal. But Your Highness,
(with slight vexation)
I did not keep her name a secret.
MARSCHALLIN
Forgive me. My memory is at fault. What of
her family? They do not come from here?
*Octavian busies himself with the tray and thus gets behind the
Baron.*

BARON

    I assure Your Highness, they do come from here.

    One whom Her Majesty the Empress has raised to the nobility.

    The whole provisioning of our armies in the Netherlands is in his hands.

    The Marschallin makes impatient signs to Octavian to withdraw. The Baron completely misunderstands her expression.

    I see that Your Highness shows upon her brow disdain at the mésalliance.

    And yet, although I say it, the girl's as pretty as an angel from above.

    She comes straight from a convent. She's an only child.

    (more emphatically)

    Her father possesses twelve houses in the city and has a palace, too.

    He's not over healthy,

    (chuckling)

    or so I've heard it said.

MARSCHALLIN

    Ah, my dear cousin, I can see now which way the wind is blowing.

    She signals to Octavian to withdraw.

BARON

    And if Your Highness will allow me,

    it seems to me I come of such a highly born and noble family that you can say

    my blood is blue enough for two, *corpo di Bacco!*

    I'll see to it that the social standing that my wife should have,

    she'll have with a question, and as regards our children, if the Empress should refuse them the golden keys of nobility—*va bene!*

    They'll still possess the twelve iron keys

    to their twelve houses in the city for their consolation.

MARSCHALLIN

    Of course. I'm sure no child of yours would ever

    find it hard to endure such consolation.

    Octavian walks backwards with the tray toward the door.

BARON

    Where are you going with that chocolate? Come back here now!

    Wait! Pst! What is it?

    Octavian hesitates, averting his face.

MARSCHALLIN
Off with you now!

BARON
If you will allow me, Your Highness,
I haven't had a bite today.

MARSCHALLIN *(resigned)*
Mariandl, bring it back and wait upon His Lordship.
Octavian comes back and serves the Baron from his right, so that the latter is again between the Marschallin and Octavian.

BARON
I'm nearly starving, my dear cousin. Sitting in my carriage since
five o'clock.
God, what a piece of flesh!
(to Octavian, softly)
Do not go yet, my child.
I've something more to tell you.
(to the Marschallin, aloud)
All my servants are here, huntsmen and grooms and footmen—
(eating voraciously)
they are all gathered in the courtyard with my almoner.

MARSCHALLIN *(to Octavian)*
You may go.

BARON *(to Octavian)*
Give me another biscuit. Stay a while!
(softly)
You are the sweetest angel, child, a proper pet.
(to the Marschallin)
We're on our way to the White Horse Inn, where I shall be staying till tomorrow evening—
(softly to Octavian)
I'll stick at no expense if we—
(to the Marschallin, very loudly)
—but till tomorrow—
(to Octavian)
—just you and I all alone together! Ah!
The Marschallin cannot help laughing at Octavian's impudent play-acting.
(to the Marschallin)
Then we're invited to stay with Faninal.
Beforehand I have to choose a fitting ambassador—

(angrily to Octavian)
Can't you wait a minute?
(to the Marschallin)
—to my highly-born and lovely bride I will send him,
with the silver rose in his hand
as the old custom is among noblemen.

MARSCHALLIN
On whom of all our kinsmen has Your Lordship's choice fallen
to act as his ambassador?

BARON
It is only because I need Your Highness's counsel on this question
that I have made so bold to come so early and to appear all
travel-stained—

MARSCHALLIN
You wish?

BARON
To beg humbly the favor that I asked for in my letter.
I hope I don't presume too much, that with my request I have
given no offense to you—

MARSCHALLIN
How so, of course not! We must find someone
to be ambassador and call upon your bride,
one of our kinsfolk—whom to choose?

BARON *(leaning back, to Octavian)*
You could do with me anything you wanted.
You're just the one for me!

MARSCHALLIN
Our cousin Preysing? Well! Or cousin Lamberg?
I wonder—

BARON
I leave it to Your Highness's absolute discretion.

MARSCHALLIN
'Tis well. Will you not come to supper, then, dear cousin?
Let's say tomorrow, will you? I'll be prepared with suggestions.

BARON
For such grace and kindness I thank Your Highness.

MARSCHALLIN *(rising)*
And now . . .

BARON *(aside)*
You must come back again! I stay until you do!

MARSCHALLIN *(to herself)*
Oho!
(aloud)
Stay where you are! And is that all now you wish to ask of me?
BARON
I hesitate to ask,
but I'd be grateful to have an introduction to your attorney
if I may.
I need advice on my marriage deed.
MARSCHALLIN
My attorney is coming this morning. Go to see, Mariandl,
if by chance he's in the anteroom and waiting.
BARON
Why send the girl away?
She really ought to be here and at your service.
I'll not allow it.
He holds Octavian back.
MARSCHALLIN
Let her be, cousin, she's not needed here.
BARON *(eagerly)*
Oh, I can't agree. Stay here now beside Her Ladyship.
'Twill not be long before a footman comes.
Can't let her go unprotected, bless my soul.
Why, God knows what my lackeys might do to her.
(caressing Octavian)
MARSCHALLIN
But Your Lordship is much too concerned.
Enter the Major-Domo.
BARON
Ah, here he is, you see!
He's come here no doubt with a message for you.
MARSCHALLIN *(to the Major-Domo)*
Struhan, tell me, is my attorney in the anteroom waiting?
MAJOR-DOMO
Yes, the attorney's waiting there, Your Highness,
likewise the steward, and likewise the chef,
then there's an alleged singer with his flute
as well, sent here by the Count Silva.
(drily)
Of course all the customary riffraff.

BARON
> *He pushes his chair behind the Major-Domo's back, and tenderly takes the hand of the supposed chambermaid; to Octavian.*
> Say, have you ever
> been with a cavalier in a tête-à-tête
> together at supper?
> *Octavian simulates embarrassment.*
> No? I bet your eyes'll open. Will you?

OCTAVIAN *(softly, in confusion)*
> I don't really know if I ought.
> *The Marschallin observes the pair as she listens inattentively to the Major-Domo, and cannot refrain from laughing. The Major-Domo bows and steps back, thus exposing the two to the Marschallin's view.*

MARSCHALLIN *(laughing, to the Major-Domo)*
> Let them wait there.
> *Exit Major-Domo; the Baron tries to appear at his ease and assumes a serious air.*
> My cousin is, I notice, not too particular.

BARON *(relieved)*
> With you, Your Highness,
> *(breathing more freely)*
> one is quite at ease. There's no silly prudery and devout pretenses,
> *(kissing her hand)*
> and no insistence on etiquette.

MARSCHALLIN *(amused)*
> Even when you have a bride-to-be?

BARON *(half rising, leaning toward her)*
> Is that any reason to live like a monk?
> For am I not like a hunting hound always pursuing quarry
> and very hot on every scent, to left or right?

MARSCHALLIN
> I see it is for you a profession to follow the chase.

BARON
> That is my pleasure.
> For the chase I know nothing to suit me better.
> Your Highness, I must commiserate with
> you, that you only know—just what shall I say—
> only know the feelings of one defending her virtue.

Parole d'honneur! But they're not in the least like the feelings
that men know.

MARSCHALLIN
I doubt it not, variety is the spice of life.

BARON
In the whole of the year, in the whole of the day, there is never—

MARSCHALLIN
Never?

BARON
—a time—

MARSCHALLIN
A time?

BARON
—a time in which little Cupid
will not grant a favor to us men.
So we men are no roosters and no stags,
rather we are lords of creation,
nor are we ruled by the moon like you women, begging your
pardon!
For example, in May it is just right for lovers' delights
(just ask any child),
but of course I say:
better in August, June, or July.
We have nights then!
To us at home in summer comes an army
of girls from Bohemia; in a swarm they cross the border:
and it's pleasant sometimes to induce
just two or three to stay with me
till the autumn falls.
They come at harvest time, nor do they refuse to work, whatever the task.
(smirking)
When 'tis done, they go home.—
And how they agree,
the active, lissome folk of Bohemia, sad and sweet,
with those of our land, of true German stock,
so different, sharp and sour
like a northern wine—
yet they agree so well!
And everywhere lovers are waiting and seeking each other,
and whispering sweet nothings in tenderest accents,

and everywhere all day
and night joyfully singing
and milking
and reaping
with a will, and dabbling in the brooks and the village pond.
MARSCHALLIN *(much amused)*
And you are everywhere keeping a watch?
BARON
Would I could be, like Jupiter, happy in a thousand disguises!
I could use the whole thousand!
MARSCHALLIN
What, even the bull? So crude would you be?
You should ride as a cloud in heaven and go sailing o'er the
  mountains
like a scented summer breeze.
BARON *(very gaily)*
That depends, yes, it depends.
For women, you know, must be wheedled and captured in a
  thousand different ways.
For one is humble and shy.
The next, a limb of the devil, straight from hell,
clouts you and beats your brains out with a broomstick.
Then the third, who giggling and sobbing will lose her head—
that one I like—
and then another—look in her eyes—there's a devil, cold and
  repelling;
bide but your time—sure 'twill come—
you'll discover how that devil is yielding
and relenting.
And when her last venomous glances she darts at me,
(with gusto)
that flavors the banquet past believing.
MARSCHALLIN
'Tis you that's a devil, on my soul!
BARON
Yet another—pray give me leave—whom no one will look at:
in tatters and rags she slinks along,
crouches 'mid ashes by the hearth—
she, if the right hour have but struck for your wooing,
she's not wanting!
A wild amazement—

stunned and bewildered, halting
'twixt fear and shame;
at last she yields, like one distraught with excess of joy,
to think that he,
the master and lord,
so far descends to look upon her lowliness!

MARSCHALLIN
You know more than your A-B-C.

BARON
Then there are others who want to be caught by stealth,
soft as the wind a-blowing through the fresh-cut hay.
The best one, by gad,
*(to Octavian, who has put the tray back on the breakfast table,
and during the foregoing come up close on the Baron's left in
amusement)*
like a tiger you jump on her back,
kick the milk-stool away,
then she lies there defenseless.
(chuckling complacently)
Let there be hay stacked for comfort close at hand.
Octavian bursts out laughing.

MARSCHALLIN
Ha! What a man! What victories!
Let go the child, I say.

BARON *(to Octavian, very forthrightly)*
Meanest of attics can never disarm me,
splendor of boudoir can never alarm me.
Fain would I clothe me in scores of disguises
for as many enterprises.
None comes amiss whether simple or cunning,
luring me on, or my company shunning,
splendor of boudoir can never alarm me,
all are for me, naught can disarm me.

OCTAVIAN *(instantly playing his role again)*
No, I won't go courtin' with you,
I do not think it right.
Mercy, what would my mother say!
Sure I should die of fright.
I don't know what you say,
I don't know why I should.
One thing I know is, 'tis for no good.

Mercy! What would my mother say!
I'd be too scared for funning,
you look too bold and cunning,
I'd be too scared for funning.
Such sport leads many a poor girl to her ruin!
(to the Marschallin)
I'm frightened, Your Highness, look what he's doin'.

MARSCHALLIN
Ha! What a man! What victories!
Ha! What a hero! Ha! What a hero!
Let that child be, I say.
But of every hundred I see each day,
there are ninety like him, 'tis still the same story,
they find there's one glory, in all that's unseemly!
And we, heaven knows! we feel all the sorrow,
we bear the hard blows,
but perchance women sin more deeply than men.
What manners are those!
(with feigned severity)
Now let the child be!

BARON
(letting go of Octavian and assuming a dignified manner again)
Pray will Your Highness give me the hussy there
to come to my intended bride as her servant?

MARSCHALLIN
What, my favorite? Tell me what for?
I'm sure your bride will have no need of her.
Such a choice she would wish to make unaided.

BARON
I never saw such a promising wench.
She has a drop of good blood in her.

OCTAVIAN *(aside)*
A drop of good blood!

MARSCHALLIN
But Your Lordship is really most observant!

BARON
Of course.
(confidentially)
I think it important that we persons of noble
birth and breeding should look for noble blood in all our servants.
I have one here who's a bastard of mine.

OCTAVIAN *(still listening with much amusement, aside)*
He's brought his own bastard?
MARSCHALLIN
What? And a girl too? I certainly hope not!
BARON *(emphatically)*
No, 'tis a son—with all the Lerchenau features in his face.
MARSCHALLIN AND OCTAVIAN
'Tis a son!
BARON
He is my private valet.
MARSCHALLIN *(laughing)*
His private valet!
OCTAVIAN
His private valet!
BARON
So if Your Highness should presently order
me to deliver the silver rose to your hands,
'tis my son who will bring it upstairs.
MARSCHALLIN
I understand. But a moment I beg.
(beckoning to Octavian)
Mariandl!
BARON
Please, will Your Highness give me this hussy? I really need her.
MARSCHALLIN
Ah! Go and bring the miniature gold medallion.
OCTAVIAN *(softly)*
Thérèse, Thérèse, beware.
MARSCHALLIN
Bring it quick! I know very well what I do.
BARON *(looking after Octavian)*
Gad, should be a young princess.
(conversationally)
I've planned for my bride that I would order a copy
of my pedigree as a wedding gift.
Also a lock of the first Lord Lerchenau, a devout support of the
    Church
and also a Lord Lieutenant and Governor
of the Carinthian March.
Octavian brings the medallion from the bed alcove.

MARSCHALLIN
Would your Lordship care to have this gallant gentleman
to take the silver rose to your lady?
BARON *(in a light conversational tone)*
Without a glance I trust Your Highness.
MARSCHALLIN *(with slight hesitation)*
It's my young cousin, the Count Octavian.
BARON *(still very courteously)*
Who could wish a more distinguished envoy?
I shall be obliged beyond all words to His Lordship.
MARSCHALLIN *(quickly)*
Look at him well!
She holds the miniature toward him.
BARON *(looking first at the miniature, then at the maid)*
How like they are!
MARSCHALLIN
Yes, yes.
BARON
It's the very spitting image.
MARSCHALLIN
It has caused me myself some surprise.
(pointing to the miniature)
Rofrano, the younger brother of the Marquis.
BARON
Octavian Rofrano? 'Tis no light thing, coming of such a house,
(pointing to the maid)
and even though it's by the kitchen door.
MARSCHALLIN
That is why I prefer her over all the rest.
BARON
Most fitting.
MARSCHALLIN
Always in waiting on me.
BARON
Quite right.
MARSCHALLIN
But get you gone now, Mariandl, off you go.
BARON
What's that? She's coming back though?
MARSCHALLIN *(intentionally ignoring the Baron)*
Admit all who are there waiting outside.

Octavian goes toward the folding door on the right.
BARON *(following him)*
Most lovely child!
OCTAVIAN *(by the door on the right)*
You can come in now!
(running to the other door)
BARON *(following him)*
I am your most humble servant. Let me have a word with you alone.
OCTAVIAN *(slamming the little door in the Baron's face)*
Be back soon.
At this moment an old chambermaid enters through the same door. The Baron retreats disappointed. Two Footmen enter from the right and bring a screen from the alcove. The Marschallin retires behind the screen, the chambermaid following her. The dressing table is brought to the center of the stage. The Footmen open the folding door on the left. Enter the Notary, the Head Cook, followed by an Assistant carrying the menu book. Then the Milliner, a Scholar with a huge tome, and the Vendor of Pets with tiny dogs and a small monkey. Valzacchi and Annina, slipping in quickly behind these, take the foremost place on the left. The Noble Widow with her Three Daughters take places on the right; all are in deep mourning. The Major-Domo leads the Singer and the Flute Player to the front. The Baron, in the background, beckons to a Footman, and gives him an order by pointing: "Here through the back door."
THREE NOBLE ORPHANS *(shrilly)*
Three poor but noble little orphans—
The Noble Widow signals to them not to shriek so and to kneel down.
Three poor but noble little orphans
lie weeping at Your Highness's feet.
MILLINER *(loudly)*
Le chapeau Paméla! La poudre à la reine de Golconde!
VENDOR OF PETS
Pretty monkeys to tease your flunkies,
bright parakeets and birds from Africa.
THREE ORPHANS
Our father in youth died a glorious death for his country,
it is our fondest wish to do the same as he.
MILLINER
Le chapeau Paméla! C'est la merveille du monde!

THE VENDOR
Cockatoo and painted jay,
from India and Africa.
Puppies quite small,
house-trained and all,
there's no mess at all.
The Marschallin steps out, all bow low. The Baron has come
forward on the left.
MARSCHALLIN *(to the Baron)*
I now present to you, dear cousin, my man of law.
The Notary, bowing toward the dressing table at which the
Marschallin has seated herself, steps toward the Baron on the
left. The Marschallin summons the youngest of the Three
Orphans to her side, takes a purse from the Major-Domo, gives
it to the girl, and kisses her on the forehead. The Scholar tries to
come forward and offer the Marschallin his book. Valzacchi
darts forward and pushes him aside.
VALZACCHI *(flourishing a black-edged newspaper sheet)*
The scandal newspaper, Your Highness!
All the latest news and scandal!
Only given to famous people,
the secret gossip.
There's a dead man in the anteroom of
one of the ministers of state!
And a doctor's wife helping her lover
to poison the husband
last night at three o'clock.
MARSCHALLIN
Take your tales to the kitchen door!
VALZACCHI
But Lady,
Tutte quante are as true as de Bible
from de great big world.
MARSCHALLIN
I will not listen! Take your tales to the kitchen door.
Valzacchi springs back with a regretful bow. The Three
Orphans prepare to withdraw, after they and their mother have
kissed the Marschallin's hand.
THREE ORPHANS *(in a whining tone)*
Joy and blessing, all confessing, lift their voices in your praise!

We shall count the high-born bounty of Your Highness all our days!
Exeunt with their mother.
The Hairdresser enters hastily, his Assistant after him with coat-tails flying. The Hairdresser scrutinizes the Marschallin and, with a solemn expression, steps back; he is studying her looks today. In the meantime the Assistant is unpacking at the dressing table. The Hairdresser pushes several persons back so as to have more room. After a little consideration he forms his plan, bustles up to the Marschallin with decision, and begins to do her hair. Enter a Footman in pink, black, and silver bearing a note. The Major-Domo is at his hand with a silver salver, on which he presents it to the Marschallin. The Hairdresser stands back to allow her to read it. His Assistant hands him new tongs. The Hairdresser waves them to and fro to cool them. After a questioning glance at the Marschallin, who nods, the Assistant hands him the note. He smiles and uses it to cool the tongs. Meanwhile the Singer has taken up his position holding his music. The Flute Player accompanies him, watching him over his shoulder. The Servants are at the front on the right, the others stand in the background.

SINGER
Di rigori armato il seno
contro amor mi ribellai,
ma fui vinto in un baleno
in mirar due vaghi rai.
Ahi! che resiste puoco
cor di gelo a stral di fuoco.
The Hairdresser hands the curling tongs to his Assistant and applauds the Singer. Then he proceeds with arranging the Marschallin's curls. In the meantime a Footman has admitted the Baron's Valet, the Almoner, and Huntsman by the small door. It is a strange trio. The Valet is a tall young fellow with a foolish, insolent expression. He carries a jewel case of red morocco under his arm. The Almoner is an unkempt village priest, four feet high, but a strong and insolent-looking imp. The Huntsman looks as if he had been carting dung before he was pushed into his ill-fitting livery. The Almoner and the Valet seem to be fighting for precedence and trip each other up. They steer a course to the left, toward their master, in whose vicinity they come to a halt.

BARON
(seated on the armchair at the front on the left, to the Notary, who is standing in front of him taking instructions; in an undertone)

As first installment, quite as a separate gift,
before the dowry, you understand me, do you not?—
the house and lands of Gaunersdorf return to me!
Redeemed of debt and with manorial rights undiminished
just as my father held them for his whole life long.

NOTARY *(short of breath)*
Your Lordship, it is my painful duty delicately to remind you
that such a compensation from the wife to the husband,
instead of from the husband to the wife
(taking a deep breath)
by contract is not in law or custom possible.

BARON
That may be so.

NOTARY
It is so—

BARON
But in a special case—

NOTARY
The law, sir, and its wise prescriptions postulate no special case.

BARON *(shouting)*
Then it is time it began to!

NOTARY *(terrified)*
Your pardon!

BARON
(quietly again, but with insistence, and full of self-importance)
If one who springs from the very noblest stock should so far
    condescend
as to take in marriage one almost of the middle classes like Miss
    Faninal—
you understand me?—take her to his bed in fact
before God and the world, and as one might say,
under the eye of the Imperial court,
(as the Flute Player begins his prelude again)
surely, *corpo di Bacco!* a first installment
would be only common justice as a sign of thanks
for the sacrifice I am making
by giving my name to her.

NOTARY *(to the Baron in a low voice)*
Perhaps, by way of a separate conveyance—

BARON *(in a low voice)*
You wretched, pettifogging fool! As first installment, I want my
    house back!

NOTARY *(as before)*
Ah, as an especial item in the marriage contract.
BARON *(a little louder)*
As first installment! Will nothing get it through your thick skull?
NOTARY *(in the same tone)*
As a *donatio inter vivos* or else—
BARON *(banging his fist on the table in a rage, and shouting)*
As first installment!
SINGER *(during the foregoing discussion)*
Ma si caro è'l mio tormento
dolce è si la piaga mia,
ch'il penare è mio contento
è'l sanarmi è tirannia.
Ahi! che resiste puoco
Cor—
At this point the Baron raises his voice to such a pitch that the
Singer breaks off abruptly, as does the Flute Player. The Notary
retires to a corner in alarm. The Marschallin summons the
Singer and gives him her hand to kiss. The Singer and the Flute
Player retire, bowing deeply. The Baron makes as if nothing had
happened, waves condescendingly to the Singer, crosses over to
his servants, straightens his Valet's tousled hair; then goes to the
small door as if looking for somebody, opens it, peeps out, is
annoyed that the chambermaid is not coming back; snoops
about the bed, shakes his head, and comes forward again.
MARSCHALLIN
(looking at herself in a hand mirror, in an undertone)
My good friend Hippolyte,
this will not do, for see how old you've made me look!
The Hairdresser falls, in consternation, on the Marschallin's coif-
fure with feverish energy and changes it again. The Marschallin
continues to wear a pensive expression. Valzacchi, followed by
Annina, has slunk behind everyone's backs to the other side of
the stage, and now presents himself to the Baron with exagger-
ated obsequiousness.
(over her shoulder to the Major-Domo)
Tell them all to go!
The Footmen, taking hands, push them all out by the door, which
they then close. Only the Scholar, whom the Major-Domo presents
to the Marschallin, remains in conversation with her until the close
of the episode between Valzacchi, Annina, and the Baron.

VALZACCHI *(to the Baron)*
De Barone needs my help I see,
de Barone is needing my service.
I can make me useful in all ways.
BARON *(drawing back)*
And what, sir, are you, sir?
VALZACCHI
De Barone 'e speak out of his eyes
like Italian marble. *Come statua di Giove.*
ANNINA
Italian marble . . . *di Giove* . . .
BARON
A most remarkable man.
VALZACCHI
My Lord Barone, we are both your obedient servants.
(falls on his knees, as does Annina)
BARON
You?
VALZACCHI, ANNINA
Together we do better work.
Per esempio: De Barone's lady is very young?
BARON
And just how do you know, you rascal, you?
VALZACCHI, ANNINA *(eagerly)*
De Barone is a jealous man: *dico per dire.*
Now or tomorrow it may be. *Affare nostro!*
Every step de lady may make,
every carriage de lady take,
every letter de lady may get—
we are there!
Up de chimney or by de fire, under de carpet—
up in de attic or in a cupboard,
in a corner, under de bed—
we are there.
*The Marschallin rises. The Hairdresser bows low and hurries
off, followed by his Assistant.*
ANNINA
De Barone will not regret it!
*They hold out their hands as if for money. The Baron pretends
not to notice them.*

BARON *(in an undertone)*
Hm! What a place it is, this old Vienna.
I'll test you now: do you know that girl Mariandl?
ANNINA *(in an undertone)*
Mariandl?
BARON *(in an undertone)*
The serving maid who waits there on Her Highness?
VALZACCHI *(in a whisper to Annina)*
Sai tu? Cosa vuole?
ANNINA *(also whispering)*
Niente!
VALZACCHI *(to the Baron)*
Surely, surely, my niece knows all about her.
Be assured of that, Your Lordship. We are there!
He holds his hand out again. The Baron ignores him.
BARON *(leaving the two Italians; to the Marschallin)*
May I now introduce
(discreetly)
the counterpart of your Mariandl to Your Highness?
(complacently)
I'm told that the likeness is unmistakable.
The Marschallin nods.
Leupold, give me the case!
The young Footman presents the case awkwardly.
MARSCHALLIN *(smiling slightly)*
He does great honor to his ancestry.
BARON
(taking the case from the lad and signalling to him to withdraw)
And here I have the silver rose.
He is about to open it.
MARSCHALLIN
Do not disturb it.
Put it down here, please, if you don't mind.
BARON
Or shall we call for your Mariandl?
Let me ring.
MARSCHALLIN
No, let her be. She has her duties too.
But this I promise, that Count Octavian shall be informed.
For me he'll consent, I know,
and will duly ride as cavalier

to your bride and present her with the silver rose.
Leave it there if you will.
And now, dear cousin, I must say adieu.
The time has come for all to leave,
or I shall be too late for church.
The Footmen open the folding doors.

BARON

Why, Your Highness, it's too much.
Your kindness and your charm have left me dumb.
*He makes an obeisance and withdraws ceremoniously. At a signal
from him, the Notary follows. The Baron's three servants shuffle
out awkwardly. The two Italians silently and obsequiously join
the train without his noticing them. The Major-Domo withdraws. The Footmen close the door. The Marschallin is left alone.*

MARSCHALLIN

And there he goes, a vain, pretentious pompous fellow,
and gets a young and pretty bride and ample dowry as reward.
(sighing)
He takes it all,
and thinks 'tis but his due; and boasts that he greatly honors her!
But why trouble myself? The world will have it so.
I remember a girl, just like this one,
who fresh from the convent was marched
off straight to the holy estate of wedlock.
She takes a hand mirror.
Where is she now? Ah,
(sighing)
go, seek the snows of yesteryear!
But can it be,
(quietly)
can it really be as I say,
that I was that young girl long ago
and that I shall one day be called the old Princess . . .
the old Princess, the Marshall's old Princess!
"Look now, there goes the old Princess Theresa!"
How can this come to pass?
Is this indeed the will of God?
For I am still I, the very same.
But if indeed it must be so,
why then must I sit here looking on,
and see it all, so clear? Why are these things not hid from me?

This all is mystery, all mystery,
and we are here on earth
(sighing)
to bear it all.
But to know "How"—
(very quietly)
in that lies all the difference.
Octavian enters from the right, in riding dress with riding boots.
(quietly, smiling)
Ah! You are back again!

OCTAVIAN *(tenderly)*
You're lost in sadness!

MARSCHALLIN
The mood has flown again. You know me, how I am.
One moment merry, one moment weeping.
My thoughts, I cannot command them, I know not how.

OCTAVIAN
I know why you have been in tears, my heart.
You were beside yourself and panic-stricken.
Am I not right? Confess to me:
you were terrified,
my angel, my loved one,
for me, for me!

MARSCHALLIN
A little perhaps,
but I recovered my courage and to myself I said: Now what
   indeed should I fear.
And does it really matter?

OCTAVIAN *(gaily)*
It was not the Feldmarschall,
but a silly clown, your cousin, and you are all mine,
you are all mine!

MARSCHALLIN *(pushing him aside)*
Dearest, embrace me not so much.
Who tries to hold too much, holds nothing fast.

OCTAVIAN *(passionately)*
Say you are mine alone, mine!

MARSCHALLIN
Oh! Do but be good, be tender and gentle and kind and wise.
Octavian is about to answer excitedly.
I beg you now, do not be like all the others are.

OCTAVIAN *(starting up suspiciously)*
Like all the others?
MARSCHALLIN *(quickly recovering herself)*
Like the Feldmarschall and my cousin Ochs.
OCTAVIAN *(still not satisfied)*
Bichette!
MARSCHALLIN *(emphatically)*
No, do not be like all the other men.
OCTAVIAN *(angrily)*
I know nothing of the other men.
(with sudden tenderness)
Only I know I love you.
Bichette, they've taken you away from me.
Bichette, where have you gone?
MARSCHALLIN *(calmly)*
I am still here, my love.
OCTAVIAN
When you are here, then I want to hold you,
to protect you from what may befall
(passionately)
and safe by my side clasp you.
Then you will know to whom you belong—
to me! For I am yours and you are mine!
MARSCHALLIN *(freeing herself from him)*
Oh, do be good, Quinquin. I feel I know
that all things earthly are but a vanity, vain, empty dreams;
deep in my heart I know
how we should grasp at naught,
how we can cling to naught,
how life and its joys slip through our fingers,
how everything alters if we but grasp it,
everything fades like shadows, like dreams.
OCTAVIAN
Oh, God, what do you say?
You only want to tell me that you love me no more.
He weeps.
MARSCHALLIN
Don't be so sad, Quinquin!
Octavian weeps more bitterly.
(quietly)
Ah, now I am the one who must console you,

for the day, be it soon, be it late, when you will leave me.
She caresses him.

OCTAVIAN
Be it soon, be it late,
(angrily)
who could have put such words into your mouth, Bichette?

MARSCHALLIN
Do my words hurt you so?
Octavian stops his ears.
The time is coming, Quinquin,
the time, be it sooner or later, what matter.
For time, how strangely, goes its own way.
We do not heed it, time has no meaning,
but there comes a moment when time is all we feel.
All the world talks of it, all our souls are filled with it,
on every face its mark will show.
Each mirror betrays it,
all through my dreams 'tis flowing,
and now between us two
it flows in silence, trickling as in an hourglass.
(earnestly)
Oh, Quinquin, sometimes I hear it flowing—
unrelenting.
(softly)
Sometimes I arise in the dead of night,
go to my clocks and stop them, every one.
And yet, to be afraid of time is useless.
For God, mindful of all His children, in His wisdom created it.

OCTAVIAN *(with quiet tenderness)*
My dearest love, why do you torture yourself so with such
    thoughts?
Now that I am here,
and my loving fingers are clasping yours so tenderly,
and my eyes look into yours to find an answer,
now that I am here,
at such a time you can feel like this?

MARSCHALLIN *(very seriously)*
Quinquin, now or tomorrow, surely,
you will go from me, leave me and choose another,
(hesitating a little)
who's younger and lovelier than I.

OCTAVIAN
So you are trying now to dismiss me
and do with words what your hands refuse?
MARSCHALLIN *(calmly)*
The day will come unbidden.
Now or tomorrow it will come, Octavian.
OCTAVIAN
Not now, not tomorrow! I love you so.
(intensely)
Not now nor tomorrow!
The sun shall not rise, that I swear, on such a day!
So dreadful a day!
That day shall never come.
(very passionately)
I cannot bear to think of it.
Why break my heart and yours, Thérèse?
MARSCHALLIN
Now or tomorrow—if not tomorrow, very soon.
I would not torture you, my love.
'Tis truth I'm speaking, 'tis as true for you as 'tis for me. . . .
Let us then lightly meet our fate.
Light must we be,
with spirits light, with gentle fingers
take all our pleasures, take them and leave them.
Unless we do much grief awaits us, and God himself won't pity us.
OCTAVIAN
Today you speak like my confessor.
Do you tell me that I may never, no,
never kiss you and love you till you are faint with rapture?
MARSCHALLIN
Quinquin, now you must go.
(softly)
Now you must leave me.
I'll go now, go to Church, and pray,
and later visit my uncle Greifenklau,
who's old and so ailing,
and dine with him: 'twill please the dear old man.
This afternoon I will send to your house a footman,
Quinquin, and he will tell you
if I plan to take the air;
and if I do

and you should wish,
you may meet me in the Prater, riding,
and you may ride beside my carriage.
And now be good. Do as I say.

OCTAVIAN *(softly)*
As you command, Bichette.
He goes; a pause.

MARSCHALLIN *(starts up passionately)*
He's gone without even a kiss.
She rings agitatedly. Footmen hurry in from the right.
Run and overtake the Count
and say I beg for a word with him.
The Footmen hurry off.
I have let him go from me, and without a single kiss!
*She sits down on the chair by the dressing table. The Footmen
enter out of breath.*

FIRST FOOTMAN
But the Count is off and away—

SECOND FOOTMAN
In a flash he seized the bridle . . .

THIRD FOOTMAN
Swung up in the stirrups . . .

FOURTH FOOTMAN
At the gate he seized the bridle like the wind.

FIRST FOOTMAN
Galloped round the corner like the wind—

SECOND FOOTMAN
We hurried after . . .

THIRD FOOTMAN
We cried ourselves hoarse . . .

FOURTH FOOTMAN
All in vain.

FIRST FOOTMAN
Galloped round the corner like the wind.

MARSCHALLIN
Very well. You may leave me.
The Footmen withdraw. The Marschallin calls after them.
Send Mohamed!
The Little Black Page enters with tinkling bells, and bows.
Take this case . . .
The Black Page quickly takes the leather jewel case.

Wait till I say where. To Count Octavian.
Give it and say,
within is the silver rose.
He will know what he must do.
*The Black Page runs off. The Marschallin props her head on
her hand and remains with a dreamlike demeanor until the end.
Here the curtain begins to fall slowly and silently.*

ACT 2

*A room in the house of Herr von Faninal. Center door leading
to the antechamber. Doors right and left. To the right a large
window. Chairs against the wall on either side of the center
door. In the rounded corners on either side are secret doors.*

HERR VON FANINAL *(on the point of saying goodbye to Sophie)*
A solemn day, a festal day!
A wondrous day, a sacred day!
Sophie kisses his hand.

MARIANNE
The new coach is there with our man at the box.
Its curtains are of sky-blue.
Four shining horses are there.

MAJOR-DOMO *(with a touch of familiarity to Faninal)*
It's high time now Your Lordship should be leaving.
It's customary for the bride's father
to have taken his
departure from the house
before the Cavalier of the Silver Rose comes here.
Footmen open the door.

FANINAL
Heaven help me.

MAJOR-DOMO
'Twould not be seemly
for you to meet him at the palace door.

FANINAL
When I come again,
I shall be leading your bridegroom-to-be by the hand.

MARIANNE
The excellent and noble Baron Lerchenau.
*Exit Faninal. Sophie comes forward alone. Marianne is at the
window.*

Up go the steps. The footmen one by one are springing up behind.
The little page has handed up the whip,
and there are faces at every house.

SOPHIE
On this most joyful day I praise Thee, my Maker,
in that Thou dost exalt me high above my worth
and bring me now to Thy altar beside the one Thou hast willed,
(controlling herself with great difficulty)
and I offer Thee now my heart, my humble heart.
My flesh is too weak to be humble,
so I must humble myself.

MARIANNE *(very excited)*
And half the town is out of doors.
See them in the cloister, the good monks one and all are at the
    windows,
and one old man sits high up on the roof.

SOPHIE *(struggling to collect her thoughts)*
Humble myself and well remember how guilty, how
vain, how little worth, how intractable Thy children are!
My mother is dead and I am all alone,
Here in prayer before Thy throne.
Here at the altar with Thy blessing I stand.

MARIANNE *(as before)*
He comes, he comes, with two great coaches.
The first one has four horses, it is empty. But the next has six
    dapple grays.
I can see him, the Rose Cavalier!

THREE FOOTMEN
(running before Octavian's carriage in the street below)
Rofrano, Rofrano!

SOPHIE *(almost losing her self-control)*
I will not be swollen with pride of station after marriage—
—after my marriage.
She can control herself no longer.
What is it they cry?

MARIANNE
They call him the Rose Cavalier and cry the names
of all the august relations of your husband, as I hear.
(with excited gestures)
Now the servants form a pathway.
The outriders are beside the door.

THREE FOOTMEN *(closer)*
Rofrano! Rofrano!
SOPHIE
Oh, but when my bridegroom comes will everyone
cry his station, and his name and titles too?
THREE FOOTMEN *(right under the window)*
Rofrano! Rofrano!
MARIANNE *(enthusiastically)*
The coach door is open and he comes,
all in silver clad, he is glittering from head to foot.
Like an archangel all on fire.
She hastily shuts the window.
SOPHIE
Merciful Heaven!
I know that pride must be a mortal sin.
But today never can I humble myself.
'Tis all in vain.
For my lot is so rare, so rare!
*Two of Faninal's Footmen quickly open the center door. Enter
Octavian, bareheaded, dressed all in white and silver, carrying the
silver rose in his hand. The Footmen, the Heiducks with crooked
Hungarian swords at their side; the Couriers in white leather with
green ostrich plumes. Immediately behind Octavian a Black
Servant carrying his hat, and another Footman who carries the
case for the silver rose in both hands. Behind these, Faninal's servants. Octavian, taking the rose in his right hand, advances with
noble grace toward Sophie; but his youthful features bear traces
of embarrassment, and he blushes. Sophie turns deathly pale with
excitement at his splendid appearance. They stand facing each
other, each disconcerted by the confusion and beauty of the other.*
OCTAVIAN *(with slight hesitation)*
It is an honor, an enchantment
to which I'll stay most deeply sensible all my days,
to come here as a messenger at
my cousin Lerchenau's bidding,
to offer you as token of his love this rose.
SOPHIE *(taking the rose)*
I am to Your Honor much indebted.
I am to Your Honor to all eternity indebted.
Momentary confusion; she smells the rose.
There is a scent in its petals of roses, like the living ones.

OCTAVIAN
Yes, there's a drop of oil of Persian roses in its heart.

SOPHIE
Like heavenly, not earthly flowers, like roses
from golden gardens of paradise. Think you not so?
*Octavian bends over the rose, which she holds out to him, then
raises his head and gazes at her lips.*
'Tis like a kiss from heaven. Oh, so sweet and rare that no one
dare breathe it again.

Drawing me on, like something that's tugging at my heart.
(softly)
Where have I been before
and felt such rapture?

OCTAVIAN
(at the same time, as though unconscious, and still more softly)
Where have I been before
and felt such rapture?

SOPHIE *(with deep expression)*
To walk those blessed fields of paradise once more. I fear not
death itself.

And yet why dream of death?
'Tis far, 'tis far, 'tis an eternity
that shines on moments of blessedness,
never to be forgotten till death close my eyes.

OCTAVIAN *(at the same time)*
I was a child,
I never heard her voice until today.
But who am I?
What fate brings me to her?
What fate brings her to me?
Feeling and sense would leave me, were I not a man;
this is a moment of blessedness,
never to be forgotten till death close my eyes.

*In the meantime Octavian's servants have taken up their posi-
tion on the left at the back, Faninal's servants with the Major-
Domo to the right. Octavian's Footman hands the jewel case to
Marianne. Sophie wakes from her reverie and gives the rose to
Marianne, who places it in the jewel case. The Footman with
the hat approaches Octavian and gives it to him. Octavian's
servants withdraw, and at the same time Faninal's servants
carry three chairs to the center, two for Sophie and Octavian,*

and one for Marianne, farther back and to one side. Faninal's Major-Domo carries the jewel case with the rose through the door to the right; the other servants immediately withdraw through the center door. Sophie and Octavian stand facing each other, partly restored to the everyday world but a little embarrassed. At a signal from Sophie, both seat themselves, and the Duenna does likewise, at the same moment as the door on the right is locked from the outside by the Major-Domo.

SOPHIE
I know you very well, *mon cousin.*

OCTAVIAN
You know me, *ma cousine?*

SOPHIE
Yes, and I've read in the court almanac, too,
"The Mirror of Nobility."
I take every evening up to bed
and read about the princes and dukes,
and the counts who will soon be my relations.

OCTAVIAN
Do you so, *ma cousine?*

SOPHIE
I know how old Your Lordship is:
seventeen and a quarter.
I know all your Christian names: Octavian, Maria Ehrenreich,
Bonaventura, Fernand, Hyacinth.

OCTAVIAN
I do not know them even half as well.

SOPHIE
I know also . . .
(blushes)

OCTAVIAN
What do you know, tell my pray, *ma cousine?*

SOPHIE *(not looking at him)*
Quinquin.

OCTAVIAN *(laughing)*
So you know that name too?

SOPHIE
Men call you Quinquin when they have your friendship,
and lovely ladies, I suppose,
with whom you are acquainted.
(slight pause; naively)

I'm happy I'll marry soon! Will you not like it too?
But perhaps you have not given thought to it, *mon cousin?*
You think it is another matter, happy and free.
OCTAVIAN *(softly, while she speaks)*
What charm she has!
SOPHIE
But then you are a man, and men are what they are.
I'll need a husband all my days, to guide my steps;
and I'll show him my thanks by doing what he tells me.
OCTAVIAN *(deeply moved and softly)*
How good and fair she is.
She confuses me quite.
SOPHIE
I never shall disgrace him, never
forget my rank and station.
(very eagerly)
Should another wife look down her nose at me
or go before me
at a christening or a funeral,
I'll show her very quickly,
if needs must be, with a slapped cheek,
that I am finer bred than she,
and I'll bear anything rather
than vulgar pride or insolence!
OCTAVIAN *(eagerly)*
Ah, do but name the wretch
who would presume to hazard such an impertinence.
For always you'll be the loveliest of all the loveliest creatures.
SOPHIE
You're making fun, *mon cousin?*
OCTAVIAN
What? And why should I laugh?
SOPHIE
You may make fun of me, if you will.
From you I gladly take all that you choose,
for I tell you, no gentleman of all I've met with,
no, nor dreamed of, has so stolen my heart away as you.
Ah, now he comes. 'Tis my bridegroom-to-be.
*The door at the back is thrown open. All three rise and step to
the right. Faninal ceremoniously conducts the Baron over the
threshold toward Sophie, giving him precedence. Lerchenau's*

servants follow in his footsteps, first the Almoner, then the Valet. Next comes the Huntsman, with another clownish bumpkin, who has a plaster over his battered nose, and two others no less uncouth, looking as if they had stepped straight from the turnip fields into their liveries. All, like their master, carry sprigs of myrtle. Faninal's servants remain in the background.

FANINAL
May I present now to Your Lordship your bride-to-be?

BARON *(bowing, then to Faninal)*
Delicious! My compliments to you.
He kisses Sophie's hand slowly, as if examining it.
A wrist so delicate, that is just what I like.
'Tis a distinction rarely found among the bourgeoisie.

OCTAVIAN *(in an undertone)*
My blood runs hot and cold.

FANINAL
Permit me my most loyal servant,
Marianne Leitmetzerin . . .
(presenting Marianne, who curtsies deeply three times)

BARON *(with a gesture of vexation)*
Some other time.
Now greet the Count, and thank him for being my ambassador.
He goes with Faninal toward Octavian, bowing. Octavian returns the bow. After having almost knocked Sophie over, Lerchenau's servants come to a standstill and withdraw a few paces.

SOPHIE
(standing on the right with Marianne, in an undertone)
How vulgar his behavior, he is like a horse-dealer
who thinks he's bought me at a country fair.

MARIANNE *(aside)*
A cavalier is always unaffected and
easy in his behavior.
Tell yourself who he is,
and the rank you will gain,
and soon you will forget your silly ways.

BARON *(to Faninal, as he leads him forward)*
It's quite astounding how the young count resembles someone
   whom I know.
He has a sister, she's a sweet little bastard.
(in a coarsely confidential tone)
That is no secret round the Imperial court.

Her Highness told me so herself.
(genially)
And since our Faninal, now that he's ennobled,
is one of us in a way,
(ever more broadly)
do not be ashamed, my dear Rofrano,
that your father once sowed his wild oats;
he's not alone in that, he stands with the elite, *(laughing)* just
    like the old Marchese.
I won't deny I've sown some, too.
(to Faninal)
Look well now at that long-legged rascal there,
the fair one, at the back.
I cannot point my finger at him,
but you will see at a glance
how he's distinguished by his high-born features.
Is he not truly a splendid fellow?
He has a noble pedigree,
but he's the greatest fool of all my household.

SOPHIE
What breeding's this, to leave me standing here!
And he is my husband that's to be.
And pockmarked also is his face, on my soul!

MARIANNE
Well, if his front displeases you so, you Mistress Haughty,
then from the back regard him well,
And then you'll find something that is good to see.

SOPHIE
Then tell me what it is that I shall find.

MARIANNE *(mimicking her)*
"Then tell me what it is that I shall find."
Why, that your patron saints have sent you this day
one of Her Majesty's
High Chamberlains as bridegroom.
That is very clear to see.
*The Major-Domo approaches Lerchenau's servants most politely
and conducts them out of the room. At the same time Faninal's
servants withdraw, except for two, who offer wine and sweets.*

FANINAL *(to the Baron)*
Perhaps you would partake? 'Tis Tokay, an old vintage.
Octavian and the Baron serve themselves.

BARON
>Good, Faninal, you know what's right and fit,
>to serve such a fine old Tokay to toast a fine young daughter.
>You've done this not too badly.
>*(to Octavian)*
>With two-bit aristocrats like this one, we must show them
>that they are not our equals, you understand me.
>Persons like us have a duty to condescend.

OCTAVIAN *(pointedly)*
>I'm all admiration for Your Lordship.
>Your Lordship's manners are so subtle.
>You should be sent as an ambassador all over Europe.

BARON *(roughly)*
>Come, let me now fetch the girl in.
>See if she's learned how to talk in company.
>I'll soon discover if she's well informed.
>*(goes over, takes Sophie by the hand, and leads her back with him)*
>*Eh bien!* Now let us hear you talk, me and your cousin Tavie,
>And to begin with, what do you fancy will please you most as a
>   bride?
>*He seats himself and tries to make her sit on his lap.*

SOPHIE *(pulling away from him)*
>What do you mean?

BARON *(comfortably)*
>Pah! What's my meaning? Let me whisper in your ear,
>and I will tell you quickly all my meaning.
>*Same caper; Sophie pulls more angrily away from him.*
>Would my lady prefer it if I were to play
>the dancing master, bowing and cavorting,
>with *"mille pardons"* and "devotion,"
>And "By your leave" and "My respects"?

SOPHIE
>Undoubtedly, yes, 'twould surely be better!

BARON *(laughing)*
>Not for me! I tell you! None of that for me, miss!
>I am an open-hearted country lad, I like a free and easy life.
>*He starts to kiss her, but she energetically pushes him away.*

FANINAL
>*(offering Octavian the second chair, which he refuses)*
>How can it be? There sits a Lerchenau,

and sets his heart upon our little Sophie, the rascals might be a
  man and wife.
And there stands a Rofrano, makes as if at home—
a Count Rofrano, nothing less—
and brother to Her Majesty's Lord High Steward.

OCTAVIAN *(angrily, aside)*
There's a rude fellow. There's nothing I'd like better
than once to take
sword in hand and no one by to watch.
No, nothing better in the world.

SOPHIE *(to the Baron)*
Do stop it now. We are not married yet!

BARON *(to Sophie)*
My dear, are you shy before Cousin Tavie?
Don't be foolish.
Why, you know in Paris,
where they have the very finest manners,
there is naught
that may be done by newly married folk,
to which 'tis not usual to invite your friends to watch you.
Even the king himself does.

*The Baron grows more and more importunate; Sophie is at her
wit's end.*

OCTAVIAN *(furiously)*
How can I bear to watch him there,
so coarse, so unashamed with her.

FANINAL *(aside)*
Would that my palace were of glass:
every pettifogging burgess in the town,
jaundiced with envy, should see them sit *en famille*.
For that pleasure, I'd give my richest house right gladly, 'pon
  my soul.

OCTAVIAN
I'm doing penance for all my sins.
Would I could up and flee from here!

BARON *(to Sophie)*
Don't be so silly now, for you belong to me!
It's all right. Now be good! It's all just as I planned it.
(half to himself, cajoling her)
Suits me exactly! Tender as a chicken!
Quite skinny though—no matter—and so white,

white as driven snow. There's nothing I like more!
I have the luck of all the Lerchenaus!
Sophie tears herself away and stamps her foot; the Baron is delighted.
Gad! She's a fine little peppery spitfire!
(rises and runs after her)
And see how hot her cheeks are burning,
hot enough to burn your hands!
SOPHIE *(flushed and then pale with anger)*
You take your hands off me!
In silent anger, Octavian crushes the glass he holds in his hand and throws the pieces to the ground. Marianne runs with affected grace toward Octavian, picks up the pieces, and confides her delight to him.
MARIANNE
He has uncommon easy ways, the Herr Baron!
He's quite enchanting, such originality!
BARON *(near Sophie)*
Nothing suits me better!
No kind of simperings or tender airs
could give me half such pleasure, on my soul!
SOPHIE *(furious, to his face)*
I hardly care if I please you or not!
BARON *(complacently)*
You please me fine, no matter if you like it or you don't.
OCTAVIAN *(aside, pale with anger)*
Ah! I must go without farewell!
Or else I cannot tell
just what I might be led to do!
Oh! I can stay no longer! I must go!
In the meantime the Notary has entered with his Clerk, introduced by Faninal's Major-Domo. He announces them in a whisper to Faninal. Faninal goes toward the Notary at the back, speaks with him, and looks through a sheaf of documents handed to him by the Clerk.
SOPHIE *(with clenched teeth)*
There is no man has ever dared to speak to me like this!
What can you think of me, and of yourself?
What are you, sir, to me?
BARON *(contentedly)*
You'll find out overnight

that you have learned
with pleasure what I am to you.
Just like the little song—you surely know it?
Lalalalala.
(very sentimentally)
"My love shall be yours all in all!
With me, with me you'll find no garret too small,
without me, without me day's terror is so strong,
(impudently and coarsely)
with me, with me night is never too long!"
*As he tries to draw Sophie still closer to him, she frees herself
and violently pushes him back.*

MARIANNE *(now hurrying to Sophie)*
He has uncommon easy ways, the Herr Baron!
He's quite enchanting, such originality!
(agitatedly trying to persuade Sophie)
Such originality, the Herr Baron!

OCTAVIAN *(without looking, yet aware of all that is occurring)*
It's more than I can stomach!
I stand on coals of fire!
I'm doing penance in an hour
for many years of sin!

BARON *(to himself, very pleased)*
I always did say, I have all the luck of all the Lerchenaus!
There is naught in the world tickles my appetite
and gives me back again my youth like a defiant wench.
*Faninal and the Notary, followed by the Clerk, have advanced
to the front on the left. As soon as he sees the Notary, the
Baron addresses Sophie eagerly, without the slightest idea what
she is thinking.*
But now there's work to do; you must do without me.
They need my help in there.
And meanwhile there's Cousin Tavie who will entertain you.

FANINAL
Is it now convenient, dear son-in-law?

BARON *(eagerly)*
Of course it's convenient.
(in passing to Octavian, embracing him familiarly)
I've no objection
if you would like to flirt a little, cousin,
now or at any time.

She's a little touch-me-not.
The more she learns from you, the better it will please me.
You can see that the girl is like an unbroken foal.
The husband has the better bargain in the end,
so long as he's wise enough to exercise his matrimonial rights.
The Baron goes to the left. The servant who had admitted the Notary has in the meantime opened the door on the left. Faninal and the Notary make for the door. The Baron fixes his eyes on Faninal and indicates to him he must keep a distance of three paces. Faninal obsequiously retreats. The Baron takes precedence, assures himself that Faninal is three paces behind him, and walks solemnly through the door on the left. Faninal follows, and after him come the Notary and his Clerk. The Footman closes the door to the left and goes out, leaving the door leading to the anteroom open. The Footman who was serving refreshments has retired. Sophie stands on the right, confused and humiliated. Marianne curtseys in the direction of the door until it closes. Octavian, quivering with excitement, hurries over to Sophie, glancing backwards to make sure that the others have gone.

OCTAVIAN
And will you really marry that bumpkin, *ma cousine?*
SOPHIE *(taking a step toward him, softly)*
Not for the world!
(glancing at her Duenna)
Oh, God! Could we but be alone,
that I might beg of you! that I might beg of you!
OCTAVIAN *(quickly, in an undertone)*
What is it you would beg of me? Tell me now, quick!
SOPHIE *(taking another step toward him)*
Oh, my God, I implore your aid! And you will not help me because
he is your cousin and your friend.
OCTAVIAN *(vehemently)*
He is cousin by courtesy;
praised be God above,
I never saw him in my life until this time yesterday!
Some of the servant girls rush headlong across the anteroom, hotly pursued by Lerchenau's attendants. The Valet and the servant with the plaster on his nose are at the heels of a pretty young girl and corner her close by the salon door.

MAJOR-DOMO
(running in much perturbed, calling the Duenna to help him)
His Lordship's servants, drunk as a lord, by your leave, Ma'am,
are scaring our girls to death, twenty times worse than
the Turks, Ma'am, or Croatians!

MARIANNE
Fetch up our people to help you; where can they be?
*She runs off with the Major-Domo. They rescue the girl from
her assailants and lead her away. All disappear, and the anteroom stands empty.*

SOPHIE *(speaking freely, now that she is unobserved)*
My trust is in your kindness, *mon cousin*,
kindness like no one's in the world.
Ah, you could be my savior,
if you only had the will to be!

OCTAVIAN
First you must yourself take courage,
then I too will help.
Till you do that for yourself,
I can do naught for you.

SOPHIE *(confidingly, almost tenderly)*
What do you mean, what is it I must do?

OCTAVIAN *(softly)*
You know that already!

SOPHIE *(looking at him undismayed)*
And what is it that you will do for me,
ah, tell me pray!

OCTAVIAN *(with determination)*
Now must you stand alone and fight for us both!

SOPHIE
What? For us both?
Oh, say that again!

OCTAVIAN *(softly)*
For us both!

SOPHIE *(rapturously)*
In all my life I have never heard that word!

OCTAVIAN *(more firmly)*
For you and me you must be steadfast
and still be . . .

SOPHIE
Still be?

OCTAVIAN
What you are.
Sophie takes his hand, bends over it, and kisses it quickly before
he can withdraw it. He kisses her on the lips.

OCTAVIAN
(holding her in his arms as she nestles close to him, tenderly)
With eyes all veiled by your tears
you're asking my aid; your fears have pierced my heart.
Be brave! Nothing shall touch or hurt you.
Your tender heart is full of fear.
Now I must find a way to make you trust me,
and yet I know not how!
Rapture so blessed, so wondrous,
to hold you here in my arms.
Give answer, but only with silence:
Did you come here of your own free will to find me?
Say yes or no. Say yes or no!
You cannot find the words to tell it.
Say, was it done from choice?
Say, was it just your need?
Just your need that bade you offer me such marvels,
your heart, your lovely, lovely face?
Say, can it be that long ago
in some divine, remembered dream,
we lived this hour before?
Think you not so?
Say, think you not as I?
My heart and soul by your side are staying,
wheresoe'er you are,
for all eternity.

SOPHIE
What rapture! Your strong arms enfold me
and hide me ever from the world.
When I can feel your heart so close to mine,
nothing in life is harsh or dreadful.
I want to stay there, there!
In silence, and let what may befall,
deep hidden like a shy bird in the branches,
breathless beside you!
You, you are close at hand!
My heart should fail me now for fear and grief,

but no, I feel only joy and blessedness
and nothing more,
I cannot find the words to tell it!
Have I been sinful in what I did?
I sought you in my need!
Your arms were so near!
I looked upon your face,
your eyes, your manly grace,
and then I knew my place
was at hand by your side;
since that moment I know not
what I feel anymore.
Stay, stay close to me,
protect me, save me, stay beside me,
I follow where'er you guide me,
Save me, leave me not.
Protect me now and stay beside me,
with your protective arms around me—
stay near me, stay ever close by my side.

*From the secret doors in the rear corners Valzacchi and Annina
have emerged noiselessly and watched the lovers, approaching
silently on tiptoe and ducking behind the armchairs. At this
moment the two Italians are close behind them. Now they jump
forward, Annina seizing Sophie, Valzacchi taking hold of Octavian.*

VALZACCHI AND ANNINA *(shouting)*
    Herr Baron von Lerchenau! Herr Baron von Lerchenau!
    Octavian jumps aside to the right.
VALZACCHI *(holding him with difficulty, breathlessly to Annina)*
    Run and fetch de Barone!
    Now at once! I must 'old on tight to him!
ANNINA
    If I let go of her, she will be off!
VALZACCHI AND ANNINA
    Herr Baron von Lerchenau!
    Herr Baron von Lerchenau!
    Come and see your bride-to-be,
    beside her the Rose Cavalier!
    Come here quickly, come here quickly! *Ecco!*
*The Baron enters through the door on the left; the Italians let
their victims go, spring aside, bow low to the Baron with eloquent
gestures. The Baron with folded arms contemplates the group.*

Ominous pause. Sophie nestles timidly up to Octavian.

BARON

Eh bien, ma'mselle, what have you got to tell me?

Sophie remains silent. The Baron shows no signs of losing his composure.

Well, do not hesitate!

SOPHIE

Oh, God, what can I tell you?

You would not understand!

BARON *(genially)*

I'll be the judge of that!

OCTAVIAN *(moving a step nearer the Baron)*

'Tis my duty to inform Your Lordship

a most essential change has taken place

concerning Fräulein Faninal.

BARON *(genially)*

Oh, really? Change? None that I know!

OCTAVIAN

And therefore I now have to tell you!

The lady—

BARON

Hey, you're not so slow! You've learned your lesson early

for all your seventeen years—I must congratulate you!

OCTAVIAN

The lady—

BARON *(half to himself)*

I was just the same when I was your age,

you rascal! How you make me laugh, you poodle-puppy!

OCTAVIAN

The lady—

BARON

She's dumb, I presume, and so she's chosen you

to speak as her attorney.

OCTAVIAN

The lady—

He breaks off once more, as if to allow Sophie to speak.

SOPHIE *(fearfully)*

No, no! I cannot speak the word.

You speak for me!

OCTAVIAN *(with determination)*

The lady—

BARON *(mimicking him)*
> The lady! The lady, the lady, the lady!
> It's a cheap little comedy. It bores me!
> So now be off with you, before I lose my patience.

OCTAVIAN *(very resolutely)*
> The lady, in a word,
> the lady does not like you.

BARON *(still genially)*
> Never mind about that. She will like what I teach her.
> *(moving toward Sophie)*
> Come with me to the lawyer, who will need you soon to sign
> the marriage papers.

SOPHIE *(retreating)*
> No, not for all the world will I go in with you!
> How can a cavalier be so indelicate!

OCTAVIAN
> *(now between the other two and the left-hand door, very
> emphatically)*
> 'Tis clear enough! The lady's mind is now made up;
> she says she will let Your Lordship stay unmarried
> for now and evermore!

BARON
> Nonsense! Baby talk! You're puffing like a cow in labor.
> *(with the air of a man in a hurry)*
> It's time to go.
> *(taking her by the hand)*

OCTAVIAN *(planting himself firmly in front of the door)*
> If one spark you have in you
> of true gentility,
> then what I just have told you
> makes your duty quite clear.

BARON *(to Sophie, as if he had not heard)*
> Thank your lucky stars I choose to close one eye,
> as is correct and seemly in a gentleman!
> *He prepares to go past Octavian with her.*

OCTAVIAN *(striking the hilt of his sword)*
> There's a way to make my meaning
> understood by such as you are!

BARON *(not letting go of Sophie, and pushing her toward the door)*
> That I can scarce believe!

OCTAVIAN *(losing all self-control)*
　Of the name of gentleman
　you are unworthy, sir!

BARON *(pompously)*
　Indeed, were I not sure you know what is my due,
　and were you not a kinsman, I hardly could, I vow,
　restrain myself from measures of violence!
　He prepares with feigned unconcern to lead Sophie toward the
　center door, after the Italians have signalled to him energetically
　to go that way.
　Come now, go to your dear, beloved father;
　you will find him waiting in there!

OCTAVIAN *(following him, close to Sophie)*
　I trust you don't forget you've a name to defend.
　I know a most convenient garden.

BARON
　(continues in the same direction, still feigning unconcern, trying
　to lead Sophie away, and still holding her by the hand; over his
　shoulder)
　God bless my soul, it's not convenient now.
　The attorney must not be kept waiting.
　'Twould be impolite to my little bride.

OCTAVIAN *(seizing him by the sleeve)*
　By Satan, never was a hide so thick!
　And through this door I'll not let you pass!
　I tell you flatly to your face
　I think you you're a rascally knave
　and a fortune-hunter.
　You are a scoundrelly liar, a dirty old peasant,
　and a cur without honor or shame!
　If need be I'll make you learn on the spot the truth!
　Sophie has freed herself from the Baron and takes refuge behind
　Octavian. They stand to the left, almost in front of the door.

BARON *(puts two fingers into his mouth and gives a shrill whistle)*
　This little boy of ours at seventeen
　has learned a pretty turn of speech.
　(looking toward the center door)
　But God be praised that everyone in Vienna
　knows just who I am,
　and that includes Her Imperial Majesty!

All Lerchenau's servants have marched in through the center door. The Baron, glancing to the back once more, assures himself of their presence.
One is just what one is, and there's no need to prove it.
You'll allow me to bid you good day, sir, and let me pass.
The Baron now advances toward Sophie and Octavian, determined to secure both Sophie and his retreat.
I would be most upset if all my servants yonder . . .
OCTAVIAN *(furiously)*
So you have made your mind up to seek help from
your grooms and lackeys in our affair.
Then draw, sir, or commend your soul!
He draws his sword. The Baron's servants, who had already approached a few steps, hesitate when as they see what is happening and pause in their advance.
SOPHIE
Oh, God! Oh, what will happen next!
The Baron takes a step forward in order to secure Sophie.
OCTAVIAN
Draw, Satan, draw now, or on my sword I'll spit you!
BARON *(withdraws a step)*
Before a lady, shame! Come now, behave yourself!
Octavian rushes at him furiously. The Baron draws, lunges clumsily, and receives the point of Octavian's sword in his upper arm. The Baron lets his sword drop; his servants rush forward.
Help! Help! I'm stabbed, I'm bleeding! Murder! Murder! Murder!
All the servants rush toward Octavian. He springs aside to the right and keeps them at arm's length, whirling his sword about him. The Almoner, Valzacchi, and Annina hurry to the Baron and, supporting him, lead him to one of the chairs in the middle of the room. The Baron is surrounded by his servants and the Italians, who block him from the audience's view.
I'm feeling feverish! Go, call a doctor!
Some bandage! And call the police! I . . . I'm bleeding to death!
    I'm dead!
Don't let him go! And call the police! And call the police!
LERCHENAU'S SERVANTS
(closing around Octavian with more swagger than courage)
Break his crown! Lay hold there!
Spider webs! Get a sponge!
Quick, take his sword away!

Stick him dead, through the heart!
All Faninal's servants, female domestics, kitchen staff, and stable hands have streamed in through the center door.

ANNINA *(haranguing the servants)*
Yes, zis young gentleman
and ze lady, understand?
vere already in secret
familiar, understand?
Valzacchi and the Almoner divest the Baron of his coat. The latter groans uninterruptedly.

FANINAL'S SERVANTS
Somebody wounded? Who?
The stranger there?
Which one? The son-in-law?
Seize the brawler, hold him tight!
Who is it that first did draw?
That one all dressed in white!
Who, the Count that brought the rose?
For what cause, then? Just for her!
Hold him tight! Tan his hide!
Just for the bride?
They were a-courting!
We'll make him rue it!
Look at the brazen thing!
How dared she do it?

SOPHIE *(front left)*
Oh, what confusion this!
Wondrous! Quicker than lightning
he drove them all away!
I feel naught but the thrill
of his embraces still!
I feel nothing of fear,
I feel nothing of shame;
his bright glances have consumed
all my heart with their flame!
(calling to Octavian desperately)
Dearest!

OCTAVIAN *(holding his assailants at arm's length)*
Short shrift for all who come to near to me!
I will explain all
when you can hear me!

(calling to Sophie desperately)
Dearest!

LERCHENAU'S SERVANTS

*(desisting from attacking Octavian and going up to the maids
nearest them, whom they proceed to handle roughly)*
Linen bands we're needing!
Sponges to stanch the bleeding!
Bring us quickly salve and plaster,
bring them quick for our dear master!
*The Duenna clears a way for herself to the Baron. All press
around him.*

BARON

I can see other people's blood unmoved, my own makes me
    flinch!
My own makes me flinch!

MARIANNE

Such a high-born Lord! Such a cruel sword!
Such a heavy blow! Such an awful day!
*Faninal rushes in by the door to the left, followed by the Notary
and his Clerk, who remain standing by the door in great alarm.*

ANNINA

*(in front, to the left, curtseying and crossing eagerly over to
Faninal)*
The gentleman and miss
are united, Your Honor,
they have been in secrecy
plighted, Your Honor!
Full of devotion
and care for Your Honor,
we have kept respectfully
watch upon the pair, yes, sir!
*Lerchenau's Servants make as if to tear up the clothes of the
younger and prettier maidservants near them. Melee, until
Faninal begins.*

BARON

Oh, oh! Oh, oh!
(shouting at the Duenna)
Stop shouting and act for once!
Get help, for I am dying!
*The Duenna rushes out and, after a brief interlude, returns
breathless, laden with linen, followed by two maids with sponges*

and basins. They surround the Baron and busy themselves about him. Sophie, as soon as she sees her father, runs over to the right and beside Octavian, who now sheathes his sword.

FANINAL

He is at first speechless. Then he throws his hands over his head and bursts out.

Dear son-in-law! What's happening here? The saints preserve us!
What an ill-bred affray, here in my house of all things!
Has no one fetched the surgeon yet? You rogues, you!
Take my ten horses! Ride them all to death!
How is it none of you mustered the wit
to throw yourselves between them?! Do I stuff
a whole troop of liveried imbeciles only for disgrace
to fall on me, and on my brand new palace, too?
(going up to Octavian, with suppressed anger)
This is not the behavior I had expected Your Lordship would
affect!

BARON *(groaning)*

Oh! Oh!

FANINAL *(turning to the Baron)*

Oh, that such blood of priceless pedigree should run to waste
like this!
(to Octavian)
Oh, pah! Oh! what a common, vulgar butchery!

BARON

I have blood so young, so full of fire,
nothing can stanch it! Oh!

FANINAL *(venting his fury on Octavian)*

Truly from your most *(bitingly)* noble Lordship your incompa-
rable wit
should make a better show of taste and breeding!

BARON *(weakening)*

Oh! Oh!

OCTAVIAN *(courteously)*

I beg you to forgive me.
I am so deeply grieved that this thing should have happened.
But I am not to blame. I promise, in the fullness of time
Your Honor will discharge me without sentence;
you'll hear from your own daughter's lips.

FANINAL *(controlling himself with difficulty)*

'Tis well, sir. Come now, tell me!

SOPHIE *(resolutely)*
As you command me, father, I shall unfold my story.
My Lord there has not acted as a man of honor.
FANINAL *(angrily)*
Why, of whom do you speak? Of my future son-in-law?
If that is so, I beg you think ere you speak.
SOPHIE *(quietly)*
It is not so. I cannot give my hand to him.
FANINAL *(still more angrily)*
Not give your hand?
SOPHIE
No more. Look at me and forgive me, dear papa!
FANINAL *(at first muttering to himself)*
Not give your hand? No more. Look and forgive!
Run through the body. By her side, that schoolboy.
(breaking out)
How dare she! Broken the marriage of my dreams.
All the prying fools of the district and their jealous wives,
how they will jeer! The surgeon! Quick! What if he dies here?
(to Sophie, beside himself with rage)
You marry him!
The Doctor arrives and proceeds at once to attend to the Baron.
Faninal turns to Octavian, changing his anger to obsequious
civility out of respect for Rofrano's rank.
And may I now, in all humility, request
Your Lordship to retire from my poor palace, fast as may be,
and never more to show your face here!
(to Sophie)
As for you!
You marry him, and if he bleeds to death, no matter,
marry his lifeless body!
The Doctor indicates by a reassuring gesture that the wounded
man is in no danger. Octavian looks for his hat, which had
fallen under the servants' feet. A maid hands it to him with a
curtsey. Faninal makes an obeisance to Octavian of exaggerated
civility, but unmistakable significance. Octavian realizes that he
cannot stay, but is longing to speak one more word to Sophie;
he replies to Faninal's obeisance with an equally ceremonious
bow. Faninal angrily bows a second, then a third time, which
Octavian promptly returns.

SOPHIE
(hurrying to speak the following words while Octavian is still within earshot; curtseying)
Marry that man I will not living, and not dead!
I will lock myself away in my room!
FANINAL
Ah! Lock yourself in! I've men enough
to haul you to your carriage, Mistress Willful.
SOPHIE *(curtseying again)*
I'll jump out from the carriage on my way to church.
FANINAL
(continuing to exchange obeisances with Octavian, who keeps stepping toward the door but cannot tear himself from Sophie at such a moment)
Jump out from your carriage? Ha! I'll be at your side
and hold you till we get there.
SOPHIE *(curtseying again)*
I promise I shall give the priest No
and not Yes for answer.
In the meantime the Major-Domo dismisses the servants. The stage is gradually cleared. Only Lerchenau's servants remain with their master.
FANINAL *(continuing to exchange obeisances with Octavian)*
Ah! Give No and not a Yes for an answer!
I'll shut you in a nunnery as I stand here!
Go! Get you from my sight, miss. Better now than next day!
For all your life!
SOPHIE *(terrified)*
I beg you to forgive me! I am not really bad!
Forgive me, I pray you, for just this once!
FANINAL *(furious, shutting his ears)*
For all your life! For all your life!
OCTAVIAN *(quickly, in an undertone)*
Only be calm, beloved, for my sake!
You'll hear from me.
The Duenna pushes Octavian toward the door.
FANINAL
For all your life!
MARIANNE *(pulling Sophie with her to the right)*
Now go, be gone from your father's presence.

*She puts her through the door on the right and closes it.
Octavian has departed by the center door. The Baron, surrounded by his servants, the Duenna, two Maids, the Italians,
and the Doctor, is now visible lying on a couch improvised out
of several chairs.*

FANINAL *(shouting once more through the door by which Sophie left)*
For all your life!
(hurrying over to the Baron)
I kiss your hand, sir. I must embrace you, my dear Baron!

BARON *(whose arm has been hurt by the embrace)*
Oh! Oh! Jesus Maria!

FANINAL *(to the right, his rage increasing again)*
Jezebel! To a nunnery!
(to the center door)
Into prison!
For all your life!

BARON
All right! All right! A drop of something liquid.

FANINAL
Some wine? Some beer? Some hippocras with ginger?
*The Doctor makes a nervous, deprecating gesture; Faninal con-
tinues, lamenting.*
Breeding and birth! So noble in misfortune!
And in my palace, too! You'll marry him, so much the sooner.
I'm master here!

BARON *(wearily)*
All right! All right!

FANINAL *(toward the left-hand door, his anger flaring up again)*
I'm master here!
(to the Baron)
I kiss your hand for such polite indulgence.
We are yours to command. I'll run and bring you—
(to the left)
A nunnery is too good!
(to the Baron)
Be at your ease.
(very obsequiously)
I know what satisfaction is due from me.
*Faninal rushes off. The Duenna and the Maids leave at the same
time. The two Italians have slunk off during the preceding scene.*

*The Baron is left alone with his servants and the Doctor. Soon a
Footman comes with a carafe of wine and offers it to the Baron.*
BARON *(sitting up slightly)*
Well, here I am. What accidents befall a man of quality
in this old Vienna town.
It does not suit me here. We're much too clearly in the hands of
   God.
I'd rather be at home!
He tries to drink and makes a movement which hurts.
Oh! Oh! The Devil! Oh! Oh! A plague upon that boy!
Not dry yet behind the ears, and plays with swords already.
(with increasing anger)
Insolent scurvy dog! Wait, wait until I catch you. I'll kill you.
I swear I'll throw you in with the dogs to cool your heels.
In the chicken-coop—no, no, the pigsty.
That's where I'll put you. I'll make you hear the angels sing!
LERCHENAU'S SERVANTS
*(at once assuming a very dangerous and threatening attitude,
turning to the door by which Octavian left; in a muted tone)*
We will do for you,
beat you black and blue.
Wait, our time will come,
vile Italian scum!
BARON *(to Faninal's Footman, who is waiting on him)*
Give me some more wine, quick!
*The Doctor pours it out for the Baron and gives it to him. As
the Baron drinks, he is gradually in a better mood.*
I can't help laughing, just to think what fancies
a boy like that can have, he gives himself such airs:
seems to think he can arrange my affairs.
Ha, ha! Well, we'll see who laughs the longest! Not for worlds,
   though,
would I have missed the chance to see that saucy baggage spitting fire at me!
(ever more cosily)
There's nothing I know that excites me so much,
or that renews my youth so well, as a defiant wench!
LERCHENAU'S SERVANTS *(in a muted tone)*
We will do for you,
vile Italian cur,

we will do for you,
beat him black and blue!

BARON

Herr Medicus, you go now to my room!
And make my bed, of softest feather bedding!
I'll come, but first I'll have more wine. Now off with you, good
   doctor.
The Doctor goes out with the Valet. He empties the second cup.
A feather bed. Two hours before we eat.
(ever more expansively)
I'll die of boredom.
*Annina has entered through the anteroom and approaches him
discreetly, a letter in her hand.*
(quietly, to himself)
"Without me, without me, every day is so long.
With me, with me, never night is too long."
*Annina places herself so that the Baron cannot avoid seeing her
and makes mysterious signs with the letter.*
For me?

ANNINA *(approaching)*

From one you know of.

BARON

And who, pray, may that be?

ANNINA *(coming quite close)*

To your own hands only, and in secret can I give it.

BARON

Clear out!
*His servants retire, unceremoniously taking the decanter from
Faninal's servant and drinking it empty.*
Show me the thing!
*He opens the letter with his left hand and tries to read it, hold-
ing it far from his eyes.*
Look for my glasses here in my pocket.
(very suspiciously, as she is searching)
No! Better not. If you can read, let's hear it.
There!

ANNINA *(taking the letter and reading it)*

"Herr Cavalier! Tomorrow come evening I'll be free!
I liked you at once, but I
was too shy there before Her Highness,
'cause I am only a young girl. Your most loving Mariandl,

humble serving girl and sweetheart.
Hoping Herr Cavalier has not completely forgotten me
I wait an answer."
BARON *(delightedly)*
She waits an answer!
It all goes so well, just like home,
there is though quite a different style in town.
(very gaily)
I still have all the luck of the Lerchenaus.
Come back tonight, I'll give the answer and in writing.
ANNINA
Yours to command, Herr Cavalier. You won't forget your servant?
BARON *(not noticing her; to himself)*
"Without me, without me, every day is too long."
ANNINA *(more insistently)*
You won't forget your servant, Your Highness?
BARON
All right.
"With me, with me, not a night is too long."
Annina makes another begging gesture.
Later on. All in good time. Don't forget.
She waits an answer! Leave me now a moment.
Go to my room, get me my pen and ink, and I will
think of an answer to dictate.
Annina goes out, not without indicating with a threatening gesture behind the Baron's back that she will soon get even with him for his niggardliness. The Baron takes a last sip of wine.
"With me, with me, not a night is too long!"
The Baron exits slowly and quite at his ease, accompanied by his servants. The curtain falls slowly.

ACT 3

A private room in an inn. At the back, to the left, an alcove, with a bed in it. The alcove is separated from the room by a curtain, which can be drawn. In the center, toward the left, a fireplace, with a fire; over it a mirror. In front on the left a door leading to a side room. Opposite the fireplace is a table laid for two, on which stands a large, many-branched candlestick. At the back, in the center, a door leading to the corridor. Next to it, on the right, a sideboard. At the back, on the right, a blind window; in front, on the right, a window looking onto the street. Candelabra with candles on the sideboard and on the chimneypiece, and sconces on the walls. Only one candle is burning in each candlestick on the chimneypiece. The room is in semi-darkness.

Annina is standing there, dressed as a lady in mourning. Valzacchi, arranging her veil and putting her dress to rights, takes a step backwards, surveys her, takes a crayon from his pocket, and paints her eyes. The door on the left is opened cautiously; a head appears and then vanishes. Then a not unsuspicious-looking, but decently dressed, old woman slips in, opens the door silently, and respectfully introduces Octavian, in female clothes, with a cap such as middle-class girls wear.

Octavian, followed by the old woman, moves toward the two others. Valzacchi is at once aware of them, stops what he is doing, and bows to Octavian. Annina does not at once recognize him in his disguise. She cannot restrain her astonishment and curtsies low. Octavian feels in his pocket (not like a woman, but like a man, and one sees that under his skirt he is wearing riding boots without spurs) and throws a purse to Valzacchi.

Valzacchi and Annina kiss his hand. Annina puts a finishing touch to his kerchief. Five suspicious-looking men enter, very cautiously, from the left. Valzacchi makes a sign to them to wait. They stand at the left, near the door. A clock strikes the half-hour. Valzacchi takes out his watch, shows it to Octavian: it is high time. Octavian hurries out to the left, followed by the old woman, who acts as his duenna. Valzacchi leads the suspicious-looking men to the front, impressing on them with every gesture the necessity of extreme caution. Annina goes to the mirror (all the while carefully avoiding making a noise), completes her disguise; then draws from her pocket a piece of paper, from which she seems to be learning a part. Valzacchi signals to one of the suspicious-looking men to follow him noiselessly, quite noiselessly. He leads him to the wall on the right, noiselessly opens a trapdoor not far from the table, makes the man descend, closes the trapdoor again, then summons two others to his side, slinks in front of them to the door of the room, puts his head out, assures himself that they are not observed, makes a sign to them to appear to him, and lets them out. Then he closes the door, directs the two remaining men to precede him silently to the door leading to the side room, and pushes them out. He beckons to Annina to come to him, goes out with her silently, noiselessly closes the door behind them, and then returns. He claps his hands. The man who is hidden rises to his waist from the trapdoor. At the same moment heads appear above the bed and in other places. At a sign from Valzacchi they disappear as suddenly—the secret panels close without a sound. Valzacchi again looks at his watch, goes to the back, opens the door. Then he produces a tinder-box and busily lights the candles on the table. A Waiter and a Boy run in with tapers for lighting candles. They light the candles on the chimney, on the sideboard, and the numerous sconces. They have left the door open behind them; dance music is heard from the anteroom at the back. Valzacchi hurries to the center doors, opens them respectfully, and jumps aside with a low bow.

Baron Ochs appears, his arm in a sling, leading Octavian by his left, followed by his Valet. The Baron surveys the room. Octavian looks around, runs to the mirror, arranges his hair. The Baron notices the Waiter and the Boy, who are about to light more candles, and signs to them to stop. In their zeal they do not notice him.

The Baron impatiently pulls the Boy from the chair onto which he has climbed and extinguishes some of the candles nearest him with his hand. Valzacchi discreetly points out the alcove to him and, by opening the curtain, the bed. The Landlord hurries forward with several Waiters to greet their noble guest.

LANDLORD
What can my poor house still offer Your Lordship?

FOUR WAITERS
A few more candles?

LANDLORD
A better apartment?

WAITERS
A few more candles for My Lord?
More silver?

BARON
(busily occupied with a napkin which he has taken from the table and is using to extinguish all the candles he can reach)
Be off! Or you will give the girl ideas!
Who asked for music? Didn't order that.
(extinguishes more candles)

LANDLORD
Shall they be told to come and play in here?
And while you dine they'll play some music.

BARON
Leave your damned fiddlers where they are.
(noticing the blind window on the right behind the table)
What is that little window there?
(checking whether it lets in a draft)

LANDLORD
'Tis only sham, My Lord.
(bows)
Your Lordship's supper waits.
All five Waiters make as if to hurry off.

BARON
Stop! What do those black beetles want?

WAITERS *(at the door)*
To wait upon Your Lordship.

BARON *(gestures them away)*
I don't need help.
(roughly when they hesitate)
Off now! My servant shall do all the serving here,
and I can pour the wine out. D'you hear me?
Valzacchi signals to them to respect His Lordship's wishes without demur. He pushes them all out the door. The Baron continues to extinguish a number of candles, among them some high on the wall that he can only reach with difficulty.
(to Valzacchi)
You are a worthy fellow. If you can get the bill reduced a little,
something will come your way. I'm sure it costs a fortune here.
Exit Valzacchi, bowing low. Octavian has now finished. The Baron leads him to the table; they sit down. The valet at the sideboard contemplates the developments of the tête-à-tête with impudent curiosity. He places carafes of wine from the sideboard on the dining table. The Baron pours out wine. Octavian sips. The Baron kisses Octavian's hand. Octavian withdraws his hand. The Baron signals to the valets to withdraw but has to repeat the signal several times before they finally leave.

OCTAVIAN *(pushing back his glass)*
No, no, let it be! No wine for me.

BARON
Why, sweetheart, what next? Come, don't be so bashful.

OCTAVIAN
No, no, no, no, I must not stay.
He jumps up as if he were about to go.

BARON *(seizing him with his left hand)*
You drive me to despair.

OCTAVIAN
I know, sir, what you think. Oh, you naughty man.

BARON *(very loud)*
Lord strike me pink! I swear by all my patron saints!

OCTAVIAN
Feigning great terror, he runs—as if by mistake—instead of to the door, into the alcove, tears the curtains apart, and sees the bed. He pretends to be utterly astonished and returns in consternation on tiptoe.
Jesus Maria, there's a bed there, a really great big one.
Lor' bless me, who's it for?

BARON *(leading him back to the table)*
You'll know in good time. Just come now. Sit down with me.
They'll soon bring us our supper. Something wrong with your
    appetite?
(puts his arm around his waist)

OCTAVIAN
(casting languishing looks at the Baron)
Oh, Lord! What a way for a bridegroom to act.
(pushes him off)

BARON
Oh, can't you for once leave that word alone.
You sit here with a cavalier at your side,
not with some lout of a footman:
a cavalier leaves all
that is not quite to his taste
outside there by the door. Here sits no bridegroom
nor any lady's chambermaid:
Here sits at supper a man in love and with the girl who stole his
    heart.
He draws Octavian nearer to him. Octavian leans back coquettishly in his chair, with half-closed eyes. Then the Baron rises. The moment for the first kiss seems to have come. As his face comes close to that of his companion, he is forcefully struck by the likeness to Octavian. He starts back and unconsciously feels his wounded arm.
That face again! That blasted boy!
His face pursues me waking and in dreams!

OCTAVIAN
(opening his eyes and looking at him with impudent coquetry)
What do you mean?

BARON
Your face reminds me of a godforsaken boy!

OCTAVIAN
Go on! I never heard of such stuff!
The Baron, once again quite certain that it is the chambermaid, forces a smile. But he is not quite free of fear; he has to breathe deeply, and so the kiss is postponed. The man under the trapdoor opens it too soon and appears. Octavian, who is sitting opposite him, makes violent signs to him to get out of sight. He vanishes at once. The Baron, taking a few steps to shake off the unpleasant impression and about to embrace Octavian from behind, catches a last glimpse of him. He is violently alarmed and points to the spot. Octavian continues as if he did not understand.
What's wrong with you?

BARON
Lord, what was that!
(pointing to the spot where the apparition vanished)
Didn't you see something there?

OCTAVIAN
Never a thing.

BARON
Not a thing? *(again anxiously scanning Octavian's face)* No?
(passing his hand over his face)
Nothing there neither?

OCTAVIAN
Why, that's my face.

BARON *(breathing heavily, pouring out a glass of wine)*
This is your face—and nothing there—I think
my head is going to burst.
He falls heavily into a chair. He is ill at ease. The door is opened, and the music from outside can be heard again. The Valet comes in and serves.

OCTAVIAN *(very softly)*
What lovely music!

BARON *(very loud again)*
It's my favorite song, you know.

OCTAVIAN *(listening to the music)*
It makes me weepy.

BARON
What?

OCTAVIAN
'Cause it's so pretty.

BARON
What, weeping? Don't be sad.
You must enjoy yourself; the music fires the blood.
(sentimentally)
Is it clear
(signalling to the Valet to go)
now, my dear? Do you not see
How it is with me?
You now can make of me your willing slave.
The Valet goes reluctantly, then opens the door again, looks in with insolent curiosity, and does not disappear till the Baron has made another angry sign.

OCTAVIAN
(leaning back, as if speaking to himself, with exaggerated melancholy)
'Tis all one, 'tis all one, 'tis all one, 'tis all one—
all our joys, and all our bitter pain.
(as the Baron takes his hand)
In the end are they not all in vain?

BARON *(letting go of his hand)*
Why, what's this? Oh, they're not all in vain.

OCTAVIAN
(still just as melancholy, casting smoldering glances at the Baron)
As the hours do fly, as the wind blows by,
so must we too shortly pass away.
'Tis the lot of man,
(a languishing glance at the Baron)
that nothing we can.
Not an eye shall weep, not for your loss, nor for mine.

BARON
Is it wine that makes you so sad?
It must be your corset cramps your poor little heart.
Octavian, with closed eyes, does not answer. The Baron rises and tries to unlace him.
I must say I am feeling warm.
Without ado he takes off his wig, looking for a place to put it. At that moment he catches a glimpse of a face which appears above

*the alcove and stares at him. The face vanishes in a trice. He says
"Apoplexy" to himself and struggles with his fear, but has to mop
his forehead. His eyes again fall on the chambermaid, slumped
helplessly on the chair. He is overcome by this and approaches tenderly. Then he again seems to see Octavian's face close to his own.
He starts back again. Mariandl hardly stirs. Once more the Baron
wrestles with his fear, forcing himself to put a cheerful face on it.
Then his eyes again alight on a strange face, staring at him from
the wall. Now he is beside himself with terror: he gives a muffled
scream, seizes the handbell from the table, and rings it in a fury.*
There and there, and there, and there!
*Suddenly the supposedly blind window is torn open. Annina in
mourning appears and points with outstretched arms to the
Baron, who is distraught with fear.*
There and there, and there, and there!

ANNINA
My husband! Yes, it is he! 'Tis he!
She vanishes.

BARON
Lord, what was that?

OCTAVIAN
This place is all bewitched! *(crosses himself)*
*Annina, followed by Valzacchi, who makes a pretense of hold-
ing her back, rushes in at the center door with the Landlord
and three Waiters.*

ANNINA
(speaking with a Bohemian accent, but in educated tones)
I am his wife! I'll get my hands on him,
God is my witness. You be witness also!
The law, and the government, Her Majesty,
give me back my beloved!

BARON *(to the Landlord)*
What does this woman want of me, you fool?
What does he want, and he, and he, and he?
(pointing all around the room)
The devil has his home in your godforsaken third-rate coffee
house.

ANNINA
And would you dare deny me, villain!
And make pretense you do not know me?

The Baron has put a cold compress on his head, holds it in its place with his left hand, then goes right up to the Landlord, the Waiters, and Annina in turn, scanning them closely as if to convince himself that they are real.

BARON

Alive, by Heaven!

He throws the compress away.

(very emphatically)

This baggage, I protest, I never saw before!

(to the landlord)

Begone now, all of you, and let us sup in peace!

I vow I'll never more set foot in your low tavern.

ANNINA *(as if only now noticing Octavian's presence)*

Ah! It is true, what all my friends did tell me,

that he intends a second marriage, oh, the monster,

a second innocent maiden such as I once was.

The Landlord is alarmed.

LANDLORD AND THREE WAITERS

Oh! Your Lordship!

BARON

What, am I in a madhouse? Plague on you all!

He shakes Valzacchi who is standing next to him, violently.

Am I Baron Ochs of Lerchenau, tell me, or am I not?

Am I possessed?

(holding a finger in a candle)

Is that a candle,

(brandishing a napkin)

and is that a napkin?

ANNINA

Yes, yes, you are he, and as true as you are he,

I am your wife, and you know me full well.

Leupold, reflect:

Leupold Anton von Lerchenau, above us all dwells a Judge that

knoweth all!

BARON *(staring at her in bewilderment)*

Surely I know you.

(looking at Octavian again)

They all have double faces, all of them together.

LANDLORD AND THREE WAITERS

Poor ill-used lady, wretched, ill-used lady!

Four Children between the ages of four and ten rush in, prematurely, and make for the Baron.

FOUR CHILDREN
Papa! Papa! Papa!

ANNINA
At first she starts violently, so that her speech is interrupted, but she soon regains her composure.
Hear you the voices of your offspring?
Children, raise your hands to him in prayer!

BARON
He hits out at the Children with a napkin which he takes from the table.
(to the Landlord)
Take all this crew away from here at once.
Take her, take him, and him, and him!
(pointing in all directions)

OCTAVIAN *(to Valzacchi)*
Have messengers been sent for Faninal yet?

VALZACCHI *(softly)*
Ere you 'ad come 'ere: in a moment 'e is 'ere.

LANDLORD *(behind the Baron)*
Asking your pardon, go not too far,
else it might end in harm for you, harm most serious!

BARON
What? Harm to me from that biddy there?
Ne'er have I touched her, not with a pitchfork's end!

ANNINA *(screaming shrilly)*
Aah!

LANDLORD *(as before)*
For bigamy is not a trifle,
It is a hanging matter.

VALZACCHI *(softly to the Baron)*
I counsel de Barone to 'ave a care,
de police in dis town, it 'ave no mercy, sir!

BARON
Bigamy! Pooh! A fig for your police!
(mimicking the Children's voices)
Papa, Papa!
(striking his head as if in despair, then furiously)
Throw out that screaming Jezebel! Who? What? You will not?
What? The police! Won't they do anything? Are the whole lot of you

only a pack of cowards?
Are we in Paris? Or on a cannibal island?
Or in Her Majesty's own city?
He pulls open the window looking onto the street.
Hey, police!
Police there, hey, police! I call you here to help me.
I am a nobleman, my life's in danger.
Loud cries for the police are heard from the street.

LANDLORD *(lamenting)*
Oh! my old inn disgraced!
And my good reputation!

THE CHILDREN *(whining)*
Papa! Papa! Papa!
A Commissar of Police enters with two Constables of the Watch. All stand back to make room for them.

VALZACCHI
O Dio! What can we do?

OCTAVIAN
Have confidence in me and leave the rest to chance.

VALZACCHI
Your humble servant to command!

COMMISSAR *(roughly)*
Halt! Keep your places! What is wrong?
Who was it called for help? Who was it broke the peace?

BARON
(going toward him with the self-confidence of a great gentleman)
It's all in order now. I am happy to see you.
I always knew that in Vienna there's no danger.
(cheerfully)
Drive all the riffraff away, I wish to dine in private.

COMMISSAR
And who are you? What right have you to intervene?
Is this your house?
The Baron gapes; the Commissar continues brusquely.
Then keep a civil tongue and wait a moment,
till I come to question you.
The Baron retires in perplexity and begins to look for his wig, which has disappeared in the confusion and is not to be found. The Commissar sits down; the two Constables take up their position behind him.
Who is in charge?

LANDLORD *(submissively)*
  Pray let me, excellent Sir Constable, only speak for myself, sir.
COMMISSAR
  Your premises do not speak well for you.
  Now, your report. The whole truth!
LANDLORD
  It happened thus: His Lordship here—
COMMISSAR
  That great big fat man there? Where have you put your wig, sir?
BARON *(who has been looking for it all this time)*
  That's what I'm asking you!
LANDLORD
  That is His Lordship Baron Lerchenau.
COMMISSAR
  Then prove it.
BARON
  What?
COMMISSAR
  Is there a man of standing here
  whom you can call as witness?
BARON
  Right here at hand. There, my secretary, that Italian.
VALZACCHI *(exchanging a glance of understanding with Octavian)*
  I do not know this gentleman. He may
  be a baron, he may not. I do not know.
  *Octavian, having previously stood quietly on the right, now
  runs back and forth as if in despair, unable to find the way out
  and mistaking the window for the door.*
BARON *(beside himself)*
  That's the last straw, you dirty, lying scoundrel!
  *The Valet, much alarmed at the situation, suddenly has a saving
  inspiration and hastily rushes out by the center door.*
COMMISSAR *(to the Baron, sharply)*
  You'd better keep a civil tongue.
OCTAVIAN
  Oh, my God, could I sink through the floor now!
  O Holy Mother of God, you must help me!
COMMISSAR
  That young person there, who is she?
BARON
  She? No one. She stands under my protection here.

COMMISSAR
Yourself will soon find some protection very necessary.
Come now, who is the girl, and why is she here?
(looking around)
I have suspicion that you are one of those profligate men who lead
young girls astray! It would go hard with you.
Once more, how come you by her? Answer quickly.

OCTAVIAN
Farewell. The river.
*Octavian runs toward the alcove as though to escape and tears
open the curtain, disclosing the peacefully illuminated bed.*

COMMISSAR *(rising)*
What's this, Landlord, what's this?
What business do you carry on?

LANDLORD *(confused)*
When there are persons of rank and fashion—come to dine or
    sup—

COMMISSAR
Hold you your tongue: wait till I question you.
(to the Baron)
Now I will count to three, then you must tell me
how it comes that this honest girl is here with you.
And I would have you know you had better not deceive me
    with lying answers.
*The Landlord and Valzacchi indicate with gestures to the Baron
how dangerous the situation is and how important his statement is.*

BARON
*(signalling confidently to them that they may rely on him, and
that he was not born yesterday)*
The Captain of the Watch, for sure, will think no harm
if men of quality with their affianced brides
should choose to sit at supper at nine o'clock here in this inn.
He glances around him to see the effect of his explanation.

COMMISSAR
She your affianced bride? Then state her father's name
and tell me where she lives. And if you've spoke the truth,
you'll be free with the girl at once to leave us.

BARON
Pray, do you know to whom you speak? I'm not accustomed—

COMMISSAR *(sharply)*
Answer without ado, else I will sing quite another tune.

BARON
All right, I'll tell you. This is Fräulein Faninal,
Sophie Anna Barbara, daughter to that
most distinguished nobleman, Herr von Faninal,
who lives in his palace quite near at hand.
The inn servants, other guests, and some of the musicians from
the other room have crowded around the door and are looking
on curiously. Herr von Faninal forces a way through them,
hastily attired in hat and coat.

FANINAL
The same, sir. What do you wish of me?
(to the Baron)
How strange you look!
I scarce expected you'd desire my presence
at this untimely hour here in a common tavern.

BARON *(very astonished and taken aback)*
Why have you stuck your nose in here in the devil's mischief?

FANINAL *(in an undertone)*
A damn stupid question indeed, Sir Son-in-law,
when your excited servant all but broke my door down
to tell me I
must come at once and save you from a horrid situation,
in which, through no fault of yours, you had found yourself.
The Baron clutches his head.

COMMISSAR
Who is this man? What is he doing here?

BARON
He's not important, only an acquaintance.
Come to this place by sheer coincidence.

COMMISSAR
Your name, and tell me why you're here!

FANINAL
I am the Baron von Faninal.

COMMISSAR
And this young lady's father?

BARON
(coming between them so as to hide Octavian from Faninal;
eagerly)
What, he her father? No, a distant kinsman.
A cousin, it may be. The father
is full twice as fat as he.

FANINAL *(much astonished)*
   What means this, pray? How strange you look. I am her father,
      surely.
BARON *(trying to get rid of him)*
   Now leave it all to me, and get you gone.
FANINAL
   What, you presume, sir—
BARON *(infuriated)*
   Get you gone, the devil take you!
FANINAL *(with growing anger)*
   To drag my name into a vulgar brawl in this low tavern!
   I'll not submit!
BARON *(trying to stop his mouth; to the Commissar)*
   It is just his fancy.
   He calls himself so as a joke.
COMMISSAR
   Yes, yes, all right then.
   (to Faninal)
   So you recognize
   this gentleman as your son-in-law?
FANINAL
   Of course, why should I fail to recognize him?
   Merely because he's lost his wig?
COMMISSAR *(to the Baron)*
   And you now recognize this gentleman to be,
   for good or evil, the young lady's father?
BARON
   *(taking the candlestick from the table and holding it up to
   Faninal's face)*
   Well, I'll be damned! Yes, yes, turns out to be the same.
   This evening I have not been feeling very well.
   I can no longer trust my eyes. I must tell you,
   there's something in this place that gives one apoplectic turns.
COMMISSAR *(to Faninal)*
   You, on the other hand, deny you are the father
   of this girl here who has been described as
   your daughter.
FANINAL *(noticing Octavian for the first time)*
   As my daughter? That, that baggage,
   says she is a child of mine?

BARON *(with a forced smile)*
A jest! A mere mistake, I vow! The landlord
has told the Captain of the Watch a tale
of me, and how I soon shall wed your daughter.
LANDLORD *(in great excitement)*
No word, no word from me, 'twas he there that told the story!
FANINAL *(beside himself)*
Arrest that shameless baggage! To the prison!
I'll have her whipped! I'll have her shut up in a convent!
I—I—I—
BARON
You'd best go home. Tomorrow I will come
and tell you all the truth. You know how much you owe to me.
FANINAL *(beside himself with rage)*
'Twas you that said it!
(taking a few steps to the rear)
Tell my daughter to come here!
Her sedan chair is below! Bid her up at once!
(pouncing on the Baron again)
You'll pay this dearly! I will go to law!
BARON
What a mighty bother you are making
about a little thing. To be your son-in-law a man must have
the patience of an ass, *parole d'honneur*!
Now bring my wig here!
(shaking the Landlord)
Find my wig! Find me my wig!
In his wild hunt for his wig, he seizes some of the Children and pushes them aside.
THE FOUR CHILDREN *(automatically)*
Papa! Papa! Papa!
FANINAL *(starting back)*
Whose brats are these?
BARON
He at least succeeds in finding his hat and hits out at the Children with it.
Nothing! A swindle! I don't know this woman!
She lies, she says that she's my lawful wife!
Damn it to hell! I am like Daniel in the lions' den.
Sophie hurries in in her coat. They make room for her. Faninal's Footmen can be seen through the door, each with a pole of the

*sedan in his hand. The Baron tries to conceal his bald pate from
Sophie with his hat, while she goes up to her father.*

CHORUS OF ONLOOKERS

The bride! Oh, what a sore disgrace!

FANINAL *(to Sophie)*

Now, look around. See, there your noble suitor stands.
And there His Gracious Lordship's family!
The wife and all her children! She's his, too,
but a morganatic wife! No, that is you, as he himself has said!
Does not the shame o'erwhelm you? What? Me, too.

SOPHIE *(with a sigh of joy)*

I'm overjoyed. I never looked on him as mine.

FANINAL

Not look on him as yours? Not look on him as yours?
(with growing desperation)
My name and fame! I'll be the mock of all the city!
No dog would even take a bone from me.
(almost in tears)

CHORUS OF ONLOOKERS

The disgrace! The disgrace!

FANINAL

I'll never face the town!
The scandal paper!

CHORUS OF ONLOOKERS

The disgrace for Herr von Faninal!

CHORUS

(heads popping out of the wall and floor, with muted voices)
The disgrace! The disgrace!
For Herr von Faninal!

FANINAL

There! From the cellar! From the air! How can I face the town?
(to the Baron, clenching his fist)
Oh, scoundrel, you! I am not well! A chair!

*Footmen rush toward him and prevent him from falling. Two of
them had previously thrown their poles to bystanders. Sophie
busies herself about him anxiously. The Landlord also hastens to
his aid. They lift him up and carry him into the next room.
Several Waiters go before them, showing them the way and opening the door. At this moment the Baron catches sight of his wig,
which has reappeared as if by magic. He rushes to it, claps it on
his head, and sets it straight before a mirror. With this change he*

regains some of his lost dignity, but he contents himself with turning his back on Annina and the Children, whose presence makes him uneasy, in spite of everything. The door is closed behind Herr von Faninal and his servants. The Landlord and Waiters soon return quietly, fetch drugs, bottles, water, and other things, which they carry to the door, and Sophie takes them in the doorway.

BARON
(his former self-confidence now completely restored, to the Commissar)
You don't need me any longer. I'll pay, I'll go!
(to Octavian)
And now I'll take you home.

COMMISSAR
That's where you're wrong. I have some questions for you still.
At a sign from the Commissar, the two Constables remove the bystanders from the room. Only Annina and the Children remain standing by the wall to the left.

BARON
Leave well alone now, 'twas a jest, I'll tell you later who she truly is.
I pledge my word: I'll marry her. I'll tell you in good time.
The wench back there has already calmed down.
You'll know now what I am and what I am not!
(about to lead Octavian off)

OCTAVIAN *(shaking him off)*
I will not go with him!

BARON *(in an undertone)*
I'll marry you if you keep well with me.
So vastly do you please me, you'll be my Baroness!

OCTAVIAN *(freeing himself from the Baron's grip, speaking)*
Herr Commissar, I have something to tell you,
but out of the hearing of the Baron.
At a sign from the Commissar, the two Constables force the Baron to the front right. Octavian seems to be telling the Commissar something which surprises him very much. The Commissar accompanies Octavian to the alcove. Octavian disappears behind the curtains.

BARON
(aside to the Constables, in a familiar tone, pointing to Annina)
God knows who she may be, I swear. We were at supper.
I've not a notion what she wants, else I would never call on you
for help.

The Commissar seems to be much entertained and stands close to the opening of the curtains without embarrassment.

BARON
(noticing the Commissar's amusement; suddenly much excited by the strange incident)
What's happening there? Can it be possible? The villain!
No, no, he can't do that to me! She is a maiden! She is a virgin!
He is restrained with difficulty.
I am her guardian, as you see. I warn you!
You will pay for this behavior!
He frees himself and goes toward the alcove. They pursue him and seize him again. Mariandl's clothes are thrown out of the alcove, piece by piece. The Commissar makes a bundle of them. The Baron struggles with his two captors. They are having much trouble holding him when Octavian's head appears at the opening of the curtains.
You'd better let me go.
Waiters enter and open the doors.

LANDLORD *(rushing in)*
Gentlemen, Her Serene Highness, the Princess von Werdenberg!
First servants in the Marschallin's livery enter, then the Baron's Valet. They form a line. Then the Marschallin enters, the Little Black Page carrying her train.

BARON
Having shaken off his captors, he wipes the perspiration from his brow and hurries over to the Marschallin.
I'm glad beyond all measure. This is more than I deserve.
Your intervention here shows me a kindness quite unequalled.

OCTAVIAN
(putting his head out from between the curtains)
Marie Thérèse, how come you here?
The Marschallin stands motionless, not answering. She looks around with a questioning glance. The Valet, proud and pleased with himself, goes up to the Baron. The Baron indicates his satisfaction with him.

COMMISSAR *(going toward the Marschallin, at attention)*
May't please Your Highness, your most humble servant.
I'm the Commissar of this district.

BARON
You see, Herr Commissar, Her Highness comes in person to my aid.
You see with whom you have to deal.

MARSCHALLIN *(to the Commissar)*
You know me?
And I think I know you too?
I think I do.
COMMISSAR
Yes, well!
MARSCHALLIN
I remember now, you were my husband's orderly?
COMMISSAR
Yes, Your Highness, to command!
Octavian again pops his head through the curtains.
BARON
(signalling to Octavian to disappear, at the same time in great anxiety lest the Marschallin should notice anything; in an undertone)
Stay there, confound you, out of sight!
The Baron hears steps approaching the door on the left to the front, rushes there, and places himself with his back to the door, trying by means of deferential gestures in the, Marschallin's direction to appear quite at ease. The Marschallin steps over to the left and looks at the Baron expectantly.
OCTAVIAN
(coming from behind the curtains in male attire, as soon as the Baron has turned his back)
Our plan has gone astray, Marie Thérèse, so strangely!
The Marschallin ignores Octavian and fixes a courteous, expectant look on the Baron, who is dividing his attention in the utmost perplexity between the Marschallin and the door. The door on the left is forced open, so that the Baron, who had been leaning against it in a vain attempt to keep it closed, is angrily forced to step back. Two of Faninal's servants now stand aside to let Sophie enter.
SOPHIE *(not seeing the Marschallin, who is hidden by the Baron)*
My father, sir, has bidden me inform you—
BARON *(interrupting her, in an undertone)*
Oh, fiddlesticks, my girl, I have no time!
Will you not wait until I come and call for you?
Can you suppose that I'd
present you in a tavern here?
OCTAVIAN
(who now comes quietly forward from the alcove, in an undertone to the Marschallin)
That is the lady—who—to whom you sent me—

MARSCHALLIN *(to Octavian, over her shoulder, in an undertone)*
You seem a little too concerned, Rofrano.
Who she is I can surely guess. She has great charm.
Octavian slips back between the curtains.

SOPHIE
*(with her back to the door, so angrily that the Baron instinctively
starts back a step)*
I must inform Your Lordship you'll present me to no one.
For I would have you know I have done with you, once and
for all.
The Marschallin converses in a low voice with the Commissar.
And this my father bids me tell you: should you carry your
unmannerly presumption only just so far
as to be seen within a hundred yards of where our palace stands,
you'll have yourself alone to thank for what will then befall you.
That, sir, is what my father bids me to say to you.

BARON *(angrily)*
Corpo di Bacco!
What a shocking use of disrespectful language!

SOPHIE
To match your own.

BARON *(beside himself, trying to pass her and reach the door)*
Hey, Faninal, I must—

SOPHIE
Stand back, sir! Do not dare!
*Faninal's two Footmen come forward, bar his passage, and
push him back. Sophie passes through the door, which is closed
behind her.*

BARON *(shouting through the door)*
I am willing to forget what's happened.
I'll let it be forgiven and forgotten.

MARSCHALLIN
*(approaching the Baron from behind and tapping him on the
shoulder)*
Leave well alone now, and go quickly. At once now!

BARON *(turning around and staring at her)*
But madam—

MARSCHALLIN *(cheerfully, in a tone of superiority)*
Think of your dignity and take your leave!

BARON *(speechless)*
I? How?

MARSCHALLIN
Make your *bonne mine à mauvais jeu*:
now make your exit nobly, like a gentleman.
The Baron stares at her speechlessly. Sophie again enters quietly
from the other room. Her eyes seek Octavian. The Commissar
is standing at the back on the right with the two Constables.
You see, Herr Commissar,
this all has been a little farce and nothing more.

COMMISSAR
All right then. Respectfully I leave you.
(exits, followed by the two Constables)

SOPHIE *(aside, frightened)*
This all has been a little farce and nothing more.
The eyes of the two women meet; Sophie makes an embar-
rassed curtsey.

BARON
(standing between Sophie and the Marschallin)
Don't understand it!

MARSCHALLIN *(impatiently stamping her foot)*
Mon cousin, explain to him!
She turns her back on the Baron.

OCTAVIAN
(approaching the Baron from behind; in a very manly tone)
Will you permit me?

BARON *(turns on him sharply)*
Who? What?

MARSCHALLIN
(from the right, where she has now taken up her position)
Your Lordship, this is Count Rofrano, who then else?

BARON *(resignedly, after carefully studying Octavian's face)*
Just as I thought!
(aside)
That face, it makes me sick.
My eyes did not mislead me then.
It was that boy, then.
Octavian stands there looking insolent and defiant.

MARSCHALLIN *(coming one step closer)*
'Twas a harmless little masquerade and nothing more.

SOPHIE *(half sadly, half ironically to herself)*
'Twas a harmless little masquerade and nothing more.

BARON *(dumbfounded)*
  Aha!
  (aside)
  I see now they were all conspiring to defeat me!
MARSCHALLIN *(haughtily)*
  'Tis well for you it was not
  really my Mariandl whom you brought into this place here to
    seduce.
  The Baron is deep in thought as the Marschallin continues,
  without looking at Octavian.
  I feel just now against all men such a resentment—
  against all men in general!
BARON *(gradually realizing the situation)*
  Well, I'll be damned! Now I begin to see it all!
  The Feldmarschall—Octavian—Mariandl—the Marschallin—
    Octavian—
  (with a sweeping gaze, which wanders from the Marschallin to
  Octavian, from Octavian back to the Marschallin)
  How should I know what I, in my confusion, am supposed
  to think of this!
MARSCHALLIN *(fixing him with a long gaze)*
  You are surely a cavalier?
  (then with great assurance)
  So you will just refrain from thinking.
  That is what I expect from you.
  (pause)
BARON *(bowing with the grace of a man of the world)*
  I am simply delighted and charmed, beyond description
    charmed.
  No Lerchenauer ever had the heart to spoil a joke.
  (coming one step nearer)
  I like the way you've played this comedy,
  but now I must demand you intercede on my behalf.
  I promise to be discreet about it all.
  I'll let it be forgiven and forgotten.
  (pause)
  Eh bien, may I tell Faninal—
  He makes as if to go to the left-hand door.
MARSCHALLIN
  You may—you may without a word withdraw and leave us.

The Baron is dumbfounded.
Can you not tell when an affair is ended?
Your talk of marriage, that affair, and everything
connected with it
(very emphatically)
from this hour is at an end.
SOPHIE *(embarrassedly, aside)*
Connected with it, from this hour is at an end.
BARON *(aside, indignantly, quietly)*
Is at an end, an end! Is at an end, an end!
MARSCHALLIN
*She seems to be looking for a seat. Octavian hurries forward
and gives her a chair on the right, and she sits down.*
(in a significant tone to herself)
Is at an end!
SOPHIE *(on the left, pale, aside)*
Is at an end.
*The Baron fails to appreciate this new development and rolls his
eyes in anger and perplexity. At this moment the man emerges
from the trapdoor. Valzacchi enters from the left, followed by
his suspicious accomplices with modest demeanor. Annina
removes her widow's cap and veil, rubs off her make-up, reveal-
ing her natural face. The Baron's astonishment grows. The
Landlord enters by the center door, carrying a long bill, fol-
lowed by Waiters, Musicians, Boys, and Coachmen.*
BARON
*As he sees them, he realizes that the game is lost. He calls out
quickly and decidedly.*
Leupold, we go!
*He makes a low, angry bow to the Marschallin. His Valet takes a
candle from the table and prepares to lead the way for his master.*
ANNINA *(insolently barring the Baron's passage)*
"I still have all the luck of the Lerchenaus."
(pointing to the Landlord's bill)
"Come when I've dined, I'll give the answer in writing."
*The Children run between the Baron's legs. He hits out at them
with his hat.*
CHILDREN
Papa! Papa! Papa!
WAITERS *(pressing forward to the Baron)*
May't please you, Your Lordship!

There are lights to pay!

LANDLORD *(pressing forward with his bill)*
May't please you, Your Lordship!

ANNINA *(dancing backwards in front of the Baron)*
"I still have all the luck of the Lerchenaus!"

VALZACCHI *(ironically)*
"I still have all the luck of the Lerchenaus!"

MUSICIANS *(barring the Baron's passage)*
There's music, two hours and more, sir.
The Valet forces a way to the door; the Baron tries to follow him.

COACHMEN *(crowding around the Baron)*
For the coach, for the coach. Horses standing. Time is up!

BOY *(insolently bawling at the Baron)*
Don't forget, sir, I lock the house.

LANDLORD *(still presenting his bill)*
May't please you, Your Lordship.

WAITERS
Two score candles. There are the lights to pay.

BARON
(forcing his way to the exit, everyone crowding around him in a throng)
Make way, make way, out of my way!

CHILDREN
Papa! Papa! Papa!
From here on all shout in wild confusion. They reach the door. The candle is wrested from the Valet. The Baron rushes off; all storm after him. The noise grows fainter. Faninal's two Footmen have gone out by the door on the left. Sophie, the Marschallin, and Octavian are left alone.

SOPHIE *(standing on left, pale)*
Oh, God! The story was a masquerade and no more.
My God! My God!
He goes toward her, and I am no more alive for him.

OCTAVIAN *(behind the Marschallin's chair, perplexed)*
Our plan has gone astray, Marie Thérèse, so strangely!
(in extreme embarrassment)
Command me, shall I—should I not—the Lady—her father—

MARSCHALLIN
Go quickly, and do all that your heart commands.

SOPHIE *(in despair)*
No more alive! Oh, my God! Oh, my God!

OCTAVIAN
Thérèse, I do not know—
MARSCHALLIN
Go now, and pay her your court.
OCTAVIAN
I swear it—
MARSCHALLIN
'Tis no matter.
OCTAVIAN
But I do not understand.
MARSCHALLIN *(laughing angrily)*
How like a man to say that. Go to her!
OCTAVIAN
As you command.
(He goes to her. Sophie stands speechless.)
Eh bien, have you no friendly word for me?
No glance or smile, no smile to show that you care?
SOPHIE *(hesitating)*
Ah, my Lord, I had dared
to expect of you and your chivalry
a token of affection more than pity.
OCTAVIAN
What! Are you then not glad?
SOPHIE *(indignantly)*
Pray then tell me what cause I have.
OCTAVIAN
Have we not chased that wretch away that made you sad?
SOPHIE
It could have been a day of happiness and joy.
Yet all conspires to shame me. And in the smile
Her Highness turns on me I can feel all the pity and the scorn.
OCTAVIAN
I swear upon my soul it is not so!
SOPHIE
Pray let me go now!
OCTAVIAN
That cannot be!
(seizing her hand)
SOPHIE
My father needs my help.

OCTAVIAN
I need you more than he.

SOPHIE
'Tis lightly said.
The Marschallin rises abruptly, but controls herself and sits down again.

OCTAVIAN
I love you more than words can say.

SOPHIE
It is not true.
Your love is not as great as you declare.
Forget me quite!

OCTAVIAN
You are my all, you are my all!

SOPHIE
Forget me quite!

OCTAVIAN *(vehemently)*
The world may vanish for all I care!

SOPHIE *(passionately)*
Forget me quite!

OCTAVIAN
My hopes are fastened on you alone.
I'm blinded to all but your face.
(taking both her hands in his)

SOPHIE *(weakly pushing him away)*
Forget me quite!

MARSCHALLIN
(to herself, gravely, at the same time as Octavian and Sophie)
Now or tomorrow, if not tomorrow, very soon.
Did I not say the words myself?
There is no woman can escape this fate.
Did I not know the truth?
Did I not take a vow on it?
That I with all my heart must be humble
and bear the blow . . .
Now or tomorrow, if not tomorrow, very soon.
She wipes her eyes and stands up.

SOPHIE *(softly)*
Her Ladyship! She calls to you. Go speak to her!

Octavian takes a few steps toward the Marschallin and stands in indecision between the two. Sophie, in the doorway, cannot decide whether to stay or go. Octavian, between them, turns his head from one to the other. The Marschallin notices his perplexity, and a melancholy smile flits across her face. Sophie is at the door.

I must go in, I think I hear my father call.

OCTAVIAN

So much is unspoken, I have no words to speak.

MARSCHALLIN

Poor boy, look how confused he stands there between us two.

OCTAVIAN *(to Sophie)*

By all that's holy, stay.

(to the Marschallin)

What, did you say something?

MARSCHALLIN

She pays no attention to Octavian but crosses to Sophie and looks at her critically but kindly. Sophie curtsies in embarrassment. Octavian retreats a step.

So quickly have you learned to love him?

SOPHIE *(very quickly)*

Indeed, ma'am, your question I can hardly understand.

MARSCHALLIN

Your cheek so pale gives me the answer plain enough.

SOPHIE *(very timid and embarrassed, still very quickly)*

No wonder if my cheeks are pale, Your Highness.

I have been dreadfully afraid for my poor father,

not to speak also of my anger at all the

vile things that that hateful man has said and done. I am most

grateful, forever grateful to Your Highness for your help and

kindness.

MARSCHALLIN *(deprecatingly)*

No need to talk so much. You're pretty, that's enough!

And as for your dear papa's discomfort, I know just the medi-

cine for him.

I'll go, say a few words to him, and bid him

drive with me and you and Count Octavian

in my own carriage home beside me—don't you think

that will be quite enough to make him well again

and even cheer his spirits?

SOPHIE

Ah, Your Highness, you are much too kind.

MARSCHALLIN
And for your pale cheeks, I think my cousin there will know the cure.

OCTAVIAN *(with deep feeling)*
Marie Thérèse, how good are you,
Marie Thérèse, I do not know—

MARSCHALLIN *(with an enigmatic expression, softly)*
I know nothing.
(quite without expression)
Nothing.
She indicates to him to stay.

OCTAVIAN *(undecided, as if he wished to follow her)*
Marie Thérèse!
The Marschallin remains standing in the door. Octavian is beside her, Sophie farther off to the right.

MARSCHALLIN *(to herself)*
I made a vow to love him rightly, as a good woman should,
e'en to love the love he bore another,
I promised! But in truth, I did not think
(at the same time as Octavian and Sophie)
that all so soon I'd find the task await me.
(sighing)
Full many a thing is ordained in this world,
which we should scarce believe could be
if we heard others tell of them.
And only we who live them believe in them, and know not how—
There stands the boy, and here stand I, and with this pretty child of his
he will know happiness such as a man thinks
the best the world can give. Well, then, so be it.

OCTAVIAN
(together with the Marschallin and Sophie, at first to himself, then gazing into Sophie's eyes)
Can I believe it has come to pass?
(with much expression)
Would I could ask her: Can it be? And just that question
is the question that I dare not ask.
Would I could ask her: Why, oh, why am I so afraid?
What if a cruel wrong has been done? And yet of her
I may not ask the question—and then I see you by me,

Sophie, and see but you, know but you,
Sophie, and know no more than you: you, you I love.

SOPHIE

(together with the Marschallin and Octavian, at first to herself,
then gazing into Octavian's eyes)
I feel as when I'm kneeling, holy rapture mixed with fear,
and rapture that's unholy, too, I know not what I feel.
As when I'm kneeling, rapture mixed with fear.   ·
(with much expression)
I'd gladly kneel before my Lady there, yet I'd hurt her
gladly; for I feel, she gives him me
and yet robs me of part of him.
I know not how it is.
Could I understand! And yet I fear the truth!
I would know and yet not know; I am hot and cold.
(eye to eye with Octavian)
And know but you, know but this one thing: that I love you!

MARSCHALLIN

In the name of God.
The Marschallin goes quietly into the room on the left; the two
others do not notice it. Octavian comes close to Sophie. A
moment later she is in his arms.

OCTAVIAN *(together with Sophie)*
Bliss too deep to understand,
one in happiness and hand in hand!
What's to come like a dream flies
before my eyes!

SOPHIE *(together with Octavian)*
Am I dreaming that here we stand,
one in happiness and hand in hand?
Ever hand in hand to be
for all eternity!

OCTAVIAN *(more strongly)*
In a palace once upon a day,
you were waiting till I stole you away.
They let me steal the brightest jewel there,
fools that they were.

SOPHIE

You are laughing? I stand in dread,
such a tumult runs in my head.

Hold me! A weak, foolish thing,
to you I cling!
*She leans on him for support. At this moment Faninal's
Footmen open the door and enter, each carrying a candlestick.
Faninal, leading the Marschallin by the hand, enters through
the door. The two young people stand for a moment in confusion, then they make a deep bow, which Faninal and the
Marschallin return. Faninal pats Sophie on the cheek with
paternal benevolence.*

FANINAL
'Tis ever so, youth will be youth!

MARSCHALLIN
Ah, yes.
*Faninal gives the Marschallin his hand and conducts her to the
center door, which is at that moment thrown open by the
Marschallin's suite, among them the Little Black Page. Outside
the light is bright, inside it is half-dark, as the two Footmen precede the Marschallin with the candlesticks.*

OCTAVIAN *(dreamily)*
Bliss too deep to understand,
one in happiness and hand in hand!
What's to come like a dream flies
before my eyes!

SOPHIE *(dreamily)*
Am I dreaming that here we stand,
one in happiness and hand in hand?
Ever hand in hand to be
for all eternity!

OCTAVIAN AND SOPHIE
I know you alone!
*She sinks into his arms. He kisses her quickly. Her handkerchief
drops from her hand without her noticing. Then they run
quickly off, hand in hand. The stage remains empty. Then the
center door opens again. The Little Black Page comes in with a
taper in his hand, looks for the handkerchief, finds it, picks it
up, and trips out. The curtain falls quickly.*

*Translated by Alfred Kalisch
with revisions by James Steakley*

MOSES AND ARON
An Opera in Three Acts

Arnold Schönberg

DRAMATIS PERSONAE

MOSES	*Speaking Role*
ARON	*Tenor*
YOUNG GIRL	*Soprano*
INVALID WOMAN	*Alto*
YOUNG MAN	*Tenor*
NAKED YOUTH	*Tenor*
ANOTHER MAN	*Baritone*
EPHRAIMITE	*Baritone*
PRIEST	*Bass*
FOUR NAKED VIRGINS	*2 Sopranos (one of them the Young Girl) and 2 Altos*
VOICE FROM THE BURNING BUSH	*Sopranos, Boys, Altos, Tenors, Baritones, Basses, 3–6 to each part*
BEGGARS	*6–8 Altos, 6–8 Basses*
SEVERAL ELDERLY PERSONS	*Tenors*
SEVENTY ELDERS	*Basses, a third to be singers (about 25), the rest to be supernumeraries*
TWELVE TRIBAL CHIEFTAINS	*1st and 2nd Tenors, 1st and 2nd Basses*
CHORUS	*Large mixed chorus of Sopranos, Mezzo-Sopranos, Altos, Tenors, Baritones, Basses*

Six Solo Voices, *in the orchestra*   *Soprano, Mezzo-Soprano,*
                                        Alto, Tenor, Baritone, Bass
Dancers, Supernumeraries
  of All Kinds

ACT 1

Scene 1: *The Calling of Moses*

MOSES
  Only One, infinite, Thou omnipresent One,
  unperceived and inconceivable God!
VOICE FROM THE BURNING BUSH
  Here lay your shoes aside.
  You have gone far enough now.
  You stand on ground that is holy.
  Be God's prophet!
MOSES
  God of my fathers, of Abraham, Isaac, and Jacob,
  who has once more awakened their
  great thoughts in my own mind, O God,
  ask not Thy servant to be Thy prophet. I am
  old. I ask Thee, let me tend my sheep in silence.
VOICE
  You've seen your kindred enslaved, the
  truth you have known, so you can do nothing else:
  therefore you must set your folk free!
MOSES
  Who am I to combat the power and force
  of that blindness?
VOICE
  United with God in oneness,
  to him joined,
  from Pharaoh torn loose!
MOSES
  What will give them proof of my mandate?
VOICE
  The name of One holy!
  The infinite will set them free;
  they shall no longer perish in bondage.

MOSES
No one will believe me!

VOICE
Before their ears you shall do wondrous things.
And their eyes will see you and recognize you.
And by your rod will they behold you,
and admire your great wisdom!
Then by your hand
they will believe your power
and feel in the Nile waters
what their own blood commands them.

MOSES
But my tongue is not flexible:
thought is easy;
speech is laborious.

VOICE
E'en as from this bush,
in darkness, ere the light
of truth fell thereupon,
so will you perceive My message
in everything.
Aron will be enlightened,
he shall be your mouth!
From him will your own voice then issue,
as from you comes My voice!
And your people will now be blest,
for this I promise to you:
Your folk are the chosen ones
before all others.
They are the folk of the one God alone.
They are thus to know Him
and give Him alone their worship.
Also they will undergo all hardships
that have in millennia
ever come to be conceived.
And this I promise to you:
I shall conduct you forward
to where with the infinite Oneness
you'll be a model to every nation.
Now begone hence.

Aron nears you in the wasteland.
You soon will see him approach and greet him.
Of this you are to inform him.
Go forth now!

Scene 2: Moses Meets Aron in the Wasteland

ARON
    O son of my fathers,
    are you sent by mighty God?
MOSES
    O son of my father, brother in spirit,
    through whom the only One is to speak,
    now hear me, and Him, and tell me
    what you perceive.
ARON
    My brother, did the almighty One give
    you me as his vessel, that from it be
    poured forth on our brothers
    the Infinite's holy grace?
MOSES
    Grace is granted through recognition.
ARON
    O happy folk, to have one mighty God
    to belong to, against whose forces no other
    power prevails.
MOSES
    Others live within a people, only in fantasy;
    but God the almighty exists apart from men.
ARON
    O vision of highest fantasy, how glad
    it is that you've enticed it to form you.
MOSES
    How can fantasy thus picture the
    unimageable?
ARON
    Love will surely not weary of image-forming.
    Happy is this folk to revere its God so!
MOSES
    Folk set apart to know the ever-unseen One,
    to reflect on greatness unimaged.

ARON

Chosen is this folk,
thus to love one great God ever and ever,
with a thousand times more devotion
than all other earthly peoples for their many godly beings.
Not be seen, not imagined.
Folk chosen by the only One, can you
worship what you dare not even conceive?

MOSES

Dare not? Not conceived because unseen,
can never be measured,
everlasting,
eternal,
because ever present,
and almighty.
The one God is almighty.

ARON

Inconceivable God:
Thou punisheth sins of the father on his
children and children's children.

MOSES

Punish?
Are we able to originate what thou
demand'st as outcome?

ARON

O righteous God:
Thou rewardest those who are faithful to Thy commandments!

MOSES

O righteous God:
Thou has directed
how everything must befall.
Then to whom is the reward presented,
him who wants or cannot want things else?

ARON

How good Thou art!
Thou perceiv'st the pleas of the beggars,
tak'st up the off'rings made by the good.

MOSES

O almighty God,
do the off'rings of beggars then buy Thee,
who Thyself made them poor?

Purify your thinking.
Free it from worthless things.
Let it be righteous.
No other reward is giv'n your off'rings.

ARON
Only this almighty God could
select a people so weak and so downtrodden,
and to them exhibit all His might and His
great wonders,
and teach them how they should learn
to revere Him and Him alone give credence.

MOSES
Law of thought irresistible
forces fulfillment.

ARON
Almighty One,
be the God of this people;
release them from Pharaoh's
harsh bondage.

Scene 3: Moses and Aron Bring God's Message to the People

A YOUNG GIRL
I saw him afar,
just as a flame hotly glowing sprang forth
and addressed him.
He threw himself on his knees
and concealed his face in the sand.
He then went forth in the wasteland.

A YOUNG MAN
He passed by my house
as would a luminous cloud pass,
even so came he by.
He floated rather than walked.
Hardly indeed did he touch the ground.
He quickly passed from my vision.

ANOTHER MAN
I hailed him,
but he neither gave me a sign
nor tarried. And then I heard it said
a God had commanded that he

meet his brother, Moses,
in the region of the wasteland.

PRIEST
Moses?
He who murdered the guard?

CHORUS *(men and women)*
Moses!
He ran away!
We then suffered the wrath of Pharaoh!
Now returning, will he stir rebellion?

PRIEST
Are we now bound to serve a new God?

CHORUS *(women)*
Another God: other off'rings!

MAN
He'll be our protector!

PRIEST
The olden gods did also give protection.
And if one did fail,
prayers were made unto the others.

CHORUS *(women)*
O ask not the gods, then,
impossibility's fulfillment.

A YOUNG MAN
How will he look to us, the newest God?
It's certain that He soars, for Aron did.

MAN
The newest God
perhaps will be stronger than Pharaoh,
stronger than our other gods are.
The gods in the past have aided
those who oppressed us.
This God will come to our aid.

GIRL
I know that
He shall be pleasing and youthful,
handsome in His splendor,
and will gleam as did Aron.

CHORUS
If we are by this man, Moses, to judge the God,
then are some blood off'rings needed.

The newest God also will not help us!
Blood off'rings! Blood off'rings!

PRIEST

Blaspheme not!
There are gods who only punish,
and those gods who only favor.
Many often must be appeased;
others can be won over forever.

CHORUS *(in many small groups)*

Blood off'rings! Blood off'rings!

GIRL

He makes me so glad!
My heart is swelled with joy!
Joyousness fills my spirit!
O holy, worshipful God,
be Thou revealed in all Thy glory.
I serve in love of Thy greatness.

A YOUNG MAN

O God that soars high,
high in the heights of the heavens,
higher than other gods do:
O lift us up to Thee,
nigh to Thee. How quickly depart
the power and might of false images!

MAN

If He aids,
if He shields us from the men of Pharaoh
and also shields us from his false gods,
then He shall be our God
and the God of Israel,
whom we serve, to whom we make off'rings.

CHORUS *(in many groups)*

A God that will please,
revealed in his glory!
A God that can soar,
that takes us to him!
A God that will save!
He shall make us free!
Perhaps He is stronger than Pharaoh!
Heed not the lying ones!
We give Him obedience!

We want to make off'rings,
we want to worship Him.
CHORUS *(in two groups)*
O heed not the liars!
The gods do not give us love!
Who is this who'd mightier be
than Pharaoh's gods are?
Leave us in peace now!
Continue working,
lest it become harder!
He shall make us free!
We want to give worship!
We want to make off'rings!
We want to give worship!
We want to make off'rings!
GIRL
He shall make us free!
*Far in the distance Moses and Aron suddenly appear. They
approach in the manner described by the choruses.*
CHORUS
See Moses and Aron!
Moses's powerful head!
Moses, his rod in his hand,
moving slowly, reflective,
seems to stand still,
now moves somewhat.
Does he wait? Is he moving?
Moses waits!
No, he's walking slowly!
He waits!
No, he moves!
Mighty his whitened head,
and strong is his arm!
And strong is his mien!
See!
Aron, a young man no more,
moves along with a light step
far before him,
and yet stands close to him!
Is Aron close to Moses?
No, he goes before!

Is Aron at Moses's side now?
Front or in back of him?
They are moving, but not in space.
Are nearer,
are farther,
are deeper,
are higher—
have vanished wholly!
See Moses! See Aron!
They have arrived!

Scene 4

CHORUS *(all)*
Bring you good tidings,
word from the mighty new God?
Come you to lead us,
once more to make us hopeful?
We yearn to give Him
gold, goods, and living off'rings!
Take, do not ask us.
Self-love compels us, forces us
to make off'rings,
not only for His favor;
giving itself is
pleasure, the highest favor!
MOSES
The only One, infinite, all-powerful One,
the omnipresent One, invisible,
inconceivable . . .
ARON
He's chosen this folk before all
other people . . .
MOSES
. . . demands no off'ring from you.
ARON
. . . and gives you alone . .
MOSES
. . . He wants not a part,
for everything's wanted.

ARON
... His unbounded holy favor.
On your knees, then, to give Him worship!

CHORUS
To worship, whom? Where is He?
But I see Him not!
Where is He?
Has He gentle or angry mien?
Are we then to love Him or to fear Him?
Where is He?
Point Him out! We want to kneel down.
We want to bring beasts forth to him,
and gold, wheat and barley, and wine!
All will go to your God almighty,
if we're His people,
if He is our God now and
if He guards us well!
But then where is He?
Point Him out!

ARON
Close off your vision
and stop up your hearing!
For in this way shall you see and hear Him!
No living man otherwise perceives Him!

CHORUS
Can He never be seen?
Is He never visible?

CHORUS *(women)*
He, your most mighty of gods,
cannot show Himself before us?

ARON
But the righteous shall see Him.

GIRL
I saw how He gleamed!

YOUNG MAN
He soars as a God!

MAN
He must be our God!

PRIEST
Then why need the murd'rer ever
fear Him?

ARON
Who sees Him not is forsaken!

CHORUS *(men)*
Then we must all be forsaken,
since we still see Him not!
Laughter.

CHORUS
Keep away with your new God,
with this almighty One!
Through Him we do not want our freedom!
Keep far away, like your God,
the all-present Deity!
We fear not, nor love we your God;
so little does He give reward or chastise!

MOSES
Almighty One, now my strength is exhausted,
and my thought become powerless in Aron's word!
Moses more and more in the background.

SIX SOLO VOICES
Aron!

ARON
Silence!
The word is mine and the deed!
He tears the rod from Moses's hand.

CHORUS
Aron, what's happening?

ARON
Moses's rod leads you.
Look, a serpent!
(throws the rod to the ground)

CHORUS
Flee! The serpent grows!
It's twisting!
See, it's turning now 'gainst the people!

ARON
In Moses's hand a rigid rod: this, the law.
In my own hand the most supple of serpents:
discretion.
Now stand so, as it commands!

CHORUS
Move! Go farther back!

Come this way! Go that way!
Take other places!
We're helpless. It has us in bonds!
Aron takes the snake by the tail and puts it back, as a rod, into Moses's hand.

ARON
You thus know the might
that through this rod
is imparted to the leader.

CHORUS *(women, speaking)*
A marvel has filled us with terror.
The rod that did change to a serpent,
shows Aron as lord of this people.
How great is the might of this Aron!

CHORUS *(men, singing)*
Is Aron the servant of Moses?
Does Moses in turn serve this new God?
Then surely this God must be mighty,
when such mighty persons do serve Him!

CHORUS *(all)*
Is Aron the servant of Moses?
Does Moses in turn serve this new God?
Through the rod that his God gave to Moses
he's mightier even than Aron.
Then surely this God must be mighty,
who even such strength can command.
How vast is the might of this great God,
when such mighty persons do serve him!
Is Aron the servant of Moses?
Does Moses in turn serve this new God?
Then surely this God must be mighty,
when such mighty persons do serve Him!

GIRL
He shall make us free!

YOUNG MAN
We want to give worship!

MAN
We want to make off'rings!

PRIEST
Your rod compels us,
yet it does not compel Pharaoh
to give us freedom!

ARON
>Oh, your spirit has been broken
>and your pride is shrunken.
>Hoping not, you labor,
>have no faith in God
>or yourselves,
>for your heart is sick!
>This way you'll not vanquish Pharaoh!

CHORUS
>Pharaoh is powerful:
>we are weak!

ARON
>See Moses's hand.
>So hale it is, and strong.
>But now Moses's heart is like your own,
>because he knows you lack spirit.
>Placing his hand on the heart,
>that's sick just as yours is,
>see!

CHORUS
>Leprous! Flee!
>Shun his path!
>And touch him not;
>you will be sick!
>Leprous!

ARON
>Therein see yourselves:
>downcast, sick, detested,
>enslaved, tormented!
>Now, even there in Moses's bosom
>the spirit of the great God dwells,
>that soon will force
>this Pharaoh to release you.
>See!

SIX SOLO VOICES
>See!

ARON
>Moses now places that leprous hand
>upon his strong and healthy heart . . .

CHORUS
>Marvel! See! Marvel!
>The hand is now hale and strong!

ARON
Discover therein your likeness.
For your spirit shall defeat the hosts of Pharaoh.
CHORUS *(women)*
Through Aron this Moses has shown us
how he saw his God be revealed.
And now can this God be imagined,
attested by visible wonders.
CHORUS *(men)*
Oh, Aron has shown us a marvel.
The hand that can be hale or sickly
is proof of the being of this God,
who yet will not show His visage!
Through Aron this Moses has shown us
how he saw his God be revealed.
Oh, leprous the hands of the faithless,
and healthy the hearts of believers,
and now can this God be imagined.
The symbol enlarges to image Him.
The spirited heart trusts in one God,
attested by visible wonders.
Through Aron this Moses has shown us
how he saw his God be revealed.
And now can this God be imagined,
attested by visible wonders.
CHORUS
Almighty God!
MAN AND CHORUS *(men)*
Everything for freedom!
Now let us shatter the shackles!
And kill the taskmasters!
Let's kill them!
And kill all their priesthood!
Let's kill them!
Destroy all their idols!
Destroy them!
Off to the wasteland!
CHORUS *(women)*
Off to the wasteland!
PRIEST
Madmen you are!
How can the wasteland give you nurture?

MOSES

> In the wasteland pureness of thought
> will provide you nurture, sustain you
> and advance you ...

ARON

> ... and the only One lets you see
> an image of your earthly good fortune
> in every spiritual marvel.
> The all-knowing One knows that you are still
> a childlike folk
> and does not expect from a child
> what's hard for elders.
> He reasons this way: that every child grows older,
> and every elder shall be wiser.
> He grants you time to devote to the pleasure
> of preparation and the wisdom that
> agedness will bring with it.
> He never will fail to provide you with food
> in the distant wasteland.
> The almighty One can change
> mere sand to fruit,
> fruit to gold,
> gold to rapture,
> rapture to soul.
> Who feeds the Nile
> that nurtures this land?
> He, who did change rod to serpent
> and changed health to leprosy's terror.
> See the Nile's clear water within this jar.
> *(pours it out)*
> No, you are not wrong.
> What you now see is blood!
> What does this mean?
> This is your own blood that gives the land nurture
> as the flow of the Nile.
> You fatten the servants of falsehood,
> the slaves of false gods.
> But the almighty One will free
> you and free your blood.
> For He has chosen you over other peoples
> to be the people of God alone,

CHORUS

> Chosen folk,
> chosen folk!

him alone to worship,
in no other's service!
You will be free then
from toil and misery!
This is His promise:
He will then lead you to a land
where milk and honey flow.
There you shall have earthly pleasure
from what in spirit was vowed your fathers.
What for Pharaoh remains,
look here, is once more
the Nile's clear water alone.
And therein is he sure to drown.

CHORUS

We are His chosen folk before all others,
we are the chosen ones,
Him alone to worship,
Him alone to serve.
We shall be free then
from toil and misery!
This is His promise:
He will then lead us to a land
where milk and honey flow.
And we shall enjoy then
what He once did promise our fathers.
Almighty, Thou art stronger
than Egyptian gods are.
Thou wilt strike down Pharaoh and all
his servants.
Now we're freed from toil by Moses and Aron.
Infinite God, we worship Thee,
consecrate to Thee off'rings
and our devotion;
for Thou hast chosen us,
lead'st us to the promised land.
We shall be free, free!

INTERLUDE

CHORUS

Where is Moses?

(whispered)
Where is our leader?
Where is he?
It's been a long time since he was seen!
Ne'er shall we see him!
Abandoned are we!
Where is his God?
Where is the Infinite?
Where is Moses?

ACT 2

Scene 1: Aron and the Seventy Elders
before the Mountain of Revelation

THE SEVENTY ELDERS
Forty days now!
PRIEST
Forty days now, yet we're still waiting here!
SEVENTY ELDERS
When will this end?
PRIEST
How long is this to continue?
Forty days now we have awaited Moses,
and still no one knows either law or command!
Unperceivable command from One who's yet
unperceived.
AN ELDER
All of the best pastures are occupied by Judah!
ANOTHER ELDER
Far worse than in Egypt,
to toil without day of rest,
as Ephraim makes Benjamin's sons do!
A THIRD ELDER
Ephraim's women have been stolen by Benjamin's sons!
SEVENTY ELDERS
Thus might now reigns!
Lewdness knows not its punishment;
virtue knows not reward!
Forty days now we have waited vainly
before this summit!

ARON
    When Moses has left the summit, come down from there,
    from where the laws are revealed to him alone,
    you shall hear both law and command from my mouth.
    You cannot expect form before idea,
    for together they'll make their appearance.
SEVENTY ELDERS
    That is too late for us!
    The people are downcast!
    They distrust this high summit,
    for the enclosure keeps the revelation from them.
    They rage, they trust not one of us,
    think the enclosure is senseless,
    the revelation is pretext,
    Moses's silence means flight!
    (noise in the far distance)
    Hear! Hear! Too late!
    Growing sounds of shouting and raging approach quickly; then
    in furious agitation the roaring crowd rushes upon the stage
    from all directions.

Scene 2

CHORUS
    Where is Moses?
    We'll tear him asunder!
    Where is the great omnipresent One?
    How can He condone this?
    Where is the almighty One?
    Why does He now impede us?
    Have no fear! Destroy him!
    The inconceivable God did not forbid it!
    Give us back our gods to worship;
    let them bring us order,
    lest we tear you limb from limb,
    you who took command and law away from us!
THE SEVENTY ELDERS
    Aron, help us! Speak out for us!
    They'll murder us! They pay you heed!
    You have their hearts!

ARON
> O Israel,
> my brother Moses tarries
> where he always is,
> though he be near to us or far:
> he rests upon that summit,
> close to his God.
> It may be that he has left us,
> being far from us.
> Or maybe his God has now left him,
> being so near to Him.
> Perhaps he approached too near!
> That God is so severe;
> it may be that He's destroyed him!

CHORUS *(one group)*
> His God may have destroyed him!

CHORUS *(another group)*
> The gods have probably destroyed him!

CHORUS *(all)*
> The gods then have indeed destroyed him!
> The gods so mighty destroyed this offender!
> The Infinite could not protect him!
> The great unseen One will never give us assistance!
> The great unseen One lets no one behold him!
> His God is powerless!
> O slay them, kill off all this priesthood.
> O smite them and burn them,
> the priesthood, servants of this false God!

SEVENTY ELDERS
> Aron, help us. Relent!

ARON
> O Israel, I return your gods to you,
> and also give you to them,
> just as you have demanded.
> Leave distant things to One infinite,
> since to you the gods have
> ever-present and always-common substance.
> You shall provide the stuff;
> I shall give it a form:
> common and visible, imaged
> in gold forever.

Bring out your gold!
Yield it! Entreat it!
You then shall be happy!

CHORUS
Joyous Israel! Joyous Israel!
Our gods, imaged in our vision;
our gods, masters of our senses!
You are earthly and visible,
manifest, assuring our certainty.
Your extent and your finitude
do not ask for that which our hearts deny.
O gods, near to all our feelings,
O gods, we can understand you.
Virtue's prize is great ecstasy;
acts of wrong are punished by righteousness.
Show us how our deeds are answered.
O gods, let us see your power.
Joyous Israel, jubilate, Israel!
Bright is this present instant,
dismal that distant timelessness.
Pleasure shuns not its consequence,
fearlessly seeks it out willingly.
Joy borders life and also death,
heightened by each, from each partakes.
Danger inflames our love of life,
steadfastness, too, and bravery.
You have given your gods
your innermost feelings
as content and form.
Now your gods' great glory
fastens your gold.
Renounce all your wealth!
Give your gold; make them rich!
They will not let you ever hunger!
Joyous Israel!
Joyous!

Scene 3: The Golden Calf and the Altar

ARON
This gold image attests

that in all things that are, a god lives.
Unchangeable, e'en as a law,
is the stuff, the gold
that you have given.
(Seemingly changeable,
as all else must be.) Much less
matters the shape that I have provided.
Revere yourselves in this gold symbol!
During Aron's last speech processions of laden camels, asses, horses, porters, and wagons enter the stage from different directions, bringing offerings of gold, grain, skins of wine and oil, animals, and the like. At many places in the foreground and background these are unloaded and piled up. Herds of all manner of animals pass by. Simultaneously, preparations for slaughter are to be seen at many places. The animals are decorated and wreathed. Butchers with large knives enter and with wild leaps dance around the animals.

Slowly it becomes evening. The butchers now slaughter the animals and throw pieces of meat to the crowd which fights over them. Some run about with bloody pieces of meat, devouring them raw. Meanwhile large pots are brought and fires prepared. Burnt offerings are brought to the altar.

DANCE OF THE BUTCHERS

An Invalid Woman is brought in on a litter. The crowd in front makes room, and the Invalid Woman is placed before the golden calf.

INVALID WOMAN
O godly form,
your rays give warmth, you heal
as never the sun's rays have healed.
I merely placed my hand on you,
and even now the crippled limbs begin moving.
As darkness falls, fires and torches are lit and wine and oil distributed.

CHORUS *(male and female beggars, quite close to the calf)*
Here, O great gods, take the only tatters
that have protected us from desert sand and sun's blazing.
And here are the last of our morsels,
those which we have begged for tomorrow's sustenance.
Several Elderly Persons, who have laboriously dragged themselves along, stand now before the golden calf.

CHORUS *(old men)*
　The final living moments
　that are still remaining to us
　we give as off'ring.
SEVENTY ELDERS
　They've slain themselves in off'rings.
　Galloping is heard; it approaches quickly. The people, excited,
　disperse. The Tribal Leaders and the Ephraimite gallop up
　wildly before the calf and spring to the ground. Bystanders hold
　the horses.
EPHRAIMITE
　Free, under lords of their choosing,
　they'll be governed by only those gods
　who rule with power.
　Tribal leaders, swear now with me
　to this image of governing power.
TRIBAL LEADERS
　We speak for all of the tribes that name us leaders:
　O gods, see how we kneel down before you.
　We yield to a power that's higher, being highest!
CHORUS
　Free under lords of our choosing!
　The Youth has cleared a path through the crowd. He is
　shrunken to a skeleton, appears feverish. With a long rod held
　in both hands he strikes out at the bystanders, trying to force
　them to give up the idol worship.
YOUTH
　As high as thought were we once upraised,
　present afar, future at hand!
　Deep as life are we degraded.
　Annihilate this image of the temporal;
　clear be the view of eternity!
　The Ephraimite, who stands behind the Youth, seizes him by
　the neck and presses him to the ground.
EPHRAIMITE
　Here, view now eternity,
　since your present life has so little value.
　The Tribal Leaders slay the Youth, mount their horses, mingle
　with people individually and in disorder, then disappear, riding
　off unobtrusively.

After the foregoing acts of renunciation and offering there now reigns a desire for mutual giving. Women give each other jewelry, fabrics, and the like, while men give each other weapons, implements, etc. They offer each other food and drink, set wreaths upon themselves and others. Some help others with tasks, etc.

Everywhere now wine is given out in streams. A wild drunkenness overtakes everyone. Heavy stone jars are thrown about. The people shower wine and implements upon each other during extravagant dancing, whereupon quarrelling and fighting break out here and there.

ORGY OF DRUNKENNESS AND DANCING

SEVENTY ELDERS
Happy is this folk,
and great is the wonder
and the rapture, and the joy they've created.
None is untransfigured; each is exalted.
None is unaffected; each is enraptured.
Powerful human virtues are reawakened:
grave and joyful; temperate, dissolute;
cheerful, pleased, and longing, active, resting.
Repression, lust, abstention, greed,
profusion, and envy.
All of beauty, goodness, ugliness, evil,
all that can be witnessed, manifest, sensate.
Sense first gives to spirit sense.
Spirit then is sense.
Those gods who have given you spirit,
sense and spirit to affect you,
let them be exalted!
Four Naked Virgins, one of them the Girl, step before the calf.
THE GIRL
O golden of gods,
your glow streams through me with pleasure!
What gleams must be good.
Unassailable virtue of gold,
its virginity cannot be lost,
repaid as model and image.
FOUR NAKED VIRGINS
O golden of gods,
O priests who serve gods so golden,

our blood, virginal and still unblemished,
is coldly metallic as gold is,
not warmed to bear fruit.
O great ones, enrapture your priesthood,
transport us, arouse us to first and last rapture.
Enkindle our blood, let it hiss 'gainst cold gold
as forth it rushes!
O crimson gold!
The priests embrace end kiss the maidens. Behind each pair, a girl stands holding a long butcher's knife and a jug for catching the blood.

SEVENTY ELDERS
Blood off'ring!
The girls hand the priests the knives. The priests seize the virgins' throats and thrust the knives into their hearts. The girls catch the blood in receptacles. The priests pour it forth on the altar.

Destruction and suicide now begin amongst the crowd. Implements are shattered, stone jars are smashed, carts destroyed, etc. Everything possible is flung about: swords, daggers, axes, lances, jars, implements, etc. In a frenzy some throw themselves upon implements, weapons, and the like, while others fall upon swords. Still others leap into the fire and run burning across the stage. Several jump down from the high rock, etc. Wild dancing with all this.

EROTIC ORGY

A Naked Youth runs forward to a girl, tears the clothes from her body, lifts her high and runs with her to the altar.

THE NAKED YOUTH
In your godly image
we shall let our passions live.
Many men follow this example, throw their clothes aside, strip women, and bear them off the same way, toward the background, pausing at the altar.

SEVERAL OTHER NAKED MEN
Holy is the creative power!

STILL OTHERS
Holy is fertility!

MANY OTHERS
Holy is desire!
A whole succession of naked people, screaming and yelling, runs past the altar in this manner and disappears in the background.

With the departure of the naked people the stage has become emptier. The excitement, frenzy, and drunkenness now quickly pass into exhaustion and lassitude. Many sink down, falling asleep. Others withdraw quietly. From the background come music and singing, always from different places.

CHORUS
Great gods who have given you spirit . . .
Senses, spirit to affect you . . .
O golden of gods.
Gold gleams like lust!
Human virtue is gold-like!
Gold is lust!
Lust is wildness!
Gold gleams like blood!
Gold is power,
devotion,
and righteousness!
Bewildering gleam!
The fires die out gradually, until only a few remain. All motion on the stage has ceased.

Scene 4

In the background, as far back as possible, a man on one of the hillocks raises himself up, peers for a time in the direction where the mountain of revelation is supposed to be, then, gesticulating, he awakens several of those lying near him and has them look in the same direction. He cries out:

MAN
Moses is descending from the mountain!
After this cry, those sleeping awaken everywhere, arise, and from all sides people again stream in.

MOSES
Begone, you image of powerlessness
to enclose the Boundless in an image finite!
The golden calf vanishes. The crowd moves back and quickly disappears from the stage.

CHORUS
The golden rays are now quenched!
Once again our god cannot be seen.
Every joy, every pleasure, every promise is gone!
All is once more gloom and darkness!

We must now escape from his might!
Exeunt all but Moses and Aron.

Scene 5: Moses and Aron

MOSES
Aron, O what have you done?
ARON
Naught diff'rent,
just my task as it ever has been:
When your idea gave forth
no word, my word gave forth
no image for them, I worked marvels
for eyes and ears to witness.
MOSES
Commanded by whom?
ARON
As always,
I heeded the voice from within.
MOSES
But I did not instruct you.
ARON
Nevertheless, I still comprehended.
MOSES
Cease!
ARON
Your ... mouth ...
You were far away from us ...
MOSES
There with my Idea.
That must have been close to you.
ARON
When you remained apart
we believed you were dead.
And since the people had long expected
both law and commandment soon
to issue from your mouth,
I was compelled to provide an image for them.
MOSES
Your image faded at my word!

ARON
> But your word was denied image
> and marvel, which are detested by you.
> And yet was the marvel an image, not more,
> when your word destroyed my image.

MOSES
> God's eternity opposes idols' transience!
> No image this, no marvel!
> These are the commands!
> The everlasting One spoke them,
> just as these tables so temp'ral,
> in the language you are speaking.
> *He holds out the tables to Aron.*

ARON
> Israel endures, thus proving the idea
> of One timeless.

MOSES
> Grant you now the power which
> Idea has over both word and image?

ARON
> I discern only this:
> that this folk shall remain protected.
> And yet, they've naught but their feeling.
> I love this humble folk.
> I live just for them
> and want to sustain them.

MOSES
> If the Idea wills it.
> My love is for my Idea. I live just for It!

ARON
> You also would have loved this people,
> had you only seen how they lived
> when they dared to see and feel and hope.
> No folk is faithful, unless it feels.

MOSES
> You have shaken me not!
> They must comprehend the Idea!
> They live for that end!

ARON
> What a piteous people, a folk made of
> martyrs they would then be!

No folk can grasp more than just a
partial image, the perceivable part
of the whole Idea.
Be understood by all the people
in their own accustomed way.

MOSES

Am I to debase the Idea?

ARON

Let me present It then,
describing without specifying:
Restrictions,
fear-inspiring yet not too harsh,
further perseverance;
the need thus will be the clearer.
Commandments stern
give rise to new hoping
and strengthen the idea.
Unbeknown, what you want will be done.
Human wavering you'll find your people still have . . .
yet worthy of love.

MOSES

I shall not live to see it!

ARON

Go on living!
Aught else is futile!
You're bounden to your Idea so closely!

MOSES

Bounden to my Idea, as e'en do these
tables set it forth.

ARON

They're images also,
just part of the whole Idea.

MOSES

Then I smash to pieces both these tables,
and I shall also ask Him to
withdraw the task given me.
He smashes the tables.

ARON

Faint-hearted one!
You, who yet have God's message,
without or with the tables.

I, your mouth, do rightly guard your Idea
whenever I do utter It.

MOSES

In image!

ARON

Image of your Idea;
they are one, as all is that emerges from It.
I simply yield before necessity;
for it is certain this folk will be sustained
to give proof of the eternal Idea.
This is my mission: to speak It more simply
than I understand It.
Yet, the knowing ones surely will
ever again discover It!

CHORUS

(moving past in the background, led by a pillar of fire)
For He has chosen us before all others
as His folk, to serve the only God,
Him alone to worship,
serving no one else!

ARON

Look there!

MOSES

The fiery pillar!

ARON

To lead us by night—
Thus through me has God given a signal
to the people.
*In the background day arrives quickly. The pillar of fire fades
and is transformed into the pillar of cloud. The foreground
remains relatively dark.*

MOSES

The cloudlike pillar!

ARON

It leads us by day.

MOSES

Godless image!

ARON

God-sent signal, burning bush again glowing.
The Infinite thus shows not Himself,
but shows the way to Him
and the way to the promised land!

CHORUS
He will then lead us to the land
where milk and honey flow,
and we shall enjoy then
what He once did promise our fathers.
Aron slowly exits in the background.

CHORUS
Almighty,
Thou art stronger than Egyptian
gods are!

MOSES
Inconceivable God!
Inexpressible, many-sided Idea,
will You let it be so explained?
Shall Aron, my mouth, fashion this image?
Then I have fashioned an image, too, false,
as an image must be.
Thus am I defeated!
Thus, all was but madness that
I believed before,
and can and must not be given voice.
O word, thou word, that I lack!
Moses sinks to the ground in despair.

ACT 3

Scene 1

Moses enters. Aron, a prisoner in chains, follows, dragged in by two soldiers who hold him fast by the shoulders and arms. Behind him come the Seventy Elders.

MOSES
Aron, now this must cease!

ARON
Will you then kill me?

MOSES
It is not a matter of your life . . .

ARON
The promised land . . .

MOSES
An image . . .

ARON

I was to speak in images
while you spoke in ideas;
I was to speak to the heart,
you to the mind.

MOSES

You, from whom both word and image flee,
you yourself remain, you yourself live
in the images that you have provided
for the people to witness.
Having been alienated from the source, from the Idea,
then neither word nor image satisfied you.

ARON *(interrupting)*

I was to perform visible marvels
when the word and the image from the mouth failed . . . !

MOSES

. . . but you were satisfied only by the act, the deed.
You then made of the rod a leader,
of my power a liberator.
And the waters of the Nile attested the supreme Might . .
You then desired actually, physically,
to tread with your feet upon an unreal land
where milk and honey flowed.
You then struck the rock,
instead of speaking to it, as you were commanded to do
in order to make water flow forth from it . . .
The word alone was to have struck forth refreshment
from the naked rock . . .

ARON

Never did your word reach the people without meaning.
And thus did I speak to the rock
in its language, which the people also understand.

MOSES

You speak more simply than you understand,
for you know that the rock is, like the
wasteland and the burning bush—
three that give not to the body
what it needs with regard to spirit—
is, I say, an image of the soul,
whose very renunciation is sufficient for eternal life.
And the rock, even as all images,

obeys the Word,
from whence it came to be manifested.
Thus, you won the people not for the eternal One,
but for yourself . . .

ARON

For their freedom—
so that they would become a nation.

MOSES

To serve, to serve the divine Idea
is the purpose of the freedom for which
this folk has been chosen.
You, however, expose them to strange gods,
to the calf
and to the pillars of fire and cloud;
for you do as the people do,
because you feel and think as they do.
And the god that you showed to them
is an image of powerlessness,
is dependent upon a Power beyond itself,
must fulfill what it has promised,
must do what it is asked,
is bound by its word.
Just as men act—well
or badly—so must it;
it must punish their wickedness, reward their virtues.
But man is independent and does
what pleases him, according to free will.
Here images govern
the Idea, instead of expressing It.
The almighty One (and He retains that quality forever)
is not obliged to do anything,
is bound by nothing.
He is bound neither by the transgressor's deeds,
nor by the prayers of the good,
nor by the offerings of the penitent.
Images lead and rule this folk
that you have freed,
and strange wishes are their gods,
leading them back to the slavery
of godlessness and earthly pleasures.
You have betrayed God to the gods,

the Idea to images,
this chosen folk to others,
the extraordinary to the commonplace . . .

SOLDIERS
Shall we kill him?

MOSES *(addressing all)*
Whensoever you went forth amongst the people
and employed those gifts—
which you were chosen to possess
so that you could fight for the divine Idea—
whensoever you employed those gifts for false
and negative ends, that you might
rival and share the lowly pleasures of strange peoples,
and whensoever you had abandoned
the wasteland's renunciation
and your gifts had led you to the highest summit,
then as a result of that misuse
you were and ever shall be hurled back
into the wasteland.
(to the Soldiers)
Set him free, and if he can,
he shall live.
Aron, free, stands up and then falls down dead.

MOSES
But in the wasteland you shall be
invincible and shall achieve the goal:
unity with God.

Translated by Allen Forte,
with revisions by Paul Hamburger
and James Steakley

ACKNOWLEDGMENTS

Every reasonable effort has been made to locate the owners of rights to previously published translations printed here. We gratefully acknowledge permission to reprint the following material:

From *The Magic Flute*, Wolfgang Amadeus Mozart, ENO Guide #3, Copyright © 1980 by Michael Geliot and Anthony Besch. Reprinted by permission of Riverrun Press.

Fidelio: An Opera in Two Acts. Ludwig van Beethoven, Translation by Paul Csonka and Ariane Theslöf. Lyrics Copyright © 1969 by Edwin F. Kalmus. Used by Permission of CPP/BELWIN, INC., Miami FL. All rights reserved.

Parsifal, translation by Andrew Porter, Copyright © 1986. C/o Artellus Limited, 30 Dorset House, Gloucester Place, London NW1 5AD.

Der Rosenkavalier © 1912 by Adolph Furstner; Copyright Renewed. Copyright and Renewal assigned to Boosey & Hawkes Ltd., London, for all countries excluding Germany, Danzig, Italy, and Portugal. Reprinted by permission of Boosey & Hawkes, Inc.

Moses and Aron. Used by permission of Belmont Music Publishers, Pacific Palisades, CA 90272.